Spiritual Reflections

100 Bible Verses with Real-life Applications

Benjamin Neesham

Kingdom Publishers

Spiritual Reflections
Copyright© Benjamin Neesham

All rights reserved. No part of this book may be reproduced in any form by photocopying or any electronic or mechanical means, including information storage or retrieval systems, without permission in writing from both the copyright owner and the publisher of the book. The right of Benjamin Neesham to be identified as the author of this work has been asserted by him in accordance with the Copyright, Designs and Patents Act 1988 and any subsequent amendments thereto.

A catalogue record for this book is available from the British Library.

All Scripture Quotations have been taken from the New International Version and the King James Version of the Bible.

ISBN: 978-1-913247-88-1

1st Edition by Kingdom Publishers

Kingdom Publishers
London, UK.

You can purchase copies of this book from any leading bookstore or email **contact@kingdompublishers.co.uk**

Dedication

To Ronnie, Hazel, William and Ruth: four of the most amazing people I have ever met.

Foreword

I am extremely grateful to Dr. Jonathan Leakey, leader of the Ballymena House of Prayer, and author of 'Scam Survivor', for accepting my invitation to write the preface to these reflections.

Benjamin Neesham – Spiritual Reflections

FOREWORD by Dr Jonathan Leakey, leader of Ballymena House of Prayer and a director of Without Walls, Ballymena

I am honoured to have been asked by Benjamin Neesham to write the foreword to his *Spiritual Reflections*. The author, over the years that I have known him, has proven himself to be a man of integrity and a faithful disciple of Jesus Christ. Not many Christians take a personal, genuine and prayerful interest in a country they don't even live in! While Benjamin lives on the Isle of Lewis he has shown a genuine love for the island of Ireland and its people, is very knowledgeable about the politics and culture of both Northern Ireland (indeed of the whole of the UK) and the Republic of Ireland, has been a frequent visitor to both and regularly (whether in person, or more recently via Zoom due to the coronavirus restrictions) joins in prayer gatherings for our town and land.

Starting with a reflection on Genesis 1:1 and the creation of the universe the author pulls no punches and has our immediate attention: "if you can accept the truth of this first verse of the Bible, then you won't have any difficulty with the rest of the Book". Then, taking 100 key verses from Genesis to Revelation, the author guides us through most if not all of the core and foundational truths of the Christian faith: from the creation of the universe to the end times, God's calling on our lives and our response to God's call, finding God in the midst of suffering and adversity, the existence of a devil and demons, God's judgement and God's mercy, salvation and what really happened on the cross of Calvary, who gets to go to heaven and how? What about hell, and miracles, and faith? There's even much to help us gain a healthy perspective on 2020 and the Covid-19 pandemic.

Benjamin has produced a unique, very readable and challenging "devotional". It is, in fact, much more than a devotional, written as it has been primarily for people who have lots of questions about God, who maybe wouldn't even call themselves a Christian. It will also help many new believers. I believe it will be a great help too for those believers who are struggling with their faith. Yet even those with a strong faith will find much here to challenge, instruct, and encourage. It could well prove an excellent introduction to Bible reading as a regular life-giving habit. I believe and pray that this book will help many to get back into the Bible with fresh interest and understanding of its relevance to their lives.

So, if your mind is full of questions about God and faith and whether the Bible and the God of the Bible can be depended upon, you should read this book. If you are a believer who feels like you have lost your way a bit, read this book. If you are a Christian with a strong faith, you will also find a lot to encourage and strengthen your faith and understanding of the Scriptures.

The author has combined intellectual rigour, human honesty, a keen observation of contemporary society, with a strong and clear faith in the dependability of the Bible and in the God of the whole Bible. He has not been afraid to tackle the difficult questions such as where is God in the midst of suffering and adversity, how can God be both a God of judgement and of mercy, what role do our choices play in view of the sovereignty of God? There is both a topical and an eternal relevance here for our 21st century lives in which global challenges, such as the coronavirus pandemic and climate change, have forced us all to reassess the dependability of our world views, belief systems and moral and spiritual foundations.

Benjamin has a firm grasp on the broad sweep of the Bible and how the truths and events of the Old Testament anticipate and prepare the way for the revelation of salvation and the restoration of all things through Christ the Messiah in the New Testament. We are also challenged to revisit what we really believe about the God of the Bible and the Christian faith, and what we are prepared to do about it.

Each of the 100 reflections is followed by a few insightful questions which readers will find practical and helpful. Some of the reflections conclude with a prayer of response which hopefully will enable many to connect personally with the God of the Bible.

Spiritual Reflections: 100 Bible Verses with Real-life Applications

This book was inspired by the work many people were doing, during the extraordinary year of 2020, to articulate the Gospel message to individuals who found themselves asking whether the Christian faith might hold at least some of the answers to the questions they'd been prompted to ask, as a consequence of the chaos that was unfolding around them. It goes without saying that such a small volume doesn't contain all the answers to every question you've ever asked yourself, or that's been asked of you, but it will hopefully provide a rational explanation of the Christian message, in a way that's easy to understand. The format has a devotional style, although it differs in certain respects from a traditional devotional text; particularly in that it's primarily intended either for people who aren't yet Christians, or those who are struggling with their faith. However, this is not to say that experienced believers can't learn something from it, too!

If reading this book prompts you to ask further questions, that's no bad thing! Please feel free to contact me directly, or to speak to a trusted Christian in your circle of family or friends. Be assured that giving consideration to the validity of the Christian faith isn't a sign of weakness: it's an extremely sensible thing to do, especially as so much - in particular your eternal destiny - could be riding on the decisions you make. Speaking of eternal destiny might seem 'heavy', but I'm certainly not intending to pressurise anyone! My hope is that, by reading this book with an open and curious mind, you'll have your eyes opened to why Christians believe what they do, and perhaps be prompted to continue your own journey of exploration. For those who already know Jesus as Lord and Saviour, it is my desire that you'll come to a fuller understanding of the power of the Gospel, thereby equipping you more effectively for conversations with people who don't yet believe, and encouraging you to enter more completely into the purposes God has for you. Clearly, none of this can be done without the power of the Holy Spirit, and I'm indebted to Him for guiding me in the writing of this book.

Considerable thanks are due to those of you who've encouraged me to embark upon this enterprise, especially my friend Ruth Gregg in Portglenone, and many of my Facebook friends, who've read some of these articles as they appeared in a weekly blog format. I'd also like to extend my gratitude to my publishers and you, my readers, for giving me this opportunity to explain why I believe the Bible to be the Word of God. My hope and prayer is that what I've written will impact your hearts, leading you to a closer - or possibly entirely new - relationship with the Saviour Who it's been my privilege to serve for the past eighteen years.

Wishing you every blessing,

Benjamin

Contents

In The Beginning!	17
God's Call On Your Life	20
Divine Turnaround!	23
Passover!	27
Miraculous Deliverance!	30
Made In God's Own Image	33
Trusting The Lord's Report	36
Abundant Blessings!	39
Memorials	42
Strategy	45
Anarchy	48
Godly Disobedience!	51
A Well-kept Pledge	54
A God Without Limits!	57
Enquiring Of The Lord	61
Mourning	64
Repentance	67
Wisdom	70
Captivity	73

Be Of Good Courage!	76
A Promise And An Obligation	79
Restoration	82
Encouragement In The Face Of Opposition	85
Faith Versus Fatalism	88
Perspective	92
Rooted In The Word!	95
Living Water	98
Revival!	100
Majestic Certainty	103
God Is Good!	105
Trust In The Lord!	108
Tie Down The Tongue!	111
Training For The Journey	113
Fear God!	116
He Is Mine, And I Am His!	119
Here I Am, Lord!	122
His Forgiveness; Our Ingratitude	125
Don't Be Deceived!	128
Seek And Ye Shall Find!	131
We Have Hope!	134
Ichabod!	137
Standing In The Gap	140
Divine Revelation!	143
Spiritual Warfare!	147
Mercy In Judgement	151

Justice!	157
Beware Destruction!	160
Running From God!	163
Devastation!	170
Would You Believe It?	173
Joyous Inheritance!	176
Never Give Up!	180
Regret And Redemption	184
Prophecy, Fulfilment And Expectation	188
A Special Invitation!	191
A Different Side To Jesus!	195
Hypocrisy	198
Well Done!	202
Resurrection!	206
Come Home!	216
Thy Will Be Done!	219
Saved!	223
Overcoming Tradition	226
Abundant Life!	230
One Way!	233
The Eternal Question	236
Mission Accomplished!	240
The Comforter!	244
Responding To The Spirit	249
Religion Or Revival?	253
Almost Persuaded?	257

One Step To Heaven!	261
No Condemnation!	265
Take Heed!	268
Grace And Endurance	272
Beware Heretics!	277
Suit Up!	281
Peace And Strength!	284
Walk Worthy!	288
Our Glorious Hope!	292
Receive The Truth!	296
Pray!	300
The Reliability Of Scripture	304
Enough Is Enough!	310
Forgiven, So Forgive!	314
What Is Faith?	317
Resist And Grow!	321
Be Ready!	324
God's Will May Not Be Done!	329
The Way Back!	333
Exercise Discernment!	336
Walk In Truth!	339
Diabolic Dialogue	342
Revelation!	346
Open The Door!	350
The Final Warning	353
No More Pain!	357

In The Beginning!

"In the beginning, God created the heaven and the earth (Genesis 1:1)."

I've previously heard the view expressed that, if you can accept the truth of this first verse of the Bible, then you won't have any difficulty with the rest of the Book. There are several reasons why this assertion has merit: people who are confident in God's ability to create the universe are unlikely to doubt His capacity to part the Red Sea, heal the sick or offer them the gift of eternal life. Moreover, if people believe that they themselves were created, they'll see a far greater meaning in life than the apparent randomness which is the natural outworking of believing that we occurred as the consequence of a cosmic accident. Is it any wonder, therefore, that Genesis 1:1 has become one of the most contested Scriptural verses in history?

It surely takes far more faith to believe that something came from nothing, than it does to accept the Biblical account of creation. However, such viewpoints are frequently espoused with the dogmatic zeal of which adherents of Biblical creation are often accused. Indeed, many of these alternative viewpoints contradict one another, but their proponents are united in their refusal to countenance the possibility that there may have been a deliberate act of creation. The reason for this is clearly that acknowledgement of creation necessitates the acceptance of a Creator, and the debate is therefore seen to be far more spiritual than it is scientific.

Interestingly, the complexity of scientific discovery, particularly related to DNA, has led avowed atheists, such as the late Antony

Flew, to re-evaluate their rejection of creation, on the basis that it's implausible to believe that random chance produced the genetic code contained in a single human cell, let alone the entire universe. Of course, none of us really knows how the world came about, because we weren't here at the time: an element of faith is therefore required to accept any supposition or theory. However, the Bible's track record in terms of prophecy fulfilment, which is something we'll look to throughout our series of reflections, strongly indicates that it is a trusted source, both for peering back into history and looking forward towards the future. In Romans 1:20, Paul speaks of creation serving as a revelation of God Himself: just as we might marvel at the skill of an engineer in designing an aeroplane, we surely have to be awestruck when we think of the One Who created the mountains, rivers, meadows and seas!

Satan's strategy is always to sow doubt, as he did when confronting Eve in the Garden of Eden: "Has God indeed said....(Genesis 3:1)?" It's only natural that, as God's adversary, and ours, he'd endeavour to undermine the cornerstone of faith in a Creator; i.e., that He actually created. Paraphrasing an Australian rugby league commentator, Satan is the type of character to promise the earth and deliver a globe, so why not instead trust the God Who created the earth, formed you in His image (Genesis 1:27), and gave His Son to offer you the gift of eternal life?

Throughout this book, I'll end our reflections with a few questions, which are intended to bring what you've read closer to home, as you consider the implications for your own life. Questions just like these:

i. If you believe in creation, are you confident that you could articulate your belief, and why you hold it, in a reasoned discussion with someone who has a different perspective?

ii. If you don't believe in creation, have you stopped to consider why not, or have you simply accepted what you've always been taught?

iii. Again, for those who don't accept creation, if you were to subject your belief, regarding how the world came into existence, to the same scrutiny as has been given to creation, do you believe that it would stand up?

Let's conclude our initial reflection with a word of prayer.

> *Heavenly Father, thank You for creating the world in which we live and for loving me from before the foundation of the earth. Lord Jesus, thank You for coming to redeem the world and for giving Your life for me in an act of selfless love that I may never fully comprehend. Holy Spirit, I ask that You'll bless everyone who reads this book; revealing the love of Jesus to people who do not yet believe and strengthening the faith of those who already do. In Jesus' Name I pray. Amen.*

God's Call On Your Life

"Now the Lord had said unto Abram, Get thee out of thy country, and from thy kindred, and from thy father's house, unto a land that I will show thee: and I will make of thee a great nation, and I will bless thee, and make thy name great; and thou shalt be a blessing (Genesis 12: 1 & 2)."

What a shock Abram must have got that day! I'm sure we all wake up with thoughts of what the coming day might have in store, but I can't imagine any of us look forward to getting a call that will completely change our lives. Of course, for some of us, that's precisely what does happen: we pick up the phone or receive a text and know that things will never be the same again. This is exactly how it was for Abram, except that his call came directly from God. Prior to this time, there is no evidence of Abram having known the Creator God we were considering in the previous reflection: he lived in an area of modern-day Iraq, where deities other than the God of the Bible were to the fore. The message for us, today, is that God loves all human beings equally, irrespective of where we live or what our history might be. It may be that you've come from a place of addiction, broken relationships or rejection of God, but He still has a plan for your life, and the depth of His love is evident from the fact that He gave His Son, Jesus, to die for you on the cross at Calvary. As a consequence, the price for all our sins has been paid and, unlike Abram, who lived prior to Calvary, we don't need to rely on the sacrifices of bulls and goats! If we're willing to accept Jesus's offer of eternal life, the slate is wiped clean, and we start again, with a vista of new opportunities awaiting us. This is what happened when Abram accepted God's invitation: his past was forgotten, and he even received a new name, Abraham, signifying that he was to be a father to the nations.

For all this encouragement, there is a significant word of caution: God's call on our lives can be immensely challenging! We see, in His commissioning of Abraham, that there is an obligation on us to do something with our lives, rather than simply waiting for God to make us into a channel of blessing. Perhaps this is one reason why many believers don't enter into the fullness of what God has prepared for them: could it be that we are reluctant to take the difficult decisions and commit fully to what He is showing us? Of course, we know this is folly - nothing can be better for us than the will of the God Who gave His Son to die for us - but there's still a tendency to 'hang back', whether because of the security we feel where we are, a fear of the unknown, or the spiritual impediments the Enemy puts in our way, as he seeks to thwart God's plans for us.

One striking characteristic of the Bible is that it is a remarkably honest Book: it doesn't attempt to hide the flaws of its heroes and heroines; nor does it make a life of faith sound easier than it is. For Abraham, to leave his homeland was a difficult command, and it was one with which he didn't feel able to fully comply. Like the children of Israel, later in history, he initially travelled only to the border of his intended destination, and remained there for twelve years, during which time he didn't hear from God again! However, this, too, gives us hope: God didn't give up on Abraham and transfer his inheritance to someone else: He loves us in our failures as much as in our triumphs and, for the duration of our life on earth, is always waiting to give us another chance, as soon as we take the first step to come back to Him.

The conclusion to our reflection is found in verse 2, which shows us that God's plans for our lives are infinitely greater than anything we could possibly imagine! As hard as it was for Abraham to leave his homeland, the blessing he subsequently received was to inherit a family that grew into a nation. For us, the challenge may appear too big to contemplate: leaving behind a way of life that 'seems right' or 'feels comfortable', but the rewards are infinite, in keeping with the attributes of the God Who has called us!

Finally, here are a few questions for personal consideration:

i. What is the call that God has placed on your life? Hint: consider the talents and interests He has given you!

ii. Are you currently experiencing a time of spiritual 'dryness'? If so, could it be that you haven't yet fully responded to God's call, as was the case with Abraham?

iii. Is there anything holding you back from entering into the purposes God has for you? If so, be honest with Him, and ask His Holy Spirit to help you overcome this stumbling-block!

Divine Turnaround!

"But as for you, ye thought evil against me; but God meant it unto good, to bring to pass, as it is this day, to save much people alive (Genesis 50:20)."

Have you ever been in what appeared to be an impossible situation, only for God to turn the tables and give you a wonderful testimony? It's an amazing feeling when that happens, but it wouldn't be possible if we didn't first face the adversity! These are frequently the times when we're inclined to cry out to God, asking for deliverance, and there's certainly nothing wrong with doing so. However, it may just be that His response is along the lines of "Not yet; I'm working a special plan through this situation, which will take some time to be revealed." The ultimate example of this is our Saviour, Who prayed in the Garden of Gethsemane for the cup to pass from Him, accepting that it would ultimately be necessary for Him to be made sin for us, to give us the opportunity to inherit eternal life.

People will often say that we need to have 20/20 spiritual vision, but perhaps we'd impact the world far more if we had Genesis 50:20 vision! This verse has obvious overtones of Romans 8:28, illustrating both God's providence and the work of the Holy Spirit in knitting the Bible together into a cohesive message of love, hope and redemption. Joseph's story was an amazing one! I'm sure you'll have heard about his extraordinary coat, which marked him out as being different, and you may also be aware of the dreams that he had, which provoked considerable jealousy amongst his brothers, who, along with Joseph, were the forefathers of the twelve tribes of Israel. Standing out from the crowd was no easier in ancient Israel than it is today: jealousy can prompt us to act in cruel and irrational ways, and Joseph's siblings' hearts ultimately hardened to the extent that they plotted to kill him! However, God had a plan for Joseph, and spared his life, by prompting one of his brothers, Reuben, to speak out on his behalf. This led to Joseph being sold to passing tradesmen, who took him to Egypt (see Genesis 37 for the full story).

It must have been quite a culture shock for Joseph to suddenly be separated from his parents in an alien land, where there was no knowledge of the True God he'd worshipped all his life. However, God's ability to work out His plans for our lives isn't constrained by our location; only by our obedience. Joseph appears to have realised this: rather than complaining about his circumstances or compromising his faith, which he might have perceived as having failed him, he worked assiduously until he became a trusted servant in an aristocratic household. Another setback followed when his character was impugned, leading to a period of imprisonment, during which time Pharaoh had two dreams that defied his understanding, prompting him to enlist the help of Joseph, who'd previously demonstrated his ability to interpret dreams, while in Egypt. Joseph correctly discerned these images as relating to a coming drought, and Pharaoh rewarded him by giving him responsibility for plotting Egypt's course through the impending famine. The wisdom with which God endued Joseph enabled him to make decisions that prospered Egypt, as a result of which representatives of other nations, including his brothers from Israel, came to him for provisions! Thus, what man meant for harm (Joseph's sale into slavery), God used for good (saving millions of souls from starvation).

For us, today, what can we learn from these events? I've noted four main lessons, but I'm sure you can think of many more, drawing on your own experiences.

1. God is in control. Events in our lives, which appear random or meaningless, can be preparing us for His service, many years later. This was the case with Joseph, where his unfortunate initial experience in relation to dreams honed his ability to interpret the warning God gave to Pharaoh.

2. When our circumstances improve, then deteriorate again, it doesn't mean God has forgotten us: He's still working out His plan. It must have been demoralising for Joseph to overcome the shock of betrayal and rise to a position of respectability in his new homeland, only to end up in prison. Moreover, he was detained there two years longer than he might have been, because one of his fellow inmates, Pharaoh's cupbearer, forgot to speak out on his behalf, as he'd promised to do. However, it was this time in prison which established the connection with Pharaoh and, in reality, God didn't allow the cupbearer to remember the pledge until His appointed time for Joseph's release.

3. Our greatest victories have their roots in our most extreme adversities. God thwarted the plan Joseph's brothers had to kill him, but allowed him to be sold into captivity. The reason for this would have been hard to understand at the time but, looking back, as he did in Genesis 50:20, he realised that this was a fundamental part of God's plan. Without Calvary, there'd have been no resurrection!

4. The Enemy will inevitably try to provoke us to doubt; wondering whether our faith is futile, and questioning why a loving God would allow us to suffer so greatly, but Scripture, allied with our life's experience so far, gives us the confidence to know that "we are more than conquerors (Romans 8:37)!"

In closing, it might be appropriate to consider the following questions:

i. Can you recall a time when God's answer to your prayers took longer than you'd hoped?

ii. Has the benefit of hindsight helped you to see how things worked out better than they might have done, had God answered you immediately?

iii. Can you think of an occasion when the suffering you endured may have ultimately yielded some good, either for yourself, or for others?

Passover!

"And the blood shall be to you for a token upon the houses where ye are: and when I see the blood, I will pass over you, and the plague shall not be upon you to destroy you, when I smite the land of Egypt (Exodus 12:13)."

I'm sure many of you will recall attending a Sunday school class that featured the ten plagues which were unleashed on Egypt, before Pharaoh was finally persuaded to allow Moses to lead the Israelites out of captivity. Not everyone, however, is aware that each of these plagues were targeted against Egyptian deities; for example, the Egyptians worshipped the Nile, so in turning water into blood, God was effectively demonstrating His superiority over false idols, which couldn't deliver anyone who venerated them. In contrast, God revealed His power and compassion by withholding the final and most severe of His judgements from everybody who painted the blood of a lamb upon their doorposts.

This criterion for deliverance was a clear precursor of Calvary, and it certainly wasn't a coincidence that Jesus, the Lamb of God (John 1:29), was crucified during the celebration of Passover. The religious leaders of the day tried to ensure this didn't happen, but God is always in control: His Word prefigured the fact that the Jewish Messiah, Who became our Saviour, would give His life for us at this time of year, in order that we might inherit eternal life. There was nothing mankind could do to prevent God's plan from coming to pass, just as the grave had no power to hold Jesus, when He rose again, three days later, to triumph over sin, death and Satan!

Let's consider a few more parallels between Passover and the cross:

1. Deliverance from judgement was open to anyone, irrespective of race, nationality or social standing. If a Jew had failed to apply the blood, their family wouldn't have been spared, whereas an Egyptian family who lived in a house to which the blood was applied would have been set free. Similarly, anybody can come to Jesus: your ethnic background, place of birth or socio-economic status don't matter to God!

2. There was only one way to be saved. A household that sacrificed an animal other than a lamb, or applied the blood to the wrong part of the house, or didn't apply the blood at all, faced devastating consequences. This would be the case, irrespective of their motives, sincerity or alternative means of appealing to God, such as charity or inherent goodness. Similarly, in modern times, the only way to inherit eternal life is to accept Jesus's sacrifice at Calvary.

3. The fairness of judgement continues to be questioned. The plagues wrought upon Egypt may seem harsh, as does the potential for a human being to be separated from God eternally, but judgement wasn't, and isn't, inevitable. God is good, but He can only be good if He is just, in the same way that a magistrate wouldn't be doing a good job if she failed to enforce the law, thereby encouraging others to break it, with potentially life-threatening consequences for others. However, both in ancient Egypt and our own time, judgement can be avoided: God has provided a way for us to be spared, and it's up to us whether we take it.

I understand people questioning why a loving God would send anybody to hell, but it isn't His will for anyone to be lost (see 2 Peter 3:9). The reality is that we send ourselves to hell by not accepting the offer of atonement that's been given to us. In that respect, we genuinely do determine our own destinies: God merely implements the consequences of our decisions. If we decide not to accept Jesus's offer of salvation, we're effectively saying that we don't want to go to heaven, and as Someone Who will never override our will, God then has no option other than, with a heavy and broken heart, to pronounce the judgement from which His Son came to save us.

In conclusion, it might be thought-provoking to consider the following questions:

i. Do you believe that you'd go to heaven if you died today and, if so, why?

ii. If you haven't yet accepted Jesus as your Lord and Saviour, is there a good reason why not?

iii. Would you like to enter into a saving relationship with Jesus? If so, He's only a prayer away! Pray something like this, then tell a trusted Christian acquaintance what you've done, in order that she or he can encourage you in your new faith:

> *Heavenly Father, thank You for loving me before the world was even created. I'm sorry that my thoughts and actions haven't always honoured You but, from now on, I want to serve You and fulfil the purpose You have for my life. Lord Jesus, thank You so much for Your sacrifice at Calvary, which made my salvation possible. I repent of the things that I've done, which have offended You, and ask that You'll fill me with Your Holy Spirit. Holy Spirit, I invite You into my life: please transform me into the person You always intended me to be and guide me in my new life of faith. In Jesus' Precious Name I pray. Amen.*

What I've written isn't a special formula of words, but if you prayed something like this, and believed it in your heart, you are now assured of your place in eternity!

Miraculous Deliverance!

"And Moses stretched out his hand over the sea; and the LORD caused the sea to go back by a strong east wind all that night, and made the sea dry land, and the waters were divided. And the children of Israel went into the midst of the sea upon the dry ground: and the waters were a wall unto them on their right hand, and on their left (Exodus 14: 21 & 22)."

As with the Biblical account of creation, which we were considering at the outset of this book, the parting of the Red Sea, chronicled in Exodus, is frequently cast into doubt: not only by people who aren't yet Christians, but also by those who profess to be sympathetic to our faith. I'd strongly recommend reading the whole chapter for context, and I'll draw upon verses that precede and follow those quoted above, during the course of this reflection.

It was a tremendously exciting time in the nation of Israel: they'd been released from the tyrannical rule of Pharaoh and given the authority to return home, after a period of four hundred and thirty years. The only problem was that, as frequently happens with our own spiritual adversary, the Egyptians didn't give up easily! Instead of honouring their word to let the Israelites go, they pursued after them, and appeared to have them cornered, to the extent that they accused Moses of leading them to their deaths (verse 11)! In fact, this was all part of God's plan to deal with the wicked Egyptian Army once and for all, but to the people who were following Moses it seemed that God had abandoned them. This indeed appeared to be the case, when their circumstances were viewed through natural eyes, as opposed to spiritual ones. It can be the same in our lives today, when we experience illness, redundancy or, especially, bereavement, and wonder where God could possibly be, in the midst of our heartache.

We have the luxury of reading the historical record from the comfort of our own homes, but to the people who were living through these events, they must have been truly terrifying. However, they did have God's assurance, given to Moses, that He would fight for them (verse 14). Whenever we're going through a storm in our own lives, it's imperative that we cling onto God's promises, and the only way we can do this is to spend time in His Word, equipping ourselves for the challenges that will inevitably come. Even then, we may well doubt, but at least we'll have a firm foundation upon which to build!

Anyway, back to verses 21 & 22! Why are they so frequently disputed? The reason is primarily the same as the controversy surrounding Genesis 1:1: a desire to downplay, or perhaps completely deny, the ability of God to perform miracles. From an atheistic perspective, it's rational to accept that non-belief in God leads to a rejection of the miraculous, as one flows from the other. However, it's much harder to understand many, who claim to be Christians, but don't accept the fundamental truths of the Bible: if your 'God' isn't capable of the miraculous, then what's the point of serving 'Him' at all? Once we deny the fundamentals of the Bible, whether relating to creation, the virgin birth or the resurrection of Christ, there's nothing left, and we're not really Christians at all. It's far better to be honest, and say "I no longer believe," than to retain a form of pseudo-faith, thereby stumbling others. Obviously, however, it's infinitely better again to enjoy a genuine, living relationship with the Saviour Who died, and now lives, to give you eternal life!

As with our own trials, it's interesting to consider why God allowed this episode to happen. I can think of at least four reasons, but there are certainly many more:

1. It was a test of the Israelites' faith.

2. Deliverance of the Israelites over the Red Sea confirmed that God had gone with them; i.e., that He hadn't remained in Egypt, as was the case with the Egyptian deities, who only had local jurisdiction.

3. It was a powerful demonstration of God's power and faithfulness, which not only strengthened the faith of those who witnessed it, but also that of their children, to whom the miracle was subsequently related.

4. These events provided the means whereby God could completely destroy (verses 23 - 28) an enemy that had mercilessly persecuted the Israelites, and rejected every plea for clemency.

Here are a few questions for reflection:

i. If you're not currently a Christian, who or what are you putting your trust in?

ii. Rather than investing your hopes in people or institutions that will inevitably fail us, would you like to have faith in a God Who can deliver us from the most extreme of circumstances?

iii. If you already consider yourself to be a Christian, how big is your God? Do you genuinely believe in the omnipotent, miracle-working God of the Bible, or have you constrained Him by the limits of what you believe to be humanly possible?

Made In God's Own Image

"But the stranger that dwelleth with you shall be unto you as one born among you, and thou shalt love him as thyself; for ye were strangers in the land of Egypt: I am the Lord your God (Leviticus 19:34)."

If it hadn't been for the coronavirus, the year of 2020 would perhaps have been characterised by the racial tension that has riven societies in all corners of the globe. Given that we were created in God's own image (Genesis 1:27), it must grieve Him immeasurably to see us destroying one another, for no better reason than the colour of our skin. Tragically, attitudes of racial superiority are frequently found within the church; indeed, churches are perhaps one of the most segregated arenas we attend. Moreover, our intolerance isn't limited to issues of race, but also of dogma, preaching style and personality. As a consequence, fellowships divide and sub-divide, doing irreparable damage to our Christian witness, and breaking the heart of the God Who gave His Son to die for us.

This verse from Leviticus reminds us that, as recipients of the Law, the children of Israel were exhorted to treat incomers as they would their own countrymen and women, remembering their history of exile in Egypt. Approximately 1,300 years later, our Saviour Jesus would become a Child Refugee Himself, as His parents were forced to flee from the evil King Herod. For anyone reading this whose skin colour is the same as my own, it is worth considering the fact that Jesus was almost certainly not white!

Although God loves us all equally, He has a special heart for the impoverished and marginalised, as demonstrated by the laws of gleaning, which required agricultural workers to leave sufficient provision for those in need. In Philippians 2:3, Paul exhorts us to esteem others more than ourselves, and yet we still don't seem to get the message. Perhaps, at the root of the problem, is the fact that we haven't truly yielded ourselves to God. Once we place Him at the pinnacle of our lives, we see everything - and everyone - else in proper perspective. However, while we remain on our own personal 'throne', with God relegated to second place (if that!), everybody else will be considered of lesser importance than ourselves. Those individuals whose viewpoints and philosophies are similar to our own will be given more esteem than the rest, but anybody who differs, whether on account of race, culture or social status, is likely to be relegated to an afterthought, or completely dismissed. Once we categorise and prioritise people in this way, it's the first step to racism, from where we can easily descend into depravities such as the Armenian genocide; justifying our actions by the deplorable assertion that certain people are less than human.

Here are some challenging questions for personal consideration:

i. Are there any people groups you consider to be inferior to yourself? If you're a Christian, this is something to bring before the Lord, in a spirit of repentance!

ii. Are there any categories of individuals you find it easier to share the Gospel with than others? For most of us, the honest answer must be "Yes!" The supplementary question then is how we intend to ensure that everyone has an opportunity to hear the Good News of Jesus, remembering His Great Commission, to go into all the world.

iii. If you're not yet a Christian, have you been put off Christianity by the bigoted attitudes of those who claim to be believers? If so, I apologise, and repent of this sin of the church. However, please be assured that this isn't the heart or attitude of God, Who loves you so much that He sent His Son to die for you.

Finally, let's close in prayer:

> *Heavenly Father, please forgive me for the wrong things I've thought, done or said, as a result of my attitudes towards individuals who are different to me. Lord Jesus, thank You for the fact that You gave Your life for everyone who puts their trust in You; not merely people of a particular ethnicity or nationality. Holy Spirit, please heal the divisions within the church, repair our witness to the world around us, and help me to be the best Christian I can possibly be. In Jesus' Name. Amen.*

Trusting The Lord's Report

"And Caleb stilled the people before Moses, and said, Let us go up at once, and possess it; for we are well able to overcome it. But the men that went up with him said, We are not able to go up against the people, for they are stronger than we (Numbers 13: 30 & 31)."

If video cameras and smart-phones had been around at the time, they'd have captured a palpable sense of excitement: after their dramatic release from captivity and nerve-racking escape through the Red Sea, the twelve tribes of Israel had reached the border of the Promised Land. The background to the two verses quoted above is that Moses sent twelve emissaries to spy out the land, of whom only Joshua and Caleb expressed the view that they should claim the inheritance God had promised them. The majority view prevailed, as a consequence of which an entire generation, except for Joshua and Caleb, ultimately died in the wilderness, while everyone under the age of twenty waited a further thirty-eight years to enter Canaan.

These verses bring out some important points, amongst which we might include the following:

1. The world's report will generally be negative, aligning with the strategy of Satan. It is vital that we critically analyse whatever we hear in the media, considering it carefully and prayerfully, in order to ensure that we're not deceived by the world's agenda. In many instances, the news we hear may contain a substantial element of truth, as in this passage, where the emissaries genuinely did see potential enemies who were far bigger than they were. Of course, Joshua and Caleb saw these

giants, too: they didn't overlook them, but interpreted what they saw in the light of the promises they'd received from God.

2. The Enemy will attempt to persuade us that all is lost, whether for our family, ministry or nation, in an endeavour to dissuade us from fighting for them in prayer. If we listen unquestioningly, we are likely to pay a heavy price, as did the Israelites who failed to claim their inheritance.

3. God's servants will generally be in a minority, but He still gives us the victory, provided we fight His battle according to His plan. One of the reasons the world is currently in such a desperate state is the widespread abandonment of godly principles, as legislation is enacted in accordance with the will of the people. Of course, this is the essence of democracy, but it does mean that, when the majority are off track, they take everyone else with them! Jesus never promised us that His followers would be in a majority, so if this is what we're waiting for we'll be disappointed. Instead, we must discern the times we're living in and fight the spiritual battle that's in front of us, interceding for the release from captivity of those who do not yet know Jesus.

4. It is imperative that we see ourselves as the Lord sees us. It's instructive to consider Jesus's letters to the seven churches in Revelation: the ones that received the greatest rebuke were those that believed they were doing the best, while particular praise was bestowed upon the churches which felt they had least to offer. This can be the case in our lives, too: the occasions we feel we 'have it made' are the times when we're most likely to stumble, whereas an awareness of our weakness makes us reliant on the Lord's direction, thereby keeping us on track.

Seeing ourselves as the Lord does can have positive and negative connotations, but both are equally valid. It may be that there are aspects of our lives which are not pleasing to Him: if so, now is the right time to address these and make a new start, knowing that, if we keep short accounts with Him on this side of eternity, we will be far more effective servants in this life, and much less likely to forgo rewards in the next one. On the other hand, we must also eschew false modesty: the 'grasshopper mentality' (Numbers 13:33) can lead to us disqualifying ourselves from the ministry God has given us, just as the Israelites talked themselves out of entering the Promised Land, and suffered immeasurably as a consequence.

So then, the question is: how does the Lord see us? Well, as we've considered previously, we're precious to Him, and made in His image: indeed, Psalm 139:14 brings us the welcome news that we're "fearfully and wonderfully made!" Although this is true of all human beings, there is a special position reserved for those who put their faith in Jesus as their Saviour. At this point, God transfers Jesus's righteousness to us, meaning that our sins are forgiven, despite us being no better than anyone else. This is the nature of the 'Great Exchange', as theologians call it: Jesus took our sin upon Himself and, in its place, gave us His right-standing with God! A decision not to put our faith in Jesus means that we must be judged on our own merits, which inevitably fall short of God's standard of perfection. In this respect, it's not our sin that condemns us, but our refusal to accept the payment Jesus made on our behalf. As American pastor Greg Laurie is wont to say, "Heaven isn't for good people; it's for forgiven people!" All we have to do is accept God's offer of forgiveness!

Finally, here are three questions to ponder:

i. During this tumultuous period in world history, whose report have you been listening to?

ii. Have you been deterred from following God's plan for your life, because of fear or anxiety? If so, the good news is that it's not too late to do something about it!

iii. Is there a difference between how God sees you and the way you perceive yourself?

Abundant Blessings!

"And all these blessings shall come on thee, and overtake thee, if thou shalt hearken unto the voice of the Lord thy God (Deuteronomy 28:2)."

Just like the Law, the blessings and curses of which we read in Deuteronomy 27 - 29 were given to the nation of Israel. Please don't ever give credence to commentators who suggest that the Church has replaced Israel: this 'replacement theology' is unscriptural false teaching which, amongst other atrocities, has been used to justify the Holocaust. Taking on board these words of serious caution, we learn so much from the Old Testament: not only in terms of history and prophecy, but also the principles of sowing and reaping, which are as valid in our spiritual lives as they are in agriculture. Just as sowing sprouts won't yield turnips, defying the Word of God will ultimately lead to disillusionment, discouragement and despair, however well we may feel things are going in the short-term.

The Bible contains a multitude (estimated at around 7,000) of promises, many of which are conditional: in other words, we receive a gift or blessing, provided we comply with an instruction that's given to us. We're familiar with this concept from the time we were children, when our parents might have promised us a trip to the seaside, provided we tidied our room. When God makes a conditional promise, He's behaving in a different way to our parents: His intention isn't to bribe us to do something for Him, but to concentrate our minds on what He knows to be best for us. One of the great things about serving such a mighty God is that He is omniscient, which means He knows everything! Unlike ourselves, who always have an element of doubt when making a decision, such as moving house or changing job, God knows absolutely what is best for us, and what will do us harm. This is why, when the Bible tells us to do something, we should do it: not because God requires our help in any way, but because He knows it's what we need, even though it may not feel like it at the time. Viewing the landscape from the other direction, activities the Bible instructs us not to engage in should be avoided, because they will ultimately damage us, whether emotionally, physically or spiritually, even if it takes a considerable time for the repercussions to become evident.

The name 'Deuteronomy' means 'Second Giving of the Law', and the Book chronicles Moses's reiteration of the Law to the people, prior to their delayed entry to the Promised Land. Rather than simply giving them a list of rules to follow, God enacted a scene, whereby everyone was made aware of the blessings which would be bestowed upon them, if they incorporated His will into their lives. As New Testament believers, we have even greater promises made to us, including: every good and perfect gift (James 1:17), the peace of God, which passes all understanding (Philippians 4:7), and that all things work together for good (Romans 8:28)! As you may well be aware, each of these promises is conditional. Receipt of "every good gift" depends upon us not yielding to temptation, the peace of God is given to those who "make their requests known to the Lord with supplication and thanksgiving" and, as I'm sure you know, all things only work together for the good of those who "love God" and who are "called according to His purpose."

This is not to say that God is ever beholden to us, or that He loves us any less when we omit to fulfil a certain precondition: it's simply that His nature is to want to bless us and, if you'll forgive the clumsy anthropomorphism, He almost can't help Himself from pouring out His blessings on us, whenever we come to Him. Similarly, God isn't judging us when He withholds His blessing, as when we yield to temptation and don't receive "every good thing:" it's simply that He loves us too much to see us destroy ourselves, and therefore keeps good things back from us to bring us to our senses. If He was to openly reward us for doing wrong, it would confirm us in our disobedience, thereby posing a danger to ourselves, and contradicting God's character of holiness and purity. Of course, the most important blessing in the Bible is conditional, too! As we read in John 3:16, eternal life is only promised to those who believe in God's Son, Jesus, which is a topic we've touched on in relation to Passover, and will no doubt visit again.

Finally, for now, here are three questions for reflection:

i. Does it make sense that a God Who loves us, and knows what's best for us, would lay down boundaries for our conduct?

ii. Can you think of any blessings you might be missing out on, as a consequence of not completely yielding to God's will for your life?

iii. Why is eternal life only promised to those who accept Jesus as their Saviour? Hint: consider God's character of holiness and purity, and His obligation to be a righteous Judge.

Memorials

> *"That this may be a sign among you, that when your children ask their fathers in time to come, saying, What mean ye by these stones? Then ye shall answer them, That the waters of Jordan were cut off before the ark of the covenant of the Lord; when it passed over Jordan, the waters of Jordan were cut off: and these stones shall be for a memorial unto the children of Israel forever (Joshua 4: 6 & 7)."*

Throughout Scripture, we see that God frequently does similar things in different ways, in order to prevent us from becoming unduly prescriptive about His methods. We observe this, for example, in the recorded account of Jesus's healing ministry: blind eyes were opened and deaf ears unblocked, but never the same way twice!

When God repeats something, it's always for emphasis, and the miraculous crossing of the Jordan, as the Israelites finally entered into the Promised Land, had obvious echoes of their parents' generation's deliverance across the Red Sea, approximately four decades previously. Another characteristic of God, which is evident from His Word, is His general avoidance of shrines and memorials: where these occur, they are usually man-made, and can easily lead to forms of idolatry, whereby we worship the image instead of our Lord. The event of which we read today is therefore unusual in at least two ways: the evident parallel with the Red Sea crossing and the instruction to create a memorial.

In some respects, the parting of the Jordan River was a dramatic memorial in itself, prompting the people to reflect upon the recollections their parents had shared with them, of how they'd crossed the Red Sea. It also served to emphasise that God was with them, and their new leader Joshua: almost as if He was saying, "I know you revered Moses, but the miracles he performed were contingent on his relationship with Me, and I can work through Joshua just as easily as I could through Moses!" But what of the physical memorial of the stones on the river bank? As our chosen verses reveal, we don't have to rely on our imagination for an answer, because the Bible tells us! The stones were intended to serve as a permanent reminder to the Israelites of God's faithfulness and goodness.

I've often heard it said that we should never look back, but this strikes me as being curious advice! Certainly, we shouldn't be so bound by the failures of the past that we're unable to move forward; nor should we become so obsessed with previous successes that we don't endeavour to make a brighter future. However, if we don't remember the things God has already done for us, how can we have faith for today or tomorrow? This brings us to the substantive reason for memorials in all our lives. I've listed three; how many more can you think of?

1. Memorials help us to remember God's faithfulness in delivering us from - or through - past trials, thereby giving us the confidence that He can, and will, deliver us again. One pastor I know describes the "little faith" of which Jesus talked as failing to have faith for God to intervene in our lives to the same extent as we've previously experienced. Thus, for example, if He delivered us from depression in 1988, it would demonstrate little faith not to believe He could do the same thing again, in 2020 or beyond. Memorials therefore serve as 'faith markers' for the things we can reasonably anticipate that He might do in our lives.

2. Memorials strengthen our testimony. If we tell people a story, it can paint a picture in their minds, of what God has done in our lives. However, a tangible demonstration brings the reality to life, just as the children of Israel were given a visual symbol of how their ancestors finally came into the land.

3. Memorials remind the Enemy of past defeats! We're engaged in a spiritual battle and, just as a championship pennant reminds a team's rivals who the champions are, our monuments to God's faithfulness leave Satan in no doubt that, while we may be bloodied and wearied from time to time, we'll ultimately emerge victorious.

Finally, here are three questions for practical consideration:

i. What are the things that God has done in your life, which serve as memorials to His goodness?

ii. Have you been faithful to share these testimonies; e.g., with your children, people who aren't yet Christians, or believers who are struggling with their faith?

iii. What battle are you currently facing that, with the Lord's help, you can turn into a testimony, or memorial, of His faithfulness?

Strategy

"And it shall come to pass, that when they make a long blast with the ram's horn, and when ye hear the sound of the trumpet, all the people shall shout with a great shout; and the wall of the city shall fall down flat, and the people shall ascend up every man straight before him (Joshua 6:5)."

I'd love to have seen the officers' faces, as Joshua convened his council of war, and outlined his battle plan for capturing Jericho! As many of you will doubtless know, Joshua's army was instructed to walk around the city once a day for six days, followed by seven circuits on the final, victorious, day that features in the verse chosen for this reflection. Of course, it wasn't Joshua's own plot at all, but it was the strategy for victory given to him by God Himself. I wonder if Joshua had any doubts, as if to say, "God, I know You've delivered us from Egypt, and just enabled us to miraculously cross the Jordan, but is this really the best plan You can offer?" Perhaps more pertinently, he might have confided, during a time of private prayer, "Lord, I trust You, and know nothing is too difficult for You, but how am I going to communicate this strategy to my troops?" After all, Joshua was a new leader, following on from Moses, who the people greatly revered, despite their numerous disagreements with him.

Even outstanding men and women of faith, such as Joshua, have their doubts, but if he didn't, then I'm sure his army did! Imagine a trained fighting unit being told that there'll be no siege, nor even a battle; just a combination of marching, horn blowing and shouting! This leads us to some important practical applications for our own lives of faith, which I've outlined below.

1. We have an obligation to follow God's strategy, even when it seems unusual. Our refusal to do this will result in failure: Jericho wouldn't have been captured if Joshua's army had marched around the city thirteen times on the one day, or employed more traditional military methods, against the will of God. Our focus has to be on serving the Lord, and not on how we are perceived.

2. Spiritual leaders must remain true to Scripture, or any tested word they receive from the Lord, irrespective of the potential impact on their reputation or popularity. It would have been easy for Joshua to say, "We can't possibly do that!" However, the consequence would have been disastrous, both for the campaign against Jericho and for his own leadership.

3. We need to respect our leaders and continue to support them, until such time as they demonstrably step outside of God's will. Had Joshua's army rebelled, a division would have occurred in the nation which may not have been easily healed.

This analysis comes with an obvious word of caution: it's imperative that we're not misled by unscriptural philosophies, simply because they appear to be spiritual or exciting. The first port of call for testing whether a plan or suggestion comes from God is the Bible: He will never tell us to do something which contradicts His Word. In some instances, the Bible won't provide a definitive answer, as when we're pondering a possible change of career. In these situations, it's advisable to ask the Lord to reveal His will, by coming to Him in a spirit of prayer and fasting, in addition to seeking the counsel of trusted believers. Failure to test an apparent word from the Lord has led many to ridicule or ruin, so be careful. It wasn't the circuits of Jericho that brought the walls down, nor the blast of the ram's horn, nor even the shouts of the people. Victory was given to the people by the Lord, because they followed His strategy for success, and it will be the same in our lives, too.

Has Joshua's example inspired you sufficiently to consider some questions?

i. Can you think of a time when God directed you along a path that seemed unconventional, but which ultimately led to the receipt of blessing?

ii. What would you do if your pastor announced a plan for your church that appeared unusual, but wasn't overtly contrary to Scripture?

iii. Have you ever been led astray by something which looked alluring, but wasn't actually from God? If so, has the benefit of this experience made you less likely to be deceived next time?

Anarchy

"In those days there was no king in Israel: every man did that which was right in his own eyes (Judges 21:25)."

God's intention was always for Israel to be a theocracy: a nation governed by Him. Ultimately, they rejected this provision, and demanded a king, just like the countries around them. However, prior to this, they were ruled by judges, some of whom were faithful to the Lord, and others whose careers were distinctly chequered. The Book of Judges, which concludes with the verse quoted above, describes a pattern that society has repeated during subsequent millennia. At times of crisis, the nation turned to the Lord and received miraculous deliverance, as when Gideon defeated the Midianite Army with three hundred men, some pots and torches (see Judges 7 for the full story)! In time, deliverance gave way to complacency, as people began to rely on their own strength, drifted further from the Lord, and ultimately fell into captivity, from which they again required to be set free, at which point the cycle began again. Recent history has followed a similar pattern, as nations declared days of prayer during global conflict, emerged into materialistic success, then completely disregarded the God to Whom the previous generation had been interceding.

It's not just countries that fall into this trap: we do, too! Has this been the case in your life? I know it has in mine! A major crisis emerges, such as unemployment or a serious medical diagnosis, at which point we cling tightly to God, knowing that no-one else has the power or authority to deliver us from the existential threat that is coming close to engulfing us. Being faithful, as He is, God then delivers us, albeit not necessarily in the manner or timeframe we might have been anticipating. Although we're grateful, we start to take our new, improved circumstances for granted and, at the back of our mind, wonder whether our answer to prayer was merely a coincidence. This reinforces our sense that everything's alright now, and we begin to trust more in ourselves and less in our Saviour. That's not to say we turn completely from Him: we still attend church, sing His praises and genuinely profess our faith, but our relationship isn't as close as it was when times were hard - until the next crisis hits!

If this is a cycle you recognise, the good news is that it's not too late to do something about it! The first thing we need to do is become more intentional about our relationship with God, setting aside time for prayer and worship, outside of the regular routine of church attendance. Rather than waiting for a crisis in our own lives to provoke us to urgent prayer, let's consider the needs which exist around us, and bring them before the Lord: not as a 'shopping list', but in earnest intercession, as our hearts break for the condition of our families, nations and communities. When we begin to seriously intercede for others, I'm convinced that we'll observe a transformation - not only in the lives of the people we've been praying for, but also in ourselves! As we develop this rhythm of prevailing upon the Lord for His provision, and thanking Him for His answers to prayer, we'll learn to walk step by step with Him, and see the world from a completely different perspective, as the Holy Spirit nudges us to pray for situations in which He longs to intervene.

Three questions you might like to consider are:

i. Have you found it difficult to break the cycle described in this reflection?

ii. Is life more rewarding when you're walking more closely with the Lord?

iii. Who are the people you would pray for, if you were to urgently bring your petitions before the Lord, rather than waiting for a crisis to develop in your own life?

Let's continue this theme, by importuning the Lord in prayer:

> *Heavenly Father, thank You for loving us, even when we don't come before You, or fail to express our gratitude for the difference You've made to our lives. Lord Jesus, thank You for the fact that You died for me, and still loved me, even when my heart was far from You. Holy Spirit, please give me a heart for precious souls who do not yet know Jesus as their Saviour: to fast and pray for them, taking their salvation as seriously as I do my own. In Jesus' Name. Amen.*

Godly Disobedience!

"And Ruth said, Entreat me not to leave thee, or to return from following after thee: for whither thou goest, I will go; and where thou lodgest, I will lodge: thy people shall be my people, and thy God my God (Ruth 1:16)."

You may have been tempted to take a second look at the title for this reflection, and I certainly wouldn't have blamed you! It sounds contradictory, but Ruth's beautiful pledge of allegiance to her mother-in-law, Naomi, was actually in direct opposition to the instruction she had given her in verse 8, to go and return to her mother's house. Naomi's other daughter-in-law, Orpah, acceded to this request, but Ruth insisted that she return with Naomi to Bethlehem. In most cases in Scripture, where one person obeys and the other disobeys, the former flourishes and the latter suffers rebuke, but on this occasion it was different: Ruth was immeasurably blessed (you'll have to read the rest of this amazing love story to find out what happened, if you don't already know!), but we don't hear of Orpah again! So, the question is, whether there is ever a time for what we might call 'godly disobedience'. The answer is most definitely that there is: it's all a matter of the heart!

In the context of Ruth's story, it's instructive to consider the reason for Naomi making her request for her daughters-in-law to return to their family homes. In the recent past, Naomi's husband had died, as had her two sons, who were the husbands of Ruth and Orpah. This sequence of events not only caused devastation within the family, but also created immense financial distress, given the patriarchal nature of society at the time. Naomi's request was therefore borne out of a combination of grief and a genuine concern for the prospects of two people about whom she cared, but for whom she was unable to provide. By deciding to return with Naomi to Bethlehem, Ruth wasn't disrespectfully disregarding her mother-in-law's wishes, as is frequently the case when we disobey; rather she was making a commitment to stand by someone she loved, irrespective of the consequences. This is the determining factor in considering whether or not our actions are pleasing to God: are we behaving in a manner that's consistent with people's long-term best interests, out of a motivation of love, or are we seeking our own advancement, despite our motives outwardly appearing to be blameless? Ruth was acting out of pure love and, when her mother-in-law saw this, the two of them embarked on the sad journey to Judah, completely unaware of what God had in store for them.

There will inevitably be times in our own lives when we encounter the choice between acceding to someone's wishes, and doing something that is in their best interests, despite them not seeing it at the time. This could happen when a person we care about requires medical intervention, but tells us to leave them alone, on the basis of their belief that everything will be okay. Such a dilemma frequently arises in the spiritual realm, too. If we have a friend or family member who tells us that they don't want anything to do with the Lord, do we continue to fast and pray for them, or do we give up completely? Of course, we know that salvation is in everyone's best interests, so we hopefully don't give up, although it is a delicate situation that requires tact and diplomacy, because incessantly witnessing to someone who doesn't want to hear about Jesus will invariably be counter-productive. Although we can be confident that coming to know the Lord is consistent with His will, we can't pretend to know the best way to bring this about, which makes it imperative for us to invite the Holy Spirit into the situation; asking Him to reveal to us the right things to say, the appropriate time to say them and, just as importantly, to help us say them in the right way! In some circumstances, it may not be a case of saying anything at all: it might be that our lives are required to be a witness, demonstrating the love and compassion of God to someone who's had a negative experience of the church, or of Christians in general.

Ruth's demonstration of love towards Naomi was as selfless as it was beautiful, and it was also remarkable, as she came from the land of Moab, whose people were traditionally hostile towards the nation of Israel, from which Naomi hailed. Furthermore, it is an act for which we should all be immensely grateful, because it ultimately led to her appearing in the genealogy of our Saviour, Jesus Christ! If we were to act so selflessly today, putting the interests of others before our own, what might the consequences be?

Here are a few more questions with which to conclude:

i. Have you ever been in a situation where the right thing to do was to 'disobey'?

ii. Are you confident in knowing when to accede to the wishes of another, and when not to do so?

iii. Do you constantly seek the guidance of the Holy Spirit, inviting Him into every decision you make? If not, why not start today?

A Well-kept Pledge

"And she (Hannah) vowed a vow, and said, O Lord of hosts, if thou wilt indeed look on the affliction of thine handmaid, and remember me, and not forget thine handmaid, but will give unto thine handmaid a man child, then I will give him unto the Lord all the days of his life, and there shall no razor come upon his head (1 Samuel 1:11)."

I'm sure we've all had times when we've made a vow, or promise, to the Lord in prayer, only to break it a short while later. The pattern is generally similar to the cycle we considered in our reflection on the concluding verse of Judges: a place of desperation provokes us to ardent prayer, then deliverance comes, and we're suddenly not so keen to pay what we promised! In many of those instances, we may never have intended to pay at all, while in others our reconsideration follows an evaluation of the cost, whether in terms of our time or financial resources. How grateful we must be that God keeps His promises to us!

Hannah's prayer was a most understandable cry of the heart: in keeping with many women, she longed to have a child of her own. Moreover, the society in which she lived considered it to be a curse for a woman not to have children, so she was no doubt something of a pariah, despite the love of her husband, which was complicated by the fact that his other wife did have children! In this context, there must have been many women in Israel who besought the Lord for a son or daughter, but it is Hannah's prayer that the Holy Spirit chose to record for posterity. One reason for this is her obvious sincerity, which was frequently misunderstood, as in her conversation with the priest, Eli, which follows the verse quoted above. Sincerity allied to integrity make for a powerful combination, and Hannah's integrity is illustrated by her decision to honour the commitment she made in relation to her new son, once she received the blessing she desired. Imagine how difficult this must have been! It was hard enough not to have children in the Israel of Hannah's day, but surely almost unconscionable to give up the son you'd hoped and prayed for, to then only be able to see him once a year. Yet this is precisely what Hannah did: dedicating her son, Samuel, to live in the Temple, from where he graduated to become Israel's greatest judge, and mentor to their greatest king so far, David.

The Lord blessed Hannah with five other children, subsequent to her dedication of Samuel, but she wasn't to know this at the time: as far as she was concerned, she was giving up the only child she would ever have. Moreover, the nation of Israel was also blessed immeasurably with a man who, in large part due to the prayers and devotion of his mother, reversed the spiritual decline of previous generations. What can we learn from this moving account of one mother's prayers? There are at least four lessons I believe we can take on board:

1. It is essential that we align our will with God's: if we pray for outcomes that aren't consistent with His will for us, we can't expect positive answers, and we shouldn't want them, either!

2. As Hannah did, we need to pursue God's purpose for our lives, irrespective of the cost: this is far easier said than done, but we will lead much more rewarding lives if we're able to at least come close to this ideal.

3. We must never give up, even when others mock or discourage us, as happened to Hannah (see 1 Samuel 1:14). Satan will continually send agents to discourage us from fulfilling God's plan for our lives, but don't give him the satisfaction of denying us our inheritance!

4. Always be honest with God: He knows the truth anyway, but our failure in this point damages our relationship with Him.

Finally, here are some questions for private thought, or discussion within the family.

i. What is a more sensible option than making a vow you don't intend to pay?

ii. Is there a desire of your heart for which you'd be prepared to make the kind of sacrifice Hannah did?

iii. What is the most precious entity that you could dedicate to God?

A God Without Limits!

"And Jonathan said to the young man that bare his armour, Come, and let us go over unto the garrison of these uncircumcised: it may be that the Lord will work for us: for there is no restraint to the Lord to save by many or by few (1 Samuel 14:6)."

What an awesome demonstration of faith! The Philistines had been tormenting Israel for years but, despite his physical stature, King Saul had neither the military wherewithal nor the spiritual insight to address the situation. There was no imminent prospect of the Philistines actually mounting an invasion, but they inflicted damage in minor skirmishes from time to time, and posed what we might call today a low-grade national security threat. Issues that are left unattended in our lives will frequently develop into significant problems, robbing us of joy and distracting us from our substantive calling. Ultimately, they have to be dealt with: the longer they're left unattended, the harder they become to resolve, and the more faith is required to effect a resolution! Jonathan and his armour bearer demonstrate the depth of the faith that can be needed in such a scenario, with valuable lessons for our own lives.

In contrast to his father, King Saul, Jonathan's faith could never be questioned. He was evidently embarrassed by the nation's inability to deal with the Philistines, which not only offended his patriotism, but was also an affront to his God. However, it's important to emphasise that he acted out of faith, rather than recklessness, and there's a world of difference between the two. It's imperative that we don't tempt God by embarking on a course of action, without having first sought Him, in the expectation that He has a duty to preserve us! Jonathan wasn't presumptuous: he tested the situation to see whether the Lord was in it: had he felt His restraining hand, he would have gone back but, when no restraint came, he ventured forward and achieved a great victory, as we read further on in 1 Samuel 14. When people accomplish things for the Lord which appear remarkable, it's generally the case that those endeavours had been incubated in prayer for a considerable period previously. We cannot expect the Lord to be with us, and manifest His presence in our lives, unless we've first been with Him in prayer! It is also incumbent upon us to spend time with the Lord after victory has been achieved, giving Him the glory, as both Jonathan and his friend David did on numerous occasions.

Extending Jonathan's logic further, God could have delivered the Philistines into his hand only, rather than the joint endeavour of Jonathan and his armour bearer. Indeed, He could have done the job on His own, which is something that happened when a single angel of the Lord wiped out 185,000 of the Assyrian Army (2 Kings 19:35). There's always a danger of reading too much into these things, but there are three lessons I'm sure we can learn from this. The first is that God rejoices in using people to accomplish wonderful results, whatever their talents may be. Thus, if we're willing to be used, as Jonathan's armour bearer evidently was, He'll use us! The second is that we need to be on our guard, defending ourselves both prior and subsequent to entering battle. Our equivalent of Jonathan's armour bearer is the shield of faith and other spiritual armour referenced by Paul in Ephesians 6. The third lesson is the importance of encouragement: we will frequently encounter people, even in the church, who try to deter us from moving forward; generally because their faith has stagnated and they want everyone else to stagnate with them. A Christian life of vibrant fulfilment is terribly convicting to somebody who's content to offer the minimum requirement for entry into heaven! Behind every great leader is a great encourager: the armour bearer was to Jonathan what Barnabus was to Paul! Having said that, there's obviously a significant contrast between negativity and wise counsel. We need to know the difference, both when giving and receiving advice: shun the former and embrace the latter!

It is evident from this passage of Scripture that Jonathan's faith was in stark contrast to the attitude of his father, Saul. It's generally the case that, when the Enemy is unable to prevent us from achieving something worthwhile in the service of the Lord, he'll turn his attention to discouraging us. Discouragers are always close at hand, and they're frequently motivated by a combination of jealousy and religion, which led to Saul's admonition of Jonathan and his attempt to have his own son killed, because of his failure to observe an ill-conceived fast, of which he hadn't even been aware! Fortunately, the people wouldn't hear of it, and exulted in the victory that had been won for them by two courageous men. Naysayers are frequently characterised by laziness, unpreparedness for action and hollow words. Saul embodied these traits perfectly; not even having a sword with which to fight (1 Samuel 13:22), confirming that he had no intention of entering the battle, and relaxing under a pomegranate tree (1 Samuel 14:3)! It's particularly important in this regard for us to protect our minds with the helmet of salvation; constantly living in the light of what Jesus accomplished at Calvary, without being drawn into petty skirmishes that deflect us from the main conflict.

Happily, our own potential to serve the Lord isn't constrained by heritage or genealogy: our parents may not have set the best example, but He can still use us in a special way; all He needs is for us to dedicate our lives to Him! By the same token, a rich spiritual heritage can easily be squandered: each of us needs to dedicate our lives to God, rather than depending on the faith of our parents, or even the reputation of our own ministry. Whether or not your family modelled a life of abundant faith, it's entirely possible that you may currently be facing overwhelming circumstances. If so, don't wait for the problem to get any worse: follow Jonathan's example and commit the situation to the Lord; there's no knowing what He might do!

Finally, here are a few questions for personal reflection:

i. Is there a situation in your life that you're leaving unattended, which will require more faith to address, the longer you leave it?

ii. Have you ever acted impetuously and regretted it? I'm sure we all have, but hopefully we're learning the difference between faith and recklessness!

iii. Who do you most closely resemble in this story: the Philistines, who taunted God's people, King Saul, who discouraged the Lord's servants, Jonathan and his armour bearer, who exhibited tremendous faith, or the people of Israel, who rejoiced in the victory, but didn't contribute to it?

Enquiring Of The Lord

"Therefore David enquired of the Lord, saying, Shall I go and smite these Philistines? And the Lord said unto David, Go, and smite the Philistines, and save Keilah. And David's men said unto him, Behold, we be afraid here in Judah: how much more then if we come to Keilah against the armies of the Philistines? Then David enquired of the Lord yet again. And the Lord answered him and said, Arise, go down to Keilah; for I will deliver the Philistines into thine hand (1 Samuel 23: 2 - 4)."

Isn't it noticeable how frequently we run aground, when we take important decisions without consulting the Lord? I once heard someone describe our relationship with God as being like that of a motorist with a spare wheel: we don't give Him a second thought until we suffer a puncture! As amusing as this may sound, our failure to commit important decisions to prayer can have serious ramifications for our lives, as when we believe we've fallen in love, don't invite the Holy Spirit into the relationship, then cry out for help, once we realise we've married the wrong person.

David wasn't king at the time of the episode at the centre of our reflection, but he had been anointed by Samuel, and both of them knew that this anointing was ultimately from God. It would therefore have been very easy for David to take matters into his own hands, either by accelerating his accession to the throne or, in this instance, mounting a presumptuous attack, without seeking God's will. However, rather than imperiously reasoning that, "I'm God's chosen vessel, so He'll have no option but to bail me out," he humbled himself by seeking the Lord's direction; not once, but twice. When the Lord gave David the assurance of victory, he was obedient to His exhortation to attack the Philistines, thereby liberating Keilah.

There is a great deal that we can learn from these events, and the following observations could be valuable life lessons:

1. We should always consult the Lord before making significant decisions: as intelligent as we may think we are, we're not always the best judges of what to do, especially where our emotions are concerned.

2. Our feelings mustn't be allowed to govern how we act: in verse 3, we read that David's men were afraid, even in the relative sanctuary of Judah, but their leader had God's assurance that it was right to attack, and that's all they needed.

3. Even in the spiritual realm, we shouldn't always be on the offensive: just as in military conflict, there can be times when it is appropriate for an individual to offer support to the combatants, without becoming directly involved. This advice is particularly pertinent to taking on demonic strongholds, when we're not properly equipped to do so.

4. Entering into battle when the time isn't right, or without the appropriate armour, can recklessly endanger others, in addition to putting ourselves at risk.

Although the kingdom was promised to David, he still had to wait for it, and fight significant battles along the way. Similarly, while we have an absolute assurance of eternal life, we'll inevitably face situations where we're required to fight to release people from captivity, albeit that these will generally be spiritual battles, rather than armed conflicts! It's important to remember, however, that people who don't yet know Jesus are not the enemy: they're the prisoners we're seeking to set free, through the power of the Holy Spirit!

In closing, these three questions might make for interesting consideration:

i. Can you think of a time in your life when your failure to consult the Lord resulted in a circumstance you regretted? If so, what have you learned from this?

ii. Would you be willing to resolve to commit significant decisions to prayer, rather than proceeding to action without seeking the Lord?

iii. If you were to seek the Lord's guidance in a particular situation, how would you know what He was telling you to do?

Mourning

"And they mourned, and wept, and fasted until even, for Saul, and for Jonathan his son, and for the people of the Lord, and for the house of Israel; because they were fallen by the sword (2 Samuel 1:12)."

I've heard some extraordinary statements in relation to grief; many of them from professing Christians. For instance, I recall opening the door to a minister who had come to console me, following mum's death, only to be met by the back of his head, as he proclaimed that he was admiring the view! Perhaps this type of behaviour stems from the perspective we have, as Christians, in relation to eternity. Certainly, the attitude of this minister (who did a great deal to encourage me in my tentative first steps of faith, and to whom I remain greatly indebted) contrasted starkly to that of mum's MacMillan nurse, who wasn't a believer, despite expressing the thought that she'd like to be. Christians frequently quote Paul's statement from 1 Thessalonians 4:13, that "We do not sorrow as others who have no hope," when counselling fellow believers who are grieving the loss of a loved one. However, this analysis only applies when the person we have lost is a Christian and, even then, it probably isn't what we want to hear at the time!

In addition to providing us with the roadmap to salvation and chronicling the development of Christianity, from its origins in Judaism to Jesus's resurrection and beyond, the Bible also teaches us valuable lessons with regard to our responses to a wide range of real-life situations. So, what does the verse we're reflecting on just now have to say about our reaction to grief? I've chosen to highlight five points for consideration, but these are in no way prescriptive, so feel free to disagree, or add your own perspective!

1. Grief is an appropriate response to losing someone we care about: there is absolutely no need to apologise for the way we're feeling, although it never does any harm to explain to the people around us that we're mourning, and may therefore possibly say the wrong thing from time to time. Our emotions are given to us by God, and the naturalness of grief has its roots in the fact that we were not born to die, but that death arises from the curse which was unleashed upon the world, as a consequence of original sin. Although we have the assurance that we will, one day, be reunited with believers who we love, grieving the loss of someone we don't know to be saved is particularly difficult, as we're forced to contemplate the possibility of eternity without them, in addition to missing them immensely in the here and now. It is therefore imperative that we give ourselves time to mourn, avoiding the temptation to rush back to work too early, or to take on too much responsibility, in a quest to 'drown out' our grief.

2. It is important to be sensitive to the feelings of others, who in some instances may be feeling either more or less heartbroken, or might be expressing their grief in a different way. It will inevitably be an immensely stressful time for families or businesses, as they mourn the loss of a pivotal figure and come to terms with life without them. In addition to the sudden void at the dinner table, behind the kiosk, or in the boardroom, there can be an awkward dynamic, as some of those who've been bereaved express inconsolable grief, while the reactions of others are perhaps more measured. As best as we can in the circumstances, we need to try to remember that everyone reacts differently to shock, and that there will be as many different manifestations of grief as there are people who've been bereaved. This brings us on to point number three.

3. Our sense of mourning, or that of our friends and colleagues, won't necessarily be defined by the nature of the relationship we had with the person who died. This is illustrated by David, who grieved considerably for Saul, despite the fact that his predecessor to the throne had, on more than one occasion,

attempted to kill him! For some people, the loss of a grandparent will be a devastating event, while for others it will scarcely register, owing to the distance in the relationship, whether emotionally or geographically.

4. We mustn't allow our grief to control us. Although David, and his nation, mourned for Saul and Jonathan, they had important work to do, and couldn't allow their emotions to overwhelm them, because they would otherwise have become vulnerable to enemy attack. For this reason, David, who was Saul's anointed successor, had less opportunity to grieve than his subjects, despite the fact that he almost certainly felt the sense of loss, particularly for Jonathan, more acutely than anyone. We, too, must be vigilant: while grief is entirely natural, as considered above, it can be used by our spiritual adversary to lead us into a tailspin of depression, and it's important that we don't stop functioning entirely, for the sake both of ourselves and the people who depend on us.

5. Possibly our best response to grief, having negotiated the initial trauma, is to make our lives an enduring tribute to the person we've lost. This is something David did, when he honoured Jonathan, who was a skilful archer, by training his army in the use of the bow (2 Samuel 1:18).

I'll close with some questions for thought or discussion:

i. Do you think it's likely that Christians and people who aren't yet believers process grief in different ways?

ii. What's the best way to console a friend or colleague who is mourning? Hint: remember Job's comforters!

iii. Do you find that speaking to someone who's grieving naturally presents opportunities for sharing the Gospel? If so, what are the pitfalls of doing this, and why must we be extremely careful?

Repentance

"And David said unto Nathan, I have sinned against the Lord. And Nathan said unto David, The Lord also hath put away thy sin; thou shalt not die (2 Samuel 12:13)."

Very few words currently seem to be as unpopular in Christian circles as 'repentance'. Perhaps 'sin' might be one of the few that could compete with it, so maybe that needs to be our starting point: in considering; not in doing! Although some professing believers would like to dismiss the idea of sin, the concept is straightforward: it's anything we think, say or do that falls short of the standard of perfection set by a Holy God. Unlike transgression, which is a deliberate violation of God's will, sin can be accidental, although the two words are often used interchangeably.

The verse which forms the heart of this reflection makes the interesting point that all sin is essentially against the Lord, even though there will usually be others involved, who will be hurt by our words or actions. One reason for this is that God is holy, omniscient and omnipresent, meaning that He knows everything we do, and therefore cannot fail to be hurt when we fall short of His standards. As a God of love, He is also grieved by the pain we cause to others, especially when, as Christians, we bring reproach upon His Name.

Given that nobody who walked this earth, other than Jesus, lived a perfect life, we might be tempted to ask why sin is so serious: after all, we repeatedly fall short of our expectations of ourselves, so can't possibly hope to attain God's standard of perfection! However, a moment's thought will lead us to Calvary. When Adam and Eve sinned in Eden, they caused a separation between humankind and our Creator, which could only be bridged by a sacrifice. God's criterion for judgement is perfection, and we were no longer perfect, as a consequence of which God sent His Son, Jesus, to give His life for us on the cross at Calvary. The fact that Jesus's death was necessary is proven by the fact that He didn't receive an affirmative answer to His plea of Matthew 26:39, "If it be possible, let this cup pass from me." Jesus drank of the cup of wrath, literally becoming sin for us, because there was no other way we could be forgiven. It is impossible for us to comprehend the depth of the pain God the Father felt, watching His Son suffer so excruciatingly, but He allowed it to happen, because there was no alternative way to deal with our sin, other than for us all to be condemned to eternal judgement. That's how serious sin is, and that's why repentance is so important.

Anyone who is familiar with the four spiritual laws will know that God loves us, and has a special plan for our lives. This is certainly true, but another axiom is that Satan hates us and has a plan to ruin us! When we sin, whether deliberately or not, we align our will with Satan's, thereby running into the arms of someone who intends to destroy us. By repenting, we turn back to God, and into the arms of a loving Father, Who loves us so much that He gave His Son, in order that we may have eternal life. Whenever we genuinely repent, God will be faithful to forgive us, but that doesn't mean there won't be consequences for our actions. David's sin which led to the conversation with Nathan, described above, resulted in the death of an innocent man and caused intense heartache for many people, including himself. Moreover, his authority, both as a leader and a father, was compromised, demonstrating that our mistakes can have far-reaching consequences, even after we've come to our senses. This hopefully emphasises, as if it should need saying, that Calvary doesn't give us carte-blanche to sin: if anybody deliberately sins, thinking that God is honour-bound to forgive them, because of Jesus's sacrifice on the cross, such an individual needs to repent of their attitude, at least as much as for their actions.

Would you be willing to consider a few more questions?

i. Are there any wrong thoughts, words or deeds for which you need to repent?

ii. Is there anyone from whom you need to seek forgiveness?

iii. Have you recently thanked Jesus for the price He paid, in order that your sins could be forgiven?

Wisdom

> *"Give therefore thy servant an understanding heart to judge thy people, that I may discern between good and bad: for who is able to judge this thy so great a people (1 Kings 3:9)?"*

Solomon's petition for wisdom and discernment clearly pleased the Lord, as we go on to read in the very next verse. This isn't surprising, in view of the damage we do to ourselves, and everyone around us, when we act injudiciously; believing that we know best, instead of seeking God's direction. A God Who loves us enough to have sent His Son to die in our place surely wants the best for our lives! And what could be better than living a life in which we drink from the infinite reservoir of His wisdom, instead of the shallow pools of our own limited understanding?

King Solomon had good reason to ask for discernment: he had just acceded to the throne in place of his father, David, who had united the nation and brought it unparalleled prosperity. With David off the scene, there was the potential for factions to emerge and for divisions to occur: as every sports fan knows, it isn't easy to follow in the footsteps of a successful leader! The consequences of acting in an unwise manner are graphically illustrated by Solomon's son, Rehoboam, who behaved impetuously, rather than listening to wise counsel, thereby sparking a civil war; events that are described in 1 Kings 12.

As believers, we frequently pray for blessings such as a happy marriage, successful career or financial security, although none of these are explicitly promised to us in Scripture. However, such rewards are far more likely to come our way when, in addition to praying, we tap into God's wisdom, thereby maximising the prospect of making the right relational, professional and financial decisions. Wonderfully, for all of us who desire to have such discernment, it's actually something which is promised to us! In James 1:5, we read that, "If any of you (believers) lack wisdom, let him ask of God, that giveth to all men liberally, and upbraideth not; and it shall be given him." The type of wisdom that James speaks of is such as will confound our enemies, as described by Jesus Himself, in Luke 21:15, where He assures us of wisdom that our adversaries will not be able to gainsay nor resist.

Has there ever been a time in history when wisdom was as scarce, yet essential, a commodity, as the era in which we currently live? Governments, boards of directors, parents and church leaders are seeking to make a series of inter-related decisions in the midst of political, economic and epidemiological crises, despite the absence of concrete information. For any of us in our chosen field, or even just in everyday life, it's vital that we study the available information and seek to expand our knowledge. However, knowledge alone doesn't guarantee drawing the right conclusions: such an outcome requires the capacity to apply what we know in the appropriate way, and this is the essence of wisdom. Fortunately, we're not alone in doing this: while Solomon was a great king, who achieved remarkable success, he lived at a time prior to Jesus's beautiful gift of the Holy Spirit having been given to everyone who believes in Him. If we take James's advice, and pray for wisdom, we would do well also to ask the Holy Spirit to guide us in every decision we take. There are innumerable crossroads on the path we traverse through life, and He knows far better than any of us the route that's best for us to take.

Finally, here are some questions to ponder, in relation to wisdom:

i. Can you recall an occasion in your life when the outcome would have been different, if only you'd had more wisdom?

ii. How would our world look, if people operated in godly discernment?

iii. Would you like greater wisdom? If so, just ask the One Who has promised to give it to you!

Captivity

"In the ninth year of Hoshea the king of Assyria took Samaria, and carried Israel away into Assyria, and placed them in Halah and in Habor by the river of Gozan, and in the cities of the Medes. For so it was, that the children of Israel had sinned against the LORD their God, which had brought them up out of the land of Egypt, from under the hand of Pharaoh king of Egypt, and had feared other gods (2 Kings 17: 6 & 7)."

We've previously discussed the cycle of faith, which turns from crisis to repentance to deliverance, then to complacency and back to crisis. But what happens if we don't repent? The people of Israel learned this lesson the hard way, when they drifted so far from God that their hearts became impermeable to His attempts to correct them. Although the God of the Bible had miraculously released Israel from her Egyptian captivity, her people always had a fascination with other deities, even though these false gods could do nothing to deliver them. The situation came to a head in the days of Elijah, when the spiritual decline of the nation precipitated a showdown (1 Kings 18) between God's prophet and the prophets of Baal. This resulted in the Baal-worshippers being exposed as charlatans, while God demonstrated His power by engulfing Elijah's sacrifice in fire, even though he'd drenched it in water! Surely, such a dramatic demonstration, both of God's power, and of His absolute superiority over any perceived 'rivals', would persuade the Israelites that there was only one True God, worthy of their worship and adoration? Sadly, this wasn't to be the case and, having given the nation every opportunity to repent, God was finally left with no alternative, other than to allow them to be taken into captivity.

It's heartbreaking to read of Israel's spiritual decline, as recorded in the historical Books of the Bible, but the fact that the nation was able to disregard God for so long, prior to judgement being pronounced, is a testament to how longsuffering He is. In contrast to the Cruel Taskmaster some people portray Him as being, God is eager to give us every opportunity to repent, either for our corporate or personal sin. However, He will not be mocked indefinitely (see Galatians 6:7), and if we persist in dishonouring His Name, we will ultimately reap the judgement that we're sowing, just as did the children of Israel, when they were taken into captivity. Being unfailingly gracious and merciful, God gave Israel many warnings, each of which was an opportunity to turn back to the path of truth. Nevertheless, judgement ultimately became necessary, in order to disabuse them, and us, of the notion that it's possible to sin with impunity. This wasn't the case of an angry and vengeful God seeking retribution, but of a loving Father chastising His children, to awaken them to the damage being caused to them by their actions. In fact, the people of Israel were literally getting what they'd asked for, when they stood on Mount Ebal and agreed to the curses that would emanate from their disobedience (Deuteronomy 27:13).

We may live a long way from ancient Israel, both in terms of time and geography, but we nonetheless all face judgement in one form or another, whether in school reports, end-of-year examinations, or annual reviews at work. It's an inescapable fact of life that we face spiritual judgements, too! Those of us who have accepted Jesus as our Lord and Saviour are assured of eternal life, but this doesn't give us freedom to sin without facing the repercussions. Therefore, if we defy God for long enough, we can expect to feel the correcting rod of our Shepherd, as He seeks to bring us back on track. Ultimately, although believers will be spared the horror of the Great White Throne judgement (Revelation 20: 11 - 15), we do risk the loss of reward if we fail to judiciously utilise the talents God has given us. Loving us as much as He does, God also makes it as difficult as possible for us to go to hell! People who haven't yet placed their trust in Jesus will therefore encounter lovingly designed roadblocks along the way, in addition to experiencing what we all do, in terms of the consequences of our actions. Ultimately, however, anyone who doesn't know Jesus will have to stand before Him on the basis of their own merits, which can never meet God's standard of perfection, however good a life they may have led.

Although this is a 'heavy' message, it has an immensely positive application! Even in judgement, God shows mercy, as demonstrated by the generation from Israel that was taken into captivity: while in exile, they flourished, learned new skills and returned to their faith. This is the very reason that God reprimands us, even on an individual level: not to punish us for our sin, but to bring us to our senses, before we do irreparable damage, either to ourselves or to others. Finally, we need to remember that many people around us are in captivity: not in a foreign land, but to a spiritual adversary, who has blinded them to their need for a Saviour. It is our privilege and responsibility to intercede for their salvation.

To close, here are some questions for personal consideration:

i. Are you currently in a form of captivity? If so, is there an act of disobedience, whether in thought, word or deed, which you need to bring before the Lord?

ii. What lessons have you learned from any spiritual chastisement you've previously experienced?

iii. Can you tell the difference between God's correction and a spiritual attack from the Enemy?

Be Of Good Courage!

"Be of good courage, and let us behave ourselves valiantly for our people, and for the cities of our God: and let the Lord do that which is good in His sight (1 Chronicles 19:13)."

I don't know about you, but when I embark on my annual plan to read the Bible, it's probably fair to say that I don't look forward to the Books of Chronicles with a sense of eager anticipation! Having said this, amongst the genealogies, coronations and battles, there are some spiritual nuggets that provide welcome sustenance for today's believers, thousands of years after those words were first written. The verse quoted above is one of these, and you may have favourites of your own, which you'd like to add.

If ever there was a verse for today, this is possibly it! In the midst of unfolding global chaos and a frenzied agenda of fear, it's absolutely imperative that we continue to "be of good courage" and "behave ourselves valiantly." The obvious question is how we do this! Well, of course, as believers, we have the power of the Holy Spirit living inside of us, as well as the assurance of eternal life that stems from our decision to accept Jesus into our lives. That said, these axioms don't automatically mean we will always act courageously. The Holy Spirit clearly made a profound difference to Peter, turning him from a fearful denier of Jesus into an anointed, fearless preacher on the Day of Pentecost. However, other Spirit-filled believers, of whom the Gospel writer Mark may have been one, have allowed fear, at least for a time, to impact their ministries. This implies that we need to take a conscious decision to "bring into captivity every thought to the obedience of Christ," as we are exhorted to do in 2 Corinthians 10:5.

It's important to remember that fear in itself isn't a sin, but that allowing it to dominate our lives can lead us into sin: especially sins of omission, where we fail to step into the promises God has prepared for us. This isn't to say we're to live in denial, pretending that everything is okay, when it isn't! Courage isn't about reckless disregard for our circumstances, but a determination to view those circumstances through the prism of God's promises to us. As Christian citizens in a confused and chaotic world, we have a responsibility to help our civil authorities bring order to the chaos and, especially, to shine the light of the Gospel into people's confusion. More than any amount of preaching or witnessing, it is the peace we exhibit as believers that will make people sit up and take notice, while the institutions of this world crumble around them.

This brings us to the reason for displaying courage: it's not about making ourselves feel good, or having people think well of us but, as the verse we're reflecting on goes on to say, "for the cities of our God." Despite not needing us, God has chosen to work through us and, remarkably, the plans He has for our families, communities and nations are predicated on Him finding people of courage to work them out! This brings us to the conclusion of our verse: the plan is God's, not ours; we are required to let Him "do that which is good in His sight." This means we need to remain faithful and courageous, even when political developments might discourage us, or we hear a bad report in relation to someone we care about. God is working a plan that is greater than any of us can imagine: we may only see one piece of the jig-saw while we're working on it, but in eternity we'll see the full picture, and be glad we were faithful! This message was sufficiently important for King David to emphasise it, when he anointed Solomon as his successor: "Be strong and of good courage, and do it: fear not, nor be dismayed: for the Lord God, even my God, will be with thee; He will not fail thee, nor forsake thee, until thou hast finished all the work for the service of the house of the Lord (1 Chronicles 28:20)."

Do you have sufficient courage to face a few questions?

i. Has there been a time in your life when a lack of courage dissuaded you from doing something you felt God was calling you to do?

ii. Do you currently have any fears or anxieties that are holding you back from fulfilling your potential?

iii. Is there anything stopping you from bringing your fears to the Lord, honestly and openly, and requesting the courage to step into the purpose He has for your life?

A Promise And An Obligation

"Now my eyes shall be open, and my ears attent to the prayer that is made in this place (2 Chronicles 7:15)."

The verse in question was written during a time when bringing petitions before the Lord in prayer was a complex matter. Worshippers had to atone for their sins, by means of the sacrifices of animals which were dedicated to the Lord. Even then, they couldn't come directly to God, but could only come via the priest, who himself had to offer sacrifices for his own sins! At the time in question, Solomon had just completed building the Temple in Jerusalem, and his dedication of the building to the Lord is recorded in the opening verses of 2 Chronicles chapter 7. If all this seems far removed from our current circumstances, verse 13 speaks of locusts and pestilences, both of which have made the headlines in 2020! Verse 15 contains the wonderful assurance that God will hear the people's prayers, but as with many promises it's conditional, which is a concept we were looking at previously. What's the nature of the conditionality? This is contained in the famous verse, which explains how our pestilences can segue into promises: "If my people, which are called by my name, shall humble themselves, and pray, and seek my face, and turn from their wicked ways; then I will hear from heaven, and will forgive their sin, and will heal their land (2 Chronicles 7:14)." So, verse 15 provides the promise, but verse 14 lays upon us an obligation, which is to humble ourselves in prayer and repent of our sin.

I've often heard it said that Calvary changed everything, and to a large extent this is true: after all, if Jesus hadn't died for my sins I'd still have been destined for hell! However, many of the precepts laid down for us in the Old Testament remain true today, which isn't surprising, in view of the unchanging nature of our God. Therefore, just as humility and repentance were preconditions for people's prayers being heard in Old Testament times, we read in the Gospels that unconfessed sin and a hardened, unforgiving heart can be hindrances to our prayers receiving the answers we desire. Something else Calvary didn't change is the very need for prayer: we can't simply sit back and bask in the glory of eternal security, thinking that the battle is won! Jesus won the war with Satan when He rose from the dead, but it's our obligation, as believers, to enforce this victory. Our failure to do so results in our spiritual adversary winning innumerable battles along the way; particularly with regard to the precious souls he tragically takes with him to a lost eternity. We would perhaps do well to reflect upon the countless hours Jesus spent in heart-rending prayer, the time He invested in teaching His disciples to pray, and some of the exhortations to pray given to us in His Word, of which Luke 22:46 and 1 Thessalonians 5:17 are just two.

Of course, Calvary not only gave us the opportunity of salvation, but it also changed the nature of our relationship with God. When the veil in the Temple (not Solomon's Temple by this time, but Herod's) was torn in two, it represented God's invitation for us to come directly to Him, on the basis of Jesus's sacrifice. This is what it means to pray in Jesus's Name: it's not about a formula of words, but about relationship. If we are God's children, which we become when we accept Jesus as our Saviour, He will hear us, in the same way we respond to the call of our own family. It's reputed that the priests in the Temple immediately sewed the veil back together again and, tragically, the religious classes have been doing the same ever since: seeking to bind people in legalistic tradition, rather than allowing them to come to Jesus. One of the great tragedies of Christianity is that it's allowed itself, in many instances, to become a rules-based religion, serving the interests of the elite, when Jesus died to give us life more abundantly (John 10:10). Another contrast between Solomon's time and ours is that location is no longer a barrier to coming to God: we can enter into His presence in our homes, cars, offices or outdoors. However, the condition of 2 Chronicles 7:14 still remains: we need to come before Him with a pure heart - geography can't keep us from God, but sin still can!

If you've previously been ignoring the questions at the end of our reflections, I'd urge you to at least consider these:

i. In view of the blessings that are promised to us in Scripture, with regard to prayer, do you think it's reasonable to conclude that there must be consequences for our failure to pray?

ii. Do you have a regular rhythm of prayer: not as a legalistic exercise, but in coming before God to repent of your sins and intercede for your family, community and nation?

iii. How different might your town/village, county and country look if you engaged in earnest prayer and met with other believers to pray for national and international revival?

Restoration

"Who is there among you of all his people? His God be with him, and let him go up to Jerusalem, which is in Judah, and build the house of the Lord God of Israel, (he is the God,) which is in Jerusalem (Ezra 1:3)."

The Book of Ezra opens with this decree from Cyrus, King of Persia, authorising the people of Judah to return to Jerusalem and rebuild the Temple. The historical context is that, seventy years previously, Nebuchadnezzar had captured the area of southern Israel, known as Judah, and brought the brightest and best of her citizens back to Babylon, along with many of the ceremonial vessels used in the Temple for worship. In the meantime, the Babylonian Empire had itself fallen, and it was the Medo-Persians who were the world rulers of the day. Thus, King Cyrus wasn't just any monarch: he was the most powerful man in the world at the time. Astonishingly, the prophets Isaiah and Jeremiah had foretold these events, in considerable detail, prior to them taking place. Jeremiah 29:10 speaks of the fact that the people of Judah would be taken into Babylonian exile and released after seventy years, while Isaiah 44:28 contains this remarkable prophecy: "That saith of Cyrus, He is my shepherd, and shall perform my pleasure: even saying to Jerusalem, Thou shalt be built; and to the temple, Thy foundation shall be laid." This passage of Scripture was written around 700 BC, whereas the events of Ezra chapter 1 occurred in 536 BC, precisely seventy years after the Babylonian invasion of Judah, and more than 160 years after Isaiah spoke of Cyrus by name!

Bible critics have used these prophecies to argue that the relevant portion of Isaiah was written after the event, or that there were 'two Isaiahs', but the overwhelming preponderance of evidence is against them. The reality is that, for an omniscient God, looking forward to the future is no more of a challenge than reflecting on the past. This doesn't mean He pre-plans everything, making humans into automatons; it's simply that He knows what will happen long before it occurs! Genesis 18:14 poses the question of whether anything is too hard for the Lord, to which Jeremiah himself provides a fitting response, in Jeremiah 32:17, "Ah Lord God! Behold, thou hast made the heaven and the earth by thy great power and stretched out arm, and there is nothing too hard for thee." One of the people Nebuchadnezzar brought back to Babylon with him was Daniel, who observed in verse 21 of chapter two of his eponymous Book that, "He (God) removeth kings and setteth up kings." Thus, we see that He is ultimately in control of events, which has to be reassuring, in the context of the shaking our world is currently experiencing. As an aside, although the Books of Isaiah, Jeremiah and Daniel appear after Ezra in our Bibles, they preceded Ezra chronologically: this is because of the way the Old Testament is divided into sections, with the historical Books placed before the Books of prophecy.

The verse selected for this reflection provides more than the backdrop to a history lesson, or even an illustration of the greatness of our God: it proves the depth and breadth of His love for us! If God cares so much about the restoration of a building that He would give His prophets specific words about these events long in advance, and record them in such detail in His Book, then how much more does He care about restoring us! As New Testament believers, we're described as the temple of God, because the Spirit of God dwells within us (1 Corinthians 3:16). When we come to know the Lord, that's not the end of a process, but the beginning: He refines and develops us for His service, taking inordinate time and care to craft us into the people He always intended us to be. This process, of going through the Refiner's fire, can be painful at times, but it equips us for being salt and light to the world around us. As Jesus continues to perfect us, our actions more closely reflect His love and compassion, enabling acquaintances who may never have read the Book of Ezra to encounter Him; perhaps for the first time. This is the most compelling reason for our presence on earth: God has a wonderful plan for people who don't yet know Him - people He loves exceedingly and created in His image - and He frequently uses us to demonstrate that love to them!

In conclusion, here are a few questions, relating to restoration:

i. What has God laid on your heart to restore?

ii. Do you know anyone who's in need of restoration? If so, why not encourage them and pray for them?

iii. Are you in need of restoration yourself? If that's the case, is there anything preventing you from asking the Holy Spirit to transform you into the person He always intended you to be?

Encouragement In The Face Of Opposition

"Then said I unto them, Ye see the distress that we are in, how Jerusalem lieth waste, and the gates thereof are burned with fire: come, and let us build up the wall of Jerusalem, that we be no more a reproach (Nehemiah 2:17)."

Although King Cyrus had previously given the Jewish people authority to return to Judah, only just under fifty thousand, out of a population of approximately one million, availed of this opportunity. Prior to their captivity, the prophet Jeremiah exhorted his compatriots to settle in Babylon and make it their home, but they had perhaps become too comfortable, as a consequence of which they were reluctant to leave at God's appointed time. Those who did return faced considerable difficulty and opposition from the new inhabitants of Judah, who had been planted there by the Babylonians. This is the backdrop to Nehemiah's exhortation for the people to rebuild the walls of Jerusalem.

Anyone who has visited a walled city, such as York or Derry~Londonderry, will have an idea in their mind of what was on Nehemiah's heart. At his time in world history, more than five hundred years before Jesus's birth in Bethlehem, it was imperative for inhabitants to defend their cities from marauders, who would mercilessly exploit any weakness in a quest to invade, plunder and pillage. The city walls were a vital component of this defensive strategy, so for the walls of Jerusalem to lie in ruin left the city most vulnerable, in addition to being "a reproach," to use Nehemiah's expressive description. Curiously, despite the pride

Jews have always had in the city that King David made their capital, nobody seemed to care sufficiently about the situation to be motivated to do anything about it. However, as is often the case in these scenarios, God had His man (although often it will be a woman!) for the occasion.

When Nehemiah heard about the condition of his beloved city, he wept, mourned and fasted before God, as recorded in Nehemiah 1:4. This demonstrates that Nehemiah had God's own heart for Jerusalem, because he was a descendant of the generation which was deported to Babylon, and had therefore never lived in Jerusalem himself. Mourning is a natural reaction to seeing something that breaks God's heart, such as when we observe someone we care about destined for a Christ-less eternity. However, it should always be a motivation to action, as here, where Nehemiah fasted and prayed; no doubt seeking God's direction with regard to what role, if any, he was to have in rectifying the situation. It is a great thing to have a desire to do something for the Lord, but it's foolhardy to proceed in our own strength, without consulting Him first, and inviting His Holy Spirit into our circumstances!

Having sought the Lord, Nehemiah felt the call to travel to Jerusalem and help rebuild the city, but he couldn't just go: he was the king's cupbearer, which was a responsible position, meaning that it was necessary for him to seek permission, prior to embarking on the journey. This is an important lesson for us to take on board: it's a privilege for us to serve the Lord, but we still have a responsibility to honour people on this earth, such as our parents, teachers, spouses and managers: failure to do so can impair our witness irreparably. With permission secured, Nehemiah set off for Jerusalem, and was profoundly discouraged by what he found when he got there. The situation was perhaps worse than he feared, and he knew that there was a considerable amount of hard work ahead of him. Of course, it wasn't something he could do on his own: he needed assistance from the rulers of the city (the 'them' of Nehemiah 2:17) and also a team to perform the construction. For anyone in a position of leadership, whether in a family home, business or church, it is essential to build the right team, ensuring that everyone has a role which contributes to the desired outcome, complementing what the others are doing.

A vital component of team-building is encouragement: people who are discouraged will soon become demotivated and disinterested, leading to a situation where the team begins to disintegrate. In contrast, individuals who receive encouragement will begin to see the importance of their role, be inspired to contribute towards the success of the project and, in turn, start to encourage others. This sounds fine in theory, but isn't always easy to implement, in the face of opposition! We obviously have our spiritual adversary, as well as people who mean us harm, and Nehemiah did, too, in the form of Tobiah, Sanballat and others. It's vital that we seek the Lord's wisdom in dealing with these situations, because rising to the bait can diminish our reputation with the people we're leading, damage our witness to the world and harm the project we're working on. However, we also need to be firm; ensuring God's will prevails and that we accomplish what He's called us to do.

If you haven't done so lately, I'd thoroughly recommend reading the Book of Nehemiah to see the full story. As you do so, you might like to contemplate the following questions:

i. Is there a project the Lord has laid on your heart, which discouragement has deterred you from completing? If so, why not take heart from Nehemiah and begin again?

ii. How do you react to people who discourage you from pursuing your dreams, and how would God want you to react?

iii. Do you know anyone who could benefit from a word of encouragement today? If so, why not encourage them!

SPIRITUAL REFLECTIONS - I

Faith Versus Fatalism

> *"Go, gather together all the Jews that are present in Shushan, and fast ye for me, and neither eat nor drink three days, night or day: I also and my maidens will fast likewise; and so will I go in unto the king, which is not according to the law: and if I perish, I perish (Esther 4:16)."*

Has it ever occurred to you that there can be a very fine line between faith and fatalism? It can sound very spiritual to say, "I'm trusting in the Lord for the outcome," but are we really thinking "I'll take what comes and live with the consequences!" As we've reflected previously, prayer changes things, but we so often treat prayer as a last resort, only turning to God when all our temporal sources of assistance have been exhausted. Perhaps that's one reason why God allows desperate circumstances to develop in our lives: knowing this is the only time we're likely to come to Him for the advice and direction we so urgently need!

Esther was certainly facing a desperate situation: as a young Jewish lady, she had just heard the worst news possible; that the king, who happened to be her husband, had issued a decree for the Jews to be exterminated. Of course, King Ahasuerus didn't know that Esther was a Jew, but the situation wasn't as simple as her asking him to revoke the decree. First of all, the protocols of the royal court dictated that even the king's wife couldn't approach him, unless invited to do so; secondly, the laws of the time meant that a royal decree couldn't be reversed. Therefore, from a temporal perspective, there didn't seem to be any hope: Esther could be put to death for making an unsolicited request to speak to the king and, even if she did get an audience with him, there wasn't much he could do, should he desire to intervene! Might this resemble a scenario you're currently facing, with regard to a challenge at school or university, an apparently intractable difficulty at work, or a troublesome relationship?

Although Esther was clearly a remarkable lady, and God's chosen vessel for a particular time in history, it's reassuring to observe that she was initially anxious about the prospect of pleading before the king for the preservation of her people. Of course, we'd have been terrified, too: she had just received unconscionable news and was facing possible death on two counts; her impending meeting with the king and her own Jewish identity. However, there can be a tendency to think of the heroes and heroines of faith as being super-human, possessing characteristics we could never hope to display, thereby reaffirming our false perception that we're unable to serve the Lord, by being His representative in the classroom, boardroom or Assembly Chamber. Unlike Esther, believers today are indwelt by the Holy Spirit, Who raised Jesus from the dead, so how much more might *we* be able to achieve?!

Having overcome her initial shock and confusion, Esther did what we should all do, when confronted with challenging news. Whenever we receive a bad report, such as an adverse medical diagnosis, there will inevitably be a period of anxiety, but it's essential that we bring both our feelings, and the news which caused them, before the Lord in prayer. If we fail to do this, we will continue to be buffeted by our emotions, which the Enemy will exploit to sow fear and discouragement into our lives. When Esther fasted and prayed, she clearly expected something to change in the spiritual realm, and by enlisting the support of other Jews she was effectively leading a delegation to the corridors of heaven, in advance of her own solitary trek along the regal corridors of power. We've recently reflected on our obligation to pray, and many of the same comments apply in relation to fasting. We know from the Gospels that Jesus fasted often and, if it's something He felt the need to do, how do we believe we can have spiritual power in our lives without doing the same? As with all areas of our lives, common sense needs to be exercised: God doesn't intend for us to make ourselves ill by fasting, and there may be times in our lives when it's more beneficial for us to switch off the television than to refrain from food! Whatever we do for the Lord, it's important that it's done with the right spirit: grimly fasting until we get the result we're looking for, expecting God to somehow be impressed, is nothing other than a pseudo-spiritual hunger strike which will achieve little more than leaving us tired and demoralised! That said, fasting in the right way, and for the right reasons, leads us closer to the Lord, and it is perhaps this closer relationship, rather than the intrinsic act of fasting itself, which ultimately adds power to our prayers.

Esther's statement, "If I perish, I perish" would have been fatalistic, if it hadn't been underpinned by her trust in God. Esther's faith was manifested by her actions of prayer and fasting, but she also accepted God's sovereignty, which means that we, as human agents, do not have the authority to determine outcomes, however desperately we might want to do so. As a consequence, we must be prepared for four different types of response to our prayers:

1. God may deliver us *from* the trial, by removing it completely, as when Jesus raised Lazarus from the dead, thereby restoring Martha and Mary's family. To an extent, this is what He did for Esther, although her story also exhibits elements of observation number 2!

2. He might deliver us *through* the trial, in a way that further strengthens our faith and serves as a witness to people around us. This was the experience of Daniel, in the lions' den, and Meshach, Shadrach and Abednego, in the fiery furnace.

3. It may be the Lord's will for the trial to continue, as when He told Paul in 2 Corinthians 12:9 that, "My grace is sufficient." This is never because God doesn't care, but in order that His purposes may be accomplished, which is a point we'll return to in a future reflection.

4. In certain circumstances, the trial may, from a human perspective, appear to overcome us, as occurred with the

martyrdom of Stephen and James. It's important to remember that our journey of faith isn't all about us: we're here to serve others and, ultimately, the Lord Who saved us. It may therefore be that adverse consequences for us serve the greater good for others. (Stephen's courage in death had a profound impact on Saul of Tarsus, while James' martyrdom dispersed Christians around the world, to spread the Gospel.) Even in this event, we know that God's plan is best for us: Christians shouldn't have any fear of death, because it means finally meeting our Saviour, and if death doesn't hold any fears there's not much the world can do to us!

I'll close with a few questions for personal thought or family discussion:

i. How do you think you'd have reacted, if you'd been in Esther's position?

ii. Do you believe that your life has meaning and that, like Esther, you're here for "such a time as this (Esther 4:14)?"

iii. Is it possible that, as did King Ahasuerus, you might hold the answer to someone else's prayers?

Perspective

"Where wast thou when I laid the foundations of the earth? Declare, if thou hast understanding (Job 38:4)."

At an initial glance, God's response to Job might seem rather harsh! Job had recently lost his children, possessions and health, leaving him in a bereft, impoverished and miserable state that we could scarcely begin to imagine. He was a man who cared greatly about his relationship with God, enjoyed wealth few of us could even dream of, and was undoubtedly held in high esteem; not only by his contemporaries, but by God Himself. Job's initial misfortunes followed a dialogue between God and Satan, in which the latter made the claim that Job's obedience was merely a response to the hedge of protection God had placed around him. Remove this, he effectively said, and Job will "curse you to your face (Job 1:11)."

God responded by allowing Satan to come against Job, with the condition that he spare his physical being. This must have been music to Satan's ears, as he devised cruel and dramatic ways to claim the lives of Job's children and extinguish his wealth. However, the consequence wasn't what he was expecting: verses 20 & 21 of chapter 1 record that Job worshipped the Lord and blessed His Name. During the next recorded spiritual joust, early in chapter 2, God emphasises Job's righteousness to Satan, as if to say, "That didn't work out too well for you, did it?" Always ready with an answer, Satan responded by asserting that Job really would curse God if his health came under attack. Consent was given for Satan to inflict Job, albeit sparing his life, and Job again remained faithful.

Having endured this unimaginable grief and physical torture, Job was then confronted with three supposed friends, who initially supported him empathetically, but ultimately suggested that his woes must have emanated from unconfessed sin. We generally don't need to dig too deep to expose the wisdom of this world as being exceedingly shallow! Even in Christian circles, there can be many misconceptions about physical maladies having their root in unconfessed sin, which is something that *can* occur, but is far from invariably the case. Far more damagingly, believers are frequently told that their failure to be healed necessarily results from a lack of faith on their part; an erroneous assertion that we'll return to later in this book.

In response to these men, and also to his circumstances, Job understandably asked God why all this had been allowed to happen to him. There may be occasions when we seek an explanation from the Lord and, while we might not always get one, it isn't a sin to ask! When God did respond, it wasn't to provide a detailed explanation, even though He could easily have done so. Instead, He asked Job a sequence of questions, which emphasised the disparity that exists, in power and resources, between human beings and their Creator. Those questions begin in chapter 38, so the one we're reflecting on here is amongst the first, but the essential concept is that God created heaven and earth, along with everything that ever existed, and neither Job, nor any other human, were there at the time. This is something for us to remember next time we're tempted to question God: His knowledge, wisdom, understanding and power are infinitely greater than anything we have to offer. If we choose to fight against Him, we're destined to lose, so why not join the winning side? That's not to say we don't have legitimate questions. Losing a loved one is bound to prompt thoughts, such as "why did this have to happen?" or "why now?" However, when we ask them, it's important to remember that we're asking a God Whose love for us led Jesus to Calvary, and Who never permits anything to happen in our lives by chance. We see in Job's story that Satan required God's permission to do what he did, and it's the same in our lives, too!

My questions aren't quite as challenging, or anointed, as God's to Job, but you might like to consider them, nonetheless.

i. What can Job's experiences teach us about the reasons for suffering?

ii. Does God always answer your questions? If not, why do you think that is?

iii. What lessons can we learn from Job's comforters, with regard to consoling people who are experiencing trials?

Rooted In The Word!

"And he shall be like a tree planted by the rivers of water, that bringeth forth his fruit in his season; his leaf also shall not wither; and whatsoever he doeth shall prosper. (Psalm 1:3)."

It's an evocative image, isn't it? This is also a picture painted for us in Jeremiah 17:8: a tree growing by the riverbank, laden with fruit, offering passers-by shelter from the heat of the day. Such a promise for our lives would have conjured up a myriad of images for readers in agrarian Israel, where the ferocity of the heat can scorch plant-life and make livestock grateful for even the shallowest pool of water. However, what we're offered in this verse isn't just enough sustenance to facilitate survival, but limitless resources which will enable us to thrive, yielding abundant results and fullness of life. In order to flourish, in the way that's described, a tree requires strong, deep roots, to draw water from the available subterranean sources. Likewise, the success or otherwise of our lives as believers will be determined by the strength and depth of our roots in the Word of God. This doesn't mean legalistically reading a given amount of Scripture each and every day, thinking we've appeased God by fulfilling an obligation, but taking His guidance for our lives into our hearts, and actually living as though we believe what we're reading!

It's wonderful to have God's promises of success and productivity but, as we've discussed previously, there's invariably an element of conditionality attached to them. The abundant life, of which we read in Psalm 1:3, isn't promised to everyone, but only to those who honour and worship God. If we choose not to do this, we will forfeit the blessing, just as the children of Israel did when they chose to worship the false gods of the nations they'd conquered in battle. The further we drift from God, the more hardened our hearts become, until we resemble the description in verse 4, of people who are "like chaff which the wind driveth away."

Although it can be tempting at times to blame external factors, other people, or even God, for our circumstances, we actually get to determine the destiny of our own lives. Do we want to resemble the bounteous, well-nourished tree by the riverbank? Then we need to study God's Word and apply His principles to our lives! Alternatively, are we more concerned with what we can extract from life in this instant? If so, our decisions may lead to a short-term alleviation of thirst, but ultimately, we'll end up becoming dried out and blown away, like the chaff of verse 4!

Life is sometimes compared to a test and, if that's the case, we can't fault God for not giving us the answers! As He says in Deuteronomy 30:19, "I have set before you life and death, blessing and cursing: therefore choose life." God isn't a cold, dispassionate Invigilator, waiting to see how we get on, and He certainly isn't a hard Taskmaster, wanting us to fail, in order that He can keep us in detention! Instead, He's done everything in His power to help us make the grade. We don't have to keep a burdensome law, attend church a given number of times each week, or make a specific pilgrimage; instead, we just need to accept the sacrifice Jesus has made on our behalf, and life everlasting will be ours!

Maintaining the theme of tests, here are a few questions:

i. Is your life firmly rooted in the Word of God? If not, how likely do you think it is that you'll be blown over when the next storm comes?

ii. Are there any changes you need to make in your life to increase the prospect of becoming the person you want to be in five, ten or twenty years' time?

iii. Think of the people you really know and admire: is there anything you can learn from them, in terms of the depth of their relationship with God?

Living Water

"Oh God, thou art my God; early will I seek thee: my soul thirsteth for thee, my flesh longeth for thee in a dry and thirsty land, where no water is (Psalm 63:1)."

It is said that the early church sang Psalm 63 every morning and, if that's the case, it's easy to see why, given its combination of worshipful reverence, confidence in the defeat of our enemies and joyous anticipation of salvation. Reading words like those contained in the Psalms can be quite a challenge: we frequently sing songs of adoration to our Saviour, and pledge to give Him all of our lives, but how quickly are they forgotten, after we leave the church sanctuary, or switch off the electronic device? Just as it's exceedingly humbling to reflect on many of Paul's most encouraging epistles having been written from prison, it can be quite sobering to think that our worship experience often pales into insignificance, compared to that of our antecedents, such as the psalmists, who only had the promise of Calvary, rather than the glorious certainty we enjoy today. It seems that their foresight might have been better than our hindsight, if there's any truth in the notion of the depth of our praise being proportional to our confidence in God's provision.

To some extent, this might be explained by the relative comfort of modern life, even accepting the immense poverty that still exists in the world and the vagaries of an ongoing pandemic. It stands to reason that, if you're living in a "dry and thirsty land, where no water is," as David evidently was when he wrote this Psalm, you're going to be keen to take hold of hope, wherever you can find it. In contrast, the thought of eternity may not be so pressing to a twenty-first century, first-world Christian, returning home to a heated driveway and flat-screen television. However, Psalm 63 is more than an expression of hope for a better life: it is an impassioned exaltation of a Saviour Who had yet to be born, with prophetic anticipation of the One Who gave us Living Water, in the form of His Holy Spirit (see John 7: 37 - 39).

Could there be a better metaphor for the Holy Spirit than Living Water? Irrespective of the wealth we might manage to accumulate, water remains absolutely essential to the sustenance of human life: we simply cannot live without it. Those of us who laboured as non-believers, prior to inviting Jesus into our lives, and receiving the gift of His Holy Spirit, will be able to testify of our transformation from people desperately searching for condensation on the pipe to recipients of torrents from above. Tragically, many believers lead unfulfilled, spiritually dry lives because they overlook the Third Person of the Trinity, but for a Christian to attempt to lead a productive life of faith without Him is as futile as trying to sustain the physical body with "bread alone!"

Finally, you might like to consider a few questions for personal reflection:

i. When you sing words of praise, do you give serious thought to what you're singing?

ii. Do you praise God all the time, or only when you feel like it? (Possibly not a fair question!)

iii. Have you sidelined the Holy Spirit? If so, why not change that, by inviting Him to have a full role in your life; perhaps by praying something like this:

> *Heavenly Father, thank You for sustaining people of faith, such as the psalmists, long before Jesus came to perform His earthly ministry. Lord Jesus, thank You for the joy of salvation and for giving me the gift of Your Holy Spirit. Holy Spirit, I'm sorry for having ignored You on occasions, and for not always having given You the honour You deserve. Please fill my heart, life, home and workplace with Your presence, enabling me to become everything You want me to be. In Jesus' Name. Amen.*

Revival!

"Wilt thou not revive us again: that thy people may rejoice in thee (Psalm 85:6)?"

Shouldn't this be the cry of every believer today? For the Holy Spirit to revive His Church and usher millions who don't yet know Christ into the Kingdom of Eternal Glory! For an entity to be revived, it's necessary that it once had life, but is now listless or lethargic. Sadly, this is an apt description of the church in many parts of the world, but it has been that way before and, very often, times of spiritual darkness have been precursors to God sending lightning bolts from heaven to electrify His people with a zeal for lost souls. There are few concepts that are as misunderstood in Christian circles as that of revival, but if we take time to study Psalm 85:6, we shouldn't go far wrong! The essence of revival isn't strange sensations, an exalted position for the church or increased memberships, but that believers would rejoice in God. From our post-resurrection perspective, this means worshipping Jesus for Calvary, allowing His Spirit to control our lives and honouring God in everything we do. When the church is reignited in this way, the world won't be able to do other than take notice, because the spontaneous life exhibited by Spirit-filled believers will be too captivating to ignore. This is the criterion by which any revival should be judged: the extent to which the hitherto unbelieving world has been awakened to its need for a Saviour, and brought into His presence at the foot of the cross.

This all seems incredibly exciting, and it's something many in the church are praying for, but do we really want it? The reason I ask this question is that there is a price to pay for revival! First of all, it has to be sought in earnest prayer, with dedicated singleness of heart, as happened in Ulster in 1859 and Wales in 1904, to name but two wonderful outpourings of the Spirit. When revival comes, the nature of church is radically transformed: the car park will be full, we may not get a seat in the sanctuary, and new believers will be scrutinising our lives, to see if they're befitting of mature Christians! The depth of our desire for revival is therefore measured by the extent of our desperation to see our communities liberated from the spiritual deception that blinds our families, friends and neighbours to their need for salvation through Jesus. If this is the primary motivation which drives our lives, then we'll fast and pray for revival, counting the sacrifice as a privilege beyond compare. On the other hand, if we're happy to drift through life, content in the knowledge of our eternal security, without being too concerned about what's happening to the people around us, then revival will remain something we'd secretly prefer to read about than to experience for ourselves.

These questions might be worth contemplating if, like the psalmist, your cry is for us to be revived once again:

i. Have you been inspired by previous accounts of revival and the testimonies of those who were saved?

ii. How desperately do you want to see revival in your church, leading to a Spiritual awakening in your community?

iii. Are you willing to fast and pray for revival, offering yourself for service? If so, why not start now!

> *Heavenly Father, thank You for the wonderful works You've done around the world, beginning with servants such as Elijah, then leading to Pentecost, the great historical outpourings of the Holy Spirit, and the amazing revivals that are yet to be seen. Lord Jesus, thank You for caring so much about us here on earth*

that You voluntarily left the splendour of heaven to live amongst us and suffer the cruellest of deaths, in order that we may be revived. May Your Name, along with that of the Father, and the Spirit Who raised You from the dead, be exalted in the coming revival, rather than that of man. Holy Spirit, I ask that You'll take control of my life and use me in whatever way You consider appropriate, to reignite Your Church and lead people to Jesus, in Whose Name I pray. Amen.

Majestic Certainty

"The Lord reigneth, he is clothed with majesty; the Lord is clothed with strength, wherewith he hath girded himself: the world also is stablished, that it cannot be moved (Psalm 93:1)."

Have you ever wondered how the majority of the Jews failed to recognise their Messiah? The scribes and Pharisees came in for some severe criticism in Jesus' day, which was entirely justified, because they'd developed such a legalistic understanding of matters of faith that they were imposing grievous burdens on people, which they themselves couldn't carry (Matthew 23:4). However, they had their virtues, too; one of them being the high regard they showed for Scripture, which ensured that the Bible text we read today is effectively unchanged in meaning from the original scrolls. Given that the Old Testament contains so many precise prophecies about the Messiah, such as where He'd be born, the nature of His ministry, and how He'd die (see Psalm 22, Isaiah 53 and Micah 5, to name just three prophetic passages), we might have thought that the scribes would have checked His claims against His Word and begun to ask themselves some serious questions, as to whether Jesus may, indeed, have been The One.

Evidently, some did, especially after His resurrection and, in their defence, they faced a significant challenge in interpreting the Messianic prophecies; namely that Jesus was prophesied both to die for our sins and to reign triumphantly for all eternity! Faced with this apparent contradiction, they did what most of us do when we encounter something we don't understand: they chose the version of events which most neatly fitted their comprehension of the narrative and disregarded anything that cast doubt on it! We have the privilege of knowing Jesus from this side of Calvary, but in early first-century Judah both the priests and the people were anticipating a Saviour Who would liberate the nation from Roman occupation, rather than One Who would die on a cross to set us free from our sin. Jesus *will* reign triumphantly for all eternity, but it was first necessary for Him to crush Satan's head!

Psalm 93 is one of those passages of Scripture that relates to what is called the Millennial Kingdom: a period of one thousand years, subsequent to the Great Tribulation, when Jesus will reign on earth, enabling those of us who have placed our trust in Him to experience life here as it was always intended to be. Reading such a passage made it almost impossible for the scribes to reconcile this depiction of their Messiah with the Son of Man Who would die upon the cross. Like many of us, before the Holy Spirit shone His light into our spiritual darkness, they failed to consider the possibility of the resurrection!

Knowing that every Biblical prophecy which has had the opportunity to be fulfilled has been true to date, including all those prophecies about the Messiah, we can have absolute confidence in what God's Word says about the future. Therefore, we can take Psalm 93:1 at face value: just as God created the earth, He set it in motion, and nothing or no-one can impact it without His authority. There will come a time when this world has served its purpose, to be replaced with something new, but, until then, it is in God's hands, and so is everyone who places their trust in Him!

Finally, here are a few questions to prompt thought or conversation:

i. Have you ever encountered a situation where your understanding of the truth was clouded by your perceptions?

ii. If you don't yet know Jesus as your Saviour, are you willing to challenge your preconceptions, by meeting Him in the Gospels?

iii. If you already are a Christian, how would you use Scripture to point your family, friends and colleagues towards Jesus?

God Is Good!

"Oh give thanks unto the Lord; for he is good: because his mercy endureth forever (Psalm 118:1)."

If the analysis is performed on the basis of chapters, rather than books, Psalm 118 appears at the mid-way point of the Bible. Could there be a better way for such a pivotal chapter to begin than with a statement of two truths that are central to our faith: why we're here and Who God is? Many of us tend to struggle with the reason for our existence, but the simple fact is that we were created to worship God. The logic and rationality of this may be hard to fathom but, as we read in Isaiah 55:9, "His ways are higher than our ways," so it's His prerogative to create us for whatever reason He chooses. Of course, we have the option of not worshipping Him, but then we'll ultimately become miserable, however liberating it may feel at first. We can never be truly happy unless we're doing what we were created to do, and even psychologists would seem to agree with this. A recent study found that it was almost impossible for humans to remain despondent when they held their arms outstretched, at 45° above the horizontal, with their palms facing upwards: the position of praise!

Those of us who've invited Jesus into our hearts are living proof of the conclusion of Psalm 118:1 - that God's mercy endures forever! Remarkably, we mocked Him, doubted His Word and may even have used His Name as a profanity, but all He did in return was to shower us with His love, waiting for the day when we'd give our lives to Christ and inherit our place in His Eternal Kingdom! Having said all this, people still debate the central statement of the verse: that God is good. In fact, this is an understatement, because He is perfect, pure and holy, but even His goodness is frequently challenged, and this can often be a stumbling-block to people coming to faith. The argument is essentially how an omnipotent, loving God could allow the atrocities we see in the world, such as rape and murder, or even a pandemic.

The first point to make here is that God doesn't cause these things: He allows human beings freedom of will and conscience, meaning that, if we depart from His plan for our lives, and align our will with Satan's, there will be serious consequences, both for ourselves and everyone around us. People ask whether it would be possible for God to strike wrongdoers down, before they harm anyone, in order to protect their victims. The obvious answer is that He could, but then how many of us might have been struck down before we came to Christ? We may say that our transgressions weren't *that* bad, but once we make this determination we're usurping God's role as Judge. Moreover, our assertion that *anything* is wrong requires a standard of perfection to serve as a comparator, which is a concept we only get from the Bible: no created being - only God - could ever be perfect.

If we accept that the answer isn't for God to strike people down (although He's perfectly capable of doing so!), couldn't He simply prevent us from sinning, in the way that inhibitors prevent cars from exceeding a certain speed? Again, this is something He could certainly have done, and I'm sure He does restrain people, frequently in answer to prayer, but taking the argument to its ultimate conclusion would leave us as pre-programmed automatons, making life completely meaningless. Therefore, we're left with the sobering truth that our free will has the capacity to cause immense harm to others, just as others can do harm to us. Prayer thus becomes imperative in this regard: both that we won't become vehicles for inflicting hurt on anyone else, and also for the protection of ourselves and the ones we love. Even after the event, God has the amazing ability to heal our emotional and physical wounds, especially if we're willing to forgive. We're not expected to be superhuman in this regard: we may feel unable to even look at someone who's hurt us, but if we come to the Lord, and ask His Holy Spirit to endue us with the capacity to offer forgiveness, He won't let us down.

This might sound fine in practice but, for the person who's profoundly suffering as a consequence of an act of emotional or physical violence, there are no easy answers. I know from experience that the Holy Spirit can and does heal painful wounds, but it's perhaps only in eternity that we'll understand why we had to experience these things. Of course, there is the alternative argument: that God *isn't* good, but then where does this leave us? Perhaps in a world of random chance, where there's no eternal significance to our actions and, ultimately, no hope of redemption. I'd far prefer to take my place in a world governed by the God Who loves us so much that He gave His Son to die for our sins, and those of everyone who is willing to put their faith in Him. How about you?

The following questions are designed to encourage private thought or group discussion.

i. If you're a Christian, how do you relate your faith to friends who aren't yet believers, and who have serious reservations about the concept of God's goodness?

ii. If you came to know the Lord later in life, how did you overcome your own anxieties about whether or not you could trust the assertion that God is good?

iii. Do you consider the argument about God's goodness to be intellectual, spiritual, or a combination of the two?

Trust In The Lord!

"Trust in the Lord with all thine heart; and lean not on thine own understanding. In all thy ways acknowledge him, and he shall direct thy paths (Proverbs 3: 4 & 5)."

Wouldn't you love to have wisdom; in particular, godly wisdom? The second and third verses of the first chapter of Proverbs set out the reason for the Book having been written; namely, that we may "know wisdom and instruction" and "receive the instruction of wisdom, justice, judgement and equity." Given that King Solomon, who wrote many of these proverbs, including the verses we're currently reflecting upon, was reputed to have been the wisest man of his generation, there is clearly much we can learn from him. More significantly, the fact that the Holy Spirit has chosen to incorporate these sayings into His Word provides us with the assurance that we're dealing with discernment which comes from the Lord, and not from man. The essence of human understanding is to rely on our own strength, assay self-improvement and accrue sufficient resources to hopefully provide a safeguard against life's storms: in other words, the focus is all on us. Recent experience has demonstrated this to be futile: the financial crisis of 2008/9 eroded our assets, as well as our confidence in the institutions that manage them; the pandemics, whether of virus or fear, which swept our world in 2020, reinforced our vulnerability to circumstances outwith our control; and how much assistance do self-help books provide when the tornado makes landfall against our lives?

By way of contrast, God's wisdom seeks to change our focus - from us, to Him! We may suggest that it's selfish for God to want us to concentrate on Him: couldn't He instead spare a thought for us? The reality is that He does: not just a passing consideration, but thoughts more numerous than the grains of sand on the seashore (Psalm 139:18)! The instruction of which we read in Proverbs 3, verses 4 & 5, could perhaps have been considered selfish if God had His own best interests at heart, but the reality is that these verses were written specifically for us, and not for Him. Our thoughts about God don't have any impact on Him at all, because He's unchanging in nature, but they do make a profound difference to the people He created. Either we become more like Him, as we dwell in His presence, or we end up increasingly discouraged, desperate and dissatisfied, as we ignore His guidance, and depend instead upon our own limited understanding.

Verse 5 of Proverbs chapter 3 gives us the reason why we should trust in the Lord and acknowledge Him; i.e., that He will then direct our paths. This direction has perhaps never been more necessary than in the current age, as we seek to negotiate our path through a maze of ever-changing guidelines, interpret the megabytes of information & misinformation that daily come our way, and endeavour to provide for the emotional and material needs of our families. Left to our own devices, we will inevitably wander off track, but there's no need for us to journey on our own! All we need to do is heed the advice Jesus gave to Thomas, when His bewildered disciple asked how it was possible to know the way: His response, that "I am the way, the truth and the life (John 14:6)," is as true today as it was then. This promise of direction doesn't only apply to the countless decisions we face on a daily basis, relating to education, employment and relationships, but also to our eternal destinies. John 14:6 concludes with Jesus telling Thomas, and all those who would listen, that "no man cometh to the Father, except by me." Thus, if we offer Him control over our lives, He will not only guide us through the vagaries of our time on earth but, ultimately, lead us to a glorious future in heaven. This compelling invitation is open to everyone; the question is: do you want to follow Him?

I'm hoping that you'll trust in the Lord for the discernment to answer these questions!

SPIRITUAL REFLECTIONS - I

i. Has past experience taught you that making the wrong decisions in life can lead to pain, heartache and disappointment?

ii. If you're reading this as a Christian, have you completely yielded control of your life to the Lord, or are you still making your own decisions, and hoping He'll go along with them?

iii. If you don't yet know Jesus as your Lord and Saviour, would you like to do so? He's only a prayer away!

> *Heavenly Father, thank You for not leaving me alone to navigate my path through life, but for giving me Your Word to illuminate the way. Thank You for sending Your Son, Jesus, to die on my behalf, and rise again on the third day, in order that I may have complete victory over sin and death. Lord Jesus, I'm indebted to You for Your loving sacrifice, which is immeasurably more than I could possibly deserve. I haven't always lived for You, but now humbly ask that You will forgive me for my sins, and be my Friend and Saviour, from this day on. Holy Spirit, I invite You into my life to be my Comforter, Guide and Companion. Please give me whatever gifts You desire, and direct my paths, in order that I may make the decisions that will bring honour to my Saviour Jesus, in Whose Name I pray. Amen.*

Tie Down The Tongue!

"Death and life are in the power of the tongue: and they that love it shall eat the fruit thereof (Proverbs 18:21)."

Have you ever been terribly hurt by something someone's said to you? Isn't it amazing how an acerbic comment that only takes a moment to say can cause a lifetime of hurt? The sad reality is that we also have the devastating potential to cause immense heartache to others. So much of this could be avoided if we took the advice contained in the Book we claim to treasure, but frequently ignore! Whether in the Old or New Testament, the Bible provides godly wisdom for defusing difficult situations and preventing seemingly innocuous scenarios from becoming incendiary. Thus, the entirety of Scripture resonates with the advice given in Proverbs 15:1, that "A soft answer turneth away wrath: but grievous words stir up anger." This consistency of message isn't surprising, given that, despite its multiplicity of human authors, inspiration for our Biblical text came from the One and Only Holy Spirit! It is this Spirit Who we grieve when we inflict pain upon other people, whether out of thoughtlessness, a failure to bridle our tongue (James 1:26), or our desire for popularity with the crowd.

Saying the wrong thing, or even saying the right thing in the wrong way, can cause irreparable harm to relationships, especially with the people we care about most, who have learned to trust us and value our advice. Cruel words have led to the disintegration of families, businesses and churches, where our capacity to forgive isn't always what it might be! A harsh remark to someone who isn't yet a Christian can be particularly damaging, because it discredits our witness and diminishes our right to be heard. We must therefore pray for the Holy Spirit to give us His wisdom, both in terms of what we say and how we say it. We would be foolish not to do so and, as we read earlier on in Proverbs 18, "A fool's mouth is his destruction (Proverbs 18:7)!"

While taking all this on board, we see that it's not only in the area of what we say *to* people where we need to exercise caution, but also in what we say *about* them! Scripture has many serious warnings for those of us who might be inclined to indulge in gossip, one of which is contained in Proverbs 18 itself: "The words of a talebearer are as wounds, and they go down into the innermost parts of the belly (Proverbs 18:8)." Thus, our words have the potential to cause physical damage, even up to the point where individuals about whom we spread malicious rumours may feel they have no option, other than to end their own lives. God's Word takes this so seriously that the concluding section of Scripture includes "whosoever loveth and maketh a lie" in the list of people who will not inherit the Kingdom of Heaven (Revelation 22:15). We would do well to consider this next time we're tempted to spread a rumour, participate in office gossip or unnecessarily damage someone's reputation, by sharing something we've 'heard on the grapevine'.

Here are a few questions to conclude:

i. Can you think of a harsh word or comment that you might need to apologise for?

ii. Have you been able to forgive the people who've hurt you with cruel remarks, whether recently or in the distant past? If not, I'd urge you to consider doing this, both for your own wellbeing, and also to avoid your unforgiveness becoming a barrier to answered prayer (Matthew 5: 23 - 24).

iii. Has the pain previously inflicted on you by other people's comments caused you to be more intentional, regarding what you say to others, and how you say it?

Training For The Journey

"Train up a child in the way he should go: and when he is old, he will not depart from it (Proverbs 22:6)."

Many of the Proverbs, including this one, were written by King Solomon, but their inspiration by the Holy Spirit is evident from their undeniable wisdom, and also the love they express for children, which is a characteristic Jesus repeatedly demonstrated during His earthly ministry. With the exception of serving God, there is no higher calling than to invest time and energy in our relationships with the people we love; especially our children. One important duty we have is to train them for their journeys through life, both in terms of their rights and responsibilities, and also their relationships with God. This isn't meant so much in a didactic sense, but in terms of the example we set: after all, if we tell our children not to drop litter, but they then see us throw a sweet wrapper on the ground, what conclusion are they likely to draw?

Obviously, our responsibilities in this area aren't limited to our own children, but extend to those entrusted to our care, through our roles as friends, teachers and Sunday school leaders. Without being stuffy about it, it's important that we use our Christian influence to be salt and light, as Jesus instructed us to do (Matthew 5: 13-16), thereby sowing Scriptural seeds in the hearts and minds of the next generation. The consequences of our failure in this regard are too devastating to contemplate: children whose primary influences are television, magazines, aggressively atheistic 'role models', and a society that will take every opportunity to exploit them. Our role in 'training' children, whether by word or example, is particularly important in the context of a world where very few youngsters regularly attend church. This limited church attendance means that their perception of us, as Christians, is likely to have a significant influence on the way they perceive our faith itself. If we're observed to be harsh, uncaring, critical and judgemental, the people around us will endeavour to avoid us, and certainly won't be interested in hearing about our faith! This is true for acquaintances of all ages, but especially those who are young and impressionable.

Certain observers have doubted the veracity of this proverb: after all, many children have been instructed in the 'way they should go', only to become involved in crime or drift far from the Lord. However, this assumes the principle as being that someone so trained would never depart from the truth, whereas the clear qualification expressed in the proverb is that "when he is old, he will not depart from it." Solomon's own experience is a graphic testimony of this. His father was King David, who undoubtedly would have taught him about the Person and precepts of God, but who also set a poor example in certain areas of his family life. This confused message must, in part, have been responsible for Solomon's excesses, which ultimately led him to conclude that, "All (apart from God) is vanity (Ecclesiastes 1:2)" and that "keeping God's commandments is the whole duty of man (Ecclesiastes 12:13)." Such an inspired realisation demonstrates a turning back to God, which may not have been possible, if it hadn't been for the teaching that gave him something (or Someone!) to turn back to. This is the hope we have for our children, and those entrusted to our care: they may temporarily depart from the path of righteousness, and even appear lost for a protracted season, but our instruction, allied with our love and prayers, guided by the Holy Spirit, will ultimately bring them home to the Truth.

I'm hoping that these three questions might give our reflection personal significance.

i. Have you given serious consideration to the influence your example is having on the children in your life?

ii. Who or what were the most powerful influences (good and bad) on your life when you were growing up, and what made them so important?

iii. Is there someone you know, who was trained up in the way they should go, but who is no longer walking with the Lord, for whose salvation you might be able to pray?

Fear God!

"Let us hear the conclusion of the whole matter: Fear God, and keep his commandments: for this is the whole duty of man (Ecclesiastes 12:13)."

The first point to make about this verse is the type of fear to which it refers: it isn't the abject terror of being confronted by an armed robber, but the reverential respect that we ought to have for our Creator. There's certainly no need to be afraid of God if we've accepted Jesus as our Saviour, for there is "no condemnation to them which are in Christ Jesus (Romans 8:1)." If you haven't yet yielded your life to Christ, please be assured that God isn't an Ogre, waiting to judge you: instead, He loves you so much that He gave His Son, to set you free from judgement! Thus, there is absolutely no reason to be frightened of God: He is so approachable that even a young child can confidently come before Him, and so forgiving that even someone like Saul of Tarsus, who was a murderous persecutor of Christians, could find forgiveness and be mightily used by Him!

Life presents us with such an array of competing choices, that it can be hard to know which ones to take. We might think that we could learn a great deal from conducting a scientific experiment which enabled us to discern the decisions we ought to make, if only we could do this without damaging our lives. Of course, much harm can be done when we make decisions solely for the purpose of experimentation, but the good news is that King Solomon has already conducted the experiment for us! With unlimited wealth and power at his disposal, the King of Israel embarked upon a quest to scour the planet for intellectual, cultural and material discoveries which he hoped would enhance his life on earth. At the end of this experiment, he concluded that there was nothing better than to honour the Lord, which is the instruction his father had given him in the first place! This is still the advice God gives us today. As rebellious human beings, we seem reluctant to listen to words of experience, whether from our elders or God Himself, but we'd save ourselves, and others, a prodigious amount of pain, if only we were more willing to do so. This is because the duty Solomon talks of in the verse we're reflecting on isn't so much an obligation we have towards God, as a responsibility towards ourselves. Nothing is as good for us as God's plan for our lives: therefore, every step we take away from Him is a step towards our own unhappiness and, ultimately, our destruction.

It's an undeniable truth that the damage we do to our lives can be proportional to the resources at our disposal. We therefore mustn't be grieved if we pray for financial prosperity and God doesn't give it to us: it may be that He is preserving us from spiritual ruin. Other constraints, such as indifferent health, can also place a hedge of protection around us, limiting our potential to engage in self-destructive activities; instead focusing our minds on the Lord. We may often contemplate how wonderfully we might be able to serve the Kingdom, if we had limitless resources at our disposal, but the reality is that we may actually drift far from God. This is what happened to Solomon, despite his famed wisdom, and there's no guarantee that it wouldn't happen to us.

As I've mentioned previously, the Bible doesn't attempt to disguise the flaws of its leading characters. This truth is graphically exemplified in the biographies it provides of King David and his son, Solomon. These recollections of their weaknesses aren't incorporated in Scripture for us to dwell upon past sins, which God promises to put as far as the east is from the west (Psalm 103:12), once we bring them before Him in a spirit of repentance. Instead, they're contained in His Word to provide a framework for our lives: giving us an opportunity to learn invaluable lessons from the mistakes of others, in order that we don't ourselves have to learn by induction. Of course, being human, we won't always heed the warnings, and will end up making some of the same mistakes as people such as Samson, Solomon and Israel's first king, Saul. When we do, the Bible gives us hope, that there's always the chance of repentance, while we're still on this side of eternity. Rather than dwelling on our failures, and allowing them to define our lives, we have the glorious potential to bring them before the Lord, and allow Him to turn them into testimonies! This is what Solomon did, although not until quite late in his life. It's always better to repent sooner rather than later, in order to mitigate the consequences of our sin and renew our conscience, which can become sclerotic if we don't keep in tune with God's heart. The most important decision we can take is to give our life to Jesus, but our journey doesn't end there: we then need to live for Him, and fulfil the ministry He's entrusted to us, investing in the lives of the people around us. Only once we've done this will we be able to hear those reaffirming words of Matthew 25:21, "Well done, my good and faithful servant!"

Finally, you may like to consider some questions related to the content of our reflection:

i. Are there blessings you've requested from the Lord, which you haven't received, and that might actually have become curses, had He given them to you?

ii. Are you in a place of having explored what the world has to offer, only to realise that it's not as alluring as it first appeared?

iii. Would you like to hear Jesus's commendation, "Well done, my good and faithful servant!" Even if you're currently going backwards in the race, it's not too late to turn around and finish well!

He Is Mine, And I Am His!

"My beloved is mine, and I am his: he feedeth among the lilies (Song of Solomon 2:16)."

The Song of Solomon is a romantic drama, which serves as an allegory for our relationship, as Christian believers, with the God Who set us free from sin, suffering and death. There are those who are challenged by reading the Bible, on account of the wars, plagues and judgements that are chronicled therein. However, there's an extraordinary amount of love contained within its pages, too! The Book of Ruth is an amazing love story which, in addition to being a factual account of real-life events, prefigures Jesus's sacrifice for us, as our Kinsman Redeemer. God's love for the people He created is woven throughout Scripture and, indeed, His Word goes so far as to say, in 1 John 4:8, that He *is* love; a point that's reiterated eight verses later, in 1 John 4:16! The romantic metaphors don't end there: Revelation 21:9 describes believers as being the Bride of Christ, while Ephesians 5:25 exhorts men to love their wives as Christ loved the church; being willing to give their lives for the woman we love, as He did for us.

This verse from the Song of Solomon, also called the Song of Songs, depicts the depth of the love we ought to have for our Saviour, but which frequently eludes us, as the pressures of everyday life impinge upon our relationship with Him. Just as our love for an individual can be buffeted by our changed perceptions of them, our love for Jesus, or at least our expression of that love, has a habit of being moderated by anxieties related to prayers that don't seem to have been answered, or trials from which we believe we ought to have been spared. The reality is that love isn't exclusively about romance and excitement! Human beings need to invest considerable time and effort in order to make a relationship work, frequently subjugating their own desires to those of another. Thus, there is a significant sacrifice involved in loving someone, as we build our lives around them (hopefully putting God first!), while at the same time realising that they may hurt us in return.

This is the conundrum which lies at the heart of the allegory: Jesus Christ, Who created the earth, left the splendour of heaven to come here in a human body, knowing that He'd be rejected, beaten, and ultimately put to death. He didn't do this out of any desire for personal glory or recognition: being God, He doesn't need anything from us at all! Instead, His actions were motivated out of a pure and perfect love that led Him to excruciating suffering on our behalf, to give us the gift of eternal life. In contrast to the apparent affection of mortal humans, which may have impure motives, and unlike the gifts they might give us, which will eventually decay, Jesus's love for us is selflessly unconditional, and His gift is of eternal value. As He said Himself, "Greater love hath no man than this, that a man lay down his life for his friends (John 15:13)." The call on our hearts today is how we choose to respond to the only completely pure act of love we will ever encounter. Will we see the compassion in Jesus's eyes, as He was nailed to the cross for our sins, and accept Him into our hearts, or will we turn down His overtures and regret our decision forever? It's for good reason that the Methodist covenant prayer echoes Song of Solomon 2:16, by saying that "Thou art mine and I am thine." To Who else would we rather belong? When we give our lives to Christ, we receive infinitely more than we give: He takes our sin and shame, in exchange for which He gives us eternal life. What could be better than that?

In closing, here are a few more questions and a final reflection:

i. Has your heart grown cold towards Christ, with formal observance taking the place of your first love? If so, then heed the advice of Jesus to the church in Ephesus and repent! (See Revelation 2: 4 & 5.)

ii. Are you a married man? If so, do you love your wife enough to be willing to give your life for her?

iii. Are you a married woman? If so, do you give your husband the honour that would make it easier for him to love you in this way?

I can't imagine any of us always live up to the ideal described in questions ii. & iii., but we don't have to go it alone! If we bring our wrong attitudes before the Lord, and ask His Holy Spirit to draw alongside us in these areas, we'll see a transformation in our homes. This doesn't only apply to marriage, but to other relationships, too, such as between parents and children, which is a dynamic modelled for us by God the Father.

Here I Am, Lord!

"Also I heard the voice of the Lord, saying, Whom shall I send, and who will go for us? Then said I, Here am I; send me (Isaiah 6:8)."

The Book of Isaiah opens with vivid descriptions of various visions and dreams the prophet was given, relating to impending judgement that was imminently to befall the southern kingdom of Judah. This would inevitably have been distressing for someone who, in addition to being a prophet, was also a patriot, who didn't want to see his nation suffer any more than it already had. The heart of God's people is always to see their communities flourish, and even when they have a hard message to relate, it is always delivered with the desire that their hearers will turn back to the Lord, rather than face His correction. Isaiah was given some hope in this regard, as we read in verses 19 & 20 of chapter one: "If ye be willing and obedient, ye shall eat the good of the land: but if ye refuse and rebel, ye shall be devoured with the sword." Even so, it wouldn't have been a popular message to convey, which possibly explains Isaiah's initial reluctance.

The verse we're reflecting on follows a further vision, in which Isaiah had a revelation of God, leading to his realisation that he was "a man of unclean lips." Paraphrasing Skip Heitzig, senior pastor of Calvary Albuquerque, the receipt of a genuine revelation of God has a tendency to bring our own inadequacies into sharp refrain. This helps to keep us grounded, although we should never disqualify ourselves, as Moses nearly did! God's servants mustn't be so arrogant as to think God can't do without them, but neither should they be so self-effacing that they believe He can't use them. These attitudes, at both ends of the spectrum, are equally dishonouring to God; suggesting that His power is either dependent upon the vessels He uses or insufficient to utilise all of the instruments at His disposal. Having said this, a level of reticence is understandable, as we grapple with the realisation that we've been called to something which is humanly impossible, then invite the Holy Spirit to work His plan through us. On many occasions, it will also be necessary to count the cost: serving God can come at a profound personal price, even up to death. As Elizabeth Howells, wife of Rees, recounted in relation to a challenging decision in her own life, "I weighed the cost against Calvary, at which point I came through." God equips His people for the roles to which He commissions them, but this doesn't mean we simply float through the mission without a care in the world: the spiritual opposition we face when serving the Lord can be intense, and it's only by His grace and protection that we emerge victorious.

As was the case with Isaiah, our call will generally come at a difficult time, when there is a considerable amount of work to be done in circumstances which aren't propitious. It may have been the call we dreamed of all our life, but it won't be easy, just as a football manager usually only lands a plum job when the team is struggling and the previous incumbent has been dismissed. Our lives are a preparation for God's calling, but only if we allow them to be. For this reason, we mustn't "despise the day of small things (Zechariah 4:10)," as these are frequently the times when God sharpens us, away from the public glare, in order that we can learn from Him, and from our mistakes, without them being magnified in full view. Wonderfully, we frequently find that He even uses experiences from prior to our salvation, demonstrating that He was working His plan for our lives before we even knew Him!

Both Moses and Isaiah travelled on a journey to the point where they were willing to be sent, and it may well be the same for us. However, it's one thing to say "send me," when we know the physical or spiritual end-point, and quite another to be obedient to the call, before we know where we're going. The reality is that we don't have the luxury of deciding our destination. When we yield our lives to Christ, He guarantees our eternal security, but for the duration of our time on earth we're expected to be unconditional in our obedience to Him, rather than opting out of various assignments, like a lawyer who only takes on the cases he expects to win. It's the prerogative of the Holy Spirit to decide how He deploys us in the spiritual battle to which we've been enlisted, but we can have complete confidence that He'll equip us for whatever lies in store. However, before we ask Him for more resources, we need to be sure that we're adequately utilising the ones we already have available to us: many a spiritual harvest has been lost because the ground wasn't first ploughed with prayer.

On the face of it, Isaiah's ministry wasn't spectacularly successful: there was no wave of national repentance and judgement was ultimately pronounced. However, God is just, as we've discussed previously: He wanted to give the people an opportunity to repent, and Isaiah was His vehicle for doing this. Just as it isn't our prerogative to critically analyse the assignment before we decide whether to participate, we shouldn't judge ourselves harshly with regard to our results, or perceived lack of them. Unlike football managers, we won't be assessed on outcomes, but on our faithfulness to follow the call, pointing people to Christ!

I'll conclude with three questions for you to consider:

i. Isaiah had visions and dreams, but how does God speak to you?

ii. Is there an assignment that God has given you, which is currently lying dormant?

iii. What are the impediments that are holding you back from achieving your dreams? If you bring these before the Lord, do you believe that His Holy Spirit will help you to overcome them?

His Forgiveness; Our Ingratitude

"He is despised and rejected of men; a man of sorrows, and acquainted with grief: and we hid as it were our faces from him; he was despised, and we esteemed him not (Isaiah 53:3)."

Chapter 53 of the Book of Isaiah speaks so eloquently of the eternal sacrifice of our Saviour that Jewish rabbis have considerable difficulty dealing with it. Prior to Jesus's crucifixion, they almost unanimously considered the chapter to prophesy their coming Messiah's suffering for our sins, but when Jesus completely fulfilled these prophecies, it left them with a dilemma. All good scientists, and people of sound mind with a reasonable intellect, will look to where the evidence leads them, and for some eminent Jews the evidence was so compelling that they rightly concluded that Jesus was their Messiah. People with a revisionist perspective on history, along with those who don't want to believe the truth, need a credible alternative to reality, which is sufficiently compelling to forestall awkward questions. The alternatives constructed around Isaiah 53 are either that it allegorises the suffering of the nation of Israel or that it refers to the as yet born Messiah. The former doesn't appear to have even been suggested, prior to the first century BC, while the latter faces credibility issues, because the events described would no longer be unique if the Messiah for whom 21st century Jews are waiting was to fulfil them, two millennia after Jesus's initial fulfilment. Many rabbis who see the flaws in both of these two positions simply choose to ignore Isaiah 53 altogether!

Only in eternity, if then, will we be able to comprehend the depth of Jesus's suffering, as He took our sins upon Himself. The physical torture was horrific enough - the beatings, scourgings, and asphyxiation by crucifixion - but even worse was His separation, for the first and only time in history, from His Heavenly Father. This separation came about because Jesus was literally made sin for us, and God, Who is unable to look upon sin (Habakkuk 1:13), therefore had to turn away from His beloved Son, as He suffered the judgement we deserved. Even nature mourned the death of her Creator, as the earth was shrouded in darkness for a period of three hours - far longer than could have been explained by an eclipse, at a time when an eclipse wouldn't even have been possible - and then convulsed in a massive earthquake (see Matthew 27: 45 - 51).

It was ironic, yet it had to be this way, that the very humans Jesus came to save were responsible for crucifying Him. The Jews have frequently been blamed for this act of deicide, but it was the civil authorities who ultimately put Jesus to death, because the Jews no longer had the right to enforce capital punishment. As Isaiah 53:3 says, Jesus was "despised and rejected of men" and, sadly, this is still true today: people all around the world mock His Name, which they use as a curse word, oblivious to the fact that, just like those present in Jerusalem that day, they're actually bringing a curse upon themselves. However, Jesus isn't universally rejected: far from it! Believers from all over the globe worship Him, too, and in heaven we'll meet men and women "from every tribe, people and nation (Revelation 5:9)," who've put their trust in Jesus for salvation.

Jesus suffered many sorrows during His time on earth, but He must surely still break His heart today, as He sees people He loves so dearly, for whom He gave His life so freely, heading to a lost eternity, without even giving Him a second thought. Jesus didn't come to receive anything from us: He came to give us the most enduring and meaningful gift in history; the value of which many will only realise when it's too late. But what of those of us who do know Jesus as our Saviour? Do we give Him due regard for the price He paid for our sins (Isaiah 52:14 suggests that His face was marred to the extent that He scarcely looked human), or do we accept the gift without contemplating its significance? For someone who isn't yet a Christian to lightly esteem Jesus's sacrifice at Calvary is understandable, because their spiritual eyes are blinded to the truth, but for a believer to display such an attitude is bordering on the inexcusable. In the words of the popular worship song, "Jesus paid it all; all to Him I owe." Let's live as though we mean it, give honour to His Name and allow the Holy Spirit to work through us, as He seeks to open the blind eyes in our classrooms, homes and offices.

Here are three important questions to reflect upon:

i. What does Jesus's sacrifice mean to you?

ii. If you've already accepted Jesus as your Saviour, but have lightly esteemed His sacrifice, why not thank Him today for everything He's done for you?

iii. If you don't yet know Jesus in a real and personal way, can you at least understand, from the passage we've been looking at, the extent of His suffering and the depth of His love for you? If so, my prayer for you is that you'll embark on a journey to get to know the Person Who loves you more than anyone else ever will, and gave you more than anyone else ever could.

Don't Be Deceived!

"The heart is deceitful above all things, and desperately wicked: who can know it (Jeremiah 17:9)?"

Have you ever fallen hopelessly in love with someone, only to realise, a short time later, that they weren't actually 'the one'? It might not have been a person, but perhaps a possession, such as a car, which you eagerly saved for, prior to the dawning of the realisation that it didn't yield the happiness you were anticipating. These are modern-day examples of what Jeremiah speaks of in the verse we're currently reflecting on: we might believe we know what we need, and it may bring us enjoyment for a period of time, but eventually we realise that decisions which weren't guided by the Holy Spirit will lead to disappointment.

Has there been a discernible change in any of your acquaintances, during the pandemic? It's possible that some of your friends and colleagues have been revealed not to be the individuals you believed them to be, while others have surpassed your expectations. There's a saying in Kilkenny, and probably elsewhere, too, that a crisis doesn't build character, so much as reveal it. This is certainly the case as far as matters of faith are concerned. If the past year has revealed *you* not to be the person you believed you were, that's more than likely because you'd been relying too much on yourself, and not enough on the Lord. The good news is that it's not too late to redress the balance: in fact, this is the perfect time to get your priorities right, as God has plans to use you in a wonderful way! As we'll read later, all you need to do is to ask Him for a new heart!

Prisoners are frequently described in terms of the worst thing they've ever done: murderers, burglars, fraudsters, etc. However, what if that standard of judgement was applied to the rest of us? We naturally do our best to portray a positive image of ourselves, but our reputations would certainly take a bit of a hit, if we were branded as liars, thieves, and the rest. While we might explain away the occasional mis-statement or exaggerated expenses submission, the uncomfortable reality is that we're all capable of far greater depravity than we probably realise. We've seen this in the not-too-distant past, with atrocities such as the Rwandan genocide and the Balkan conflict, where people who for years had peacefully co-existed as neighbours inexplicably perpetrated horrendous acts of brutality against one another. We all have our tipping points, and a slight shift in circumstances can produce a radical change in our behaviour, revealing a less than savoury character lurking within.

Amazingly, God knows the very worst that we're capable of, and yet He still loves us! Furthermore, He's aware of the best that's within us, and is keen to draw that to the surface, as we take the advice given by Ezekiel to the nation of Israel, and ask the Lord to replace our hearts of stone with hearts of flesh, in order that His Spirit will guide us to do the right things for the right reasons (Ezekiel 36: 26 & 27). Self-help manuals won't make us better human beings: they'll only enable us to enhance an image that will immediately be exposed when we next come under pressure. Genuine transformation only occurs by inviting the Holy Spirit to mould us, and our hearts, into His image!

If you promise not to deceive yourselves, you might like to consider a few challenging questions!

i. How would it feel if everyone else's perception of you was based on the worst thing you've ever done?

ii. When you did this thing, whatever it was, did it shock you, to see what you were capable of?

iii. Have you unsuccessfully attempted to change your heart, without the transformative power of the Holy Spirit? If so, why not ask for His help today? He'll not only radically alter your actions, but also transform the thoughts that produce them!

Seek And Ye Shall Find!

"And ye shall seek me, and find me, when you search for me with all your heart (Jeremiah 29:13)."

Some of our previous reflections have considered the mercy that motivates God's correction: His desire isn't to punish us but, as we were reflecting last time, He knows what we need far better than we do! It may therefore be that someone who is attempting to live their life apart from Christ will encounter an obstacle of some description, to bring them to the realisation that they really do need Jesus: not just in eternity, but in this life, too. Similarly, Christians who wander off track, and aren't aware of the damage they could be doing, both to themselves and to their witness, might be confronted with a scenario which hastens their realisation that remaining close to the Lord is the only way to navigate their course through life. Jeremiah chapter 29 reveals God's heart in this respect: it was written by the prophet, as a message from God to the people of Jerusalem, who were to be taken into Babylonian captivity. Had the Lord merely been angry, He might have said something along the lines of, "You've really blown it this time; I don't want anything more to do with you," or perhaps He might not have spoken to them at all! Instead, however, He gave Jeremiah a letter for them, which emphasised both His love, and their opportunity for redemption. Aren't we glad we serve such a merciful God?

Jeremiah's correspondence contains numerous words of profound encouragement, including the promise that their captivity wasn't to be permanent, but would end after seventy years (Jeremiah 29:10). The next verse may be on a fridge magnet in your home, or perhaps inscribed on a bookmark: "For I know the thoughts that I think towards you, saith the Lord, thoughts of peace, and not of evil, to give you an expected end." Some translations render "an expected end" as "a future and a hope;" either way, these are not the words of a vengeful Cosmic Power, seeking to punish people for defying His will. In verse 12, God promises that He will hear the people's prayers, while in verse 14 He reiterates His pledge to bring the nation home again. Sandwiched between these two verses we find the key to unlocking all of these promises: they can only be fulfilled when our hearts are aligned with God's, and for this to be possible it is necessary for us to earnestly seek Him.

Are you reading this as someone who isn't yet a Christian? Perhaps you're sufficiently interested in matters of faith to pick up a book of spiritual reflections, but maybe you don't yet have a relationship with Jesus as your Lord and Saviour. It could be that you're waiting for Him to make the first move, on the basis that: He knows where I am; it's up to Him to come and get me! Alternatively, you might be looking for something more mystical, in the form of a 'sign' or a 'call' from above. It certainly isn't beyond God to work in this way, but He's already given you all the 'signs' and 'calls' that you need. Jesus's invitation to His disciples to "Come, follow me!" applies to you, today, just as much as it did to them, back then, while His death and resurrection prove His love for you and validate all the claims He ever made in Scripture. The next move, essentially, is therefore up to you: a relationship with God is as close as calling out to Him, thanking Jesus for His sacrifice, and inviting His Holy Spirit into your life. However, this must be done in all sincerity: no half-hearted applicants need respond!

Speaking of half-heartedness brings me to readers who have accepted Jesus into their hearts, but who are currently not fully walking with Him. Perhaps you've allowed the cares of this world to dampen your initial zeal, or maybe, like the people to whom Jeremiah was writing, a sequence of wrong decisions has led you progressively further from the sanctuary you found in the Lord. If this is the case, you won't have an easy life! God loves you too much to allow you to wander astray, so there'll come a point when you experience His correction; indeed, you might already be doing so! If that's the case, why not seek Him now, with all your heart? You're guaranteed to find Him: you have His Word for it!

It might be an interesting exercise to ponder the following questions:

i. If you're reading this as a Christian, how does God's heart for people who've wandered from Him compare to your own attitudes towards them?

ii. If you're not yet a Christian, are you surprised to see the heart God has towards you, as revealed in Jeremiah 29?

iii. If you're currently experiencing God's correction, but simply intend to 'ride out the storm', without turning back to Him, what do you think the outcome is likely to be? Even if you get through this storm, might another one follow?

We Have Hope!

"It is of the Lord's mercies that we are not consumed, because his compassions fail not. They are new every morning: great is thy faithfulness (Lamentations 3: 22 & 23)."

The first two and a third chapters of Lamentations are incredibly hard to read! This short Book was written by the prophet Jeremiah, who was lamenting over the destruction of his beloved Jerusalem. In the preceding Book, which bears his name, Jeremiah repeatedly warned the inhabitants of the city of the judgement that would be inevitable if they continued to harden their hearts and display outward opposition, or even indifference, to the God of their fathers. This wasn't a responsibility that Jeremiah relished (who would!), and he suffered greatly for his obedience to the call God placed on his life. In addition to being routinely ridiculed, Jeremiah was forbidden from marrying and, in Jeremiah 38, we read of him being accused of treason, for which alleged felony he was thrown into a dungeon, where he sunk into the mire (Jeremiah 38:6). What a pathetic image this is; yet it was almost prophetic in itself, given that it pictures how the people of Jerusalem must have felt, as they were carried into captivity.

If the foretaste of impending judgement was bad, witnessing it at first hand was even worse, when Jeremiah saw the city he loved being laid waste. In Lamentations, he personifies Jerusalem's suffering, speaking as though the unfolding judgement was actually consuming him, which I'd imagine is how he felt. Similar to the situation which can often pertain in our own lives, there came a point of almost total despair, but it was during this time when, as described in the verse immediately preceding those we're reflecting on, Jeremiah recalled that he had hope! His heartache then gave way to a joyous doxology, extolling all that is good, including the Lord Himself. Implicit in the premise of Lamentations 3:22 is the acknowledgement that God could consume (destroy) those who oppose Him, but we see that His unfailing compassion motivates Him to display the mercy which spares us from judgement, until such time as it becomes absolutely necessary. This section of Scripture, and in particular verse 23, inspired Thomas Chisholm's famous hymn, 'Great is thy Faithfulness'. Only a God of unfailing mercy, compassion and creativity could use circumstances as bleak as Jeremiah's to inspire, more than two and a half thousand years later, such a stirring and moving anthem!

When in times of distress, we'll inevitably look for hope, whether in the form of a new job, the reconciliation of a relationship, or an assuaging of our sense of grief. We may look within ourselves, to our own inner strength, or to external sources, such as friends or music, but very often we can hang onto mere aspirations, rather than depending upon the unfailing promises of an omnipotent, miracle-working God, Who cannot fail to deliver. Looking to ourselves will always cause disappointment, as we see our own imperfections and then begin to obsess about them. Cultivating friendships is an important thing to do, but we can never completely depend upon our friends, who have their own insecurities and weaknesses, in addition to a myriad of responsibilities that compete for the time they can devote to us. In contrast, as Jeremiah found when writing the Book of Lamentations, focusing our eyes on God inspires us to worship Him, giving proper perspective to our heartaches, which are bound to end one day! In common with Thomas Chisholm, we also have one advantage that Jeremiah didn't, in being able to give thanks for Calvary, thereby enabling us to sing of "Pardon for sin and a peace that endureth; Thine own dear presence to cheer and to guide; Strength for today and bright hope for tomorrow, Blessings all mine, with ten thousand beside!"

Will your heart stand up to a few more questions?

SPIRITUAL REFLECTIONS - I

i. Do you, like Jeremiah, grieve over men and women who are facing impending judgement?

ii. If you're a Christian, how do you demonstrate to people who don't yet know the Lord that you care about them?

iii. If you're not yet a Christian, are you tired of all the talk of possible judgement? Please be assured that these warnings are only contained in God's Word to you because He loves you, and wants you to experience joy instead of judgement!

Ichabod!

"Then the glory of the Lord departed from off the threshold of the house, and stood over the cherubim (Ezekiel 10:18)."

What a tragic condition for the house of God to be in! In 1 Kings 8, we read of the dedication of Solomon's Temple, during which the people pledged to honour the Lord and He, in turn, promised to hear their prayers. Most notably, in verses 10 and 11 of this chapter, we read: "It came to pass, when the priests were come out of the holy place, that the cloud filled the house of the Lord, so that the priests could not stand to minister because of the cloud: for the glory of the Lord had filled the house of the Lord." In the intervening years, as we have seen, the Kingdom of Judah spiralled into a state of spiritual decline, as she took her lead from rulers who forsook the True God, in favour of a myriad of empty philosophies. The rate of deterioration was arrested on occasion by kings of integrity, who attempted to institute reform, although these reforms were generally superficial exercises, rather than heartfelt moves of national repentance. In the end, however, things got so bad that even the Temple was profaned, with abominations such as those described by Ezekiel in the eighth chapter of his Book. We've previously considered Galatians 6:7, which warns us that "God will not be mocked," and this verse goes on to promise that we will reap what we sow. This can be a good thing: if we sow love, generosity and wisdom, we will reap a bounteous harvest. However, in the Jerusalem of Ezekiel's time, even God's representatives, the priests, were sowing seeds of evil and corruption. When repentance wasn't forthcoming, judgement was sure to follow.

To the people of Jerusalem, their Temple was a crowning glory, which set their city apart from any other on earth. It was a truly magnificent edifice, constructed out of the finest materials, during an epoch of opulent national wealth. However, it wasn't the gold, exotic wood or precious stones that gave the Temple its magnificence, but the indwelling of God's glory, which is something that can never be taken for granted. While God is longsuffering, He cannot be expected to dwell where sin resides, and He was ultimately obliged to leave the Temple, on account of the exceeding iniquity of the house of Israel and Judah (Ezekiel 9:9). In other words, God wasn't simply 'having a bad day, when His mercy gave way to a fit of anger'; nor did He merely take umbrage at a minor peccadillo; He was so grieved by the consistent pollution of His house on earth that He could no longer stay there. Later, in Ezekiel 11:23, we read that He departed the city of Jerusalem itself (the word 'ichabod' means 'the glory has departed'), although a reading of the text leaves us with the overwhelming impression that He did so with an immensely heavy heart.

So much for the history; what about us today? If you're a Christian, then your body is analogous to the Temple of old; indwelt by His Holy Spirit, which is the modern equivalent of God's glory. In the same way that the priests in Ezekiel's time offended God to the extent that His glory left the Temple, it is possible for us to grieve the Holy Spirit, which is something Paul urges us not to do, in Ephesians 4:30. How is it possible for us to grieve the Holy Spirit? By polluting the temple, just as the priests did! In Paul's words, we must "let no corrupt communication proceed out of our mouth (Ephesians 4:29)" and put away "all bitterness, wrath, anger, clamour, evil speaking and malice (Ephesians 4:31)." If we do this, the Holy Spirit will remain with us for as long as we want Him to, but our wilful insensitivity will cause Him to depart from us, in the same way that we don't enjoy being around people we consider to be obnoxious! It's always a good idea to 'keep short accounts with God', repenting for our sins as we become aware of them, and asking Him to "Search me, O God, and know my heart: try me, and know my thoughts (Psalm 139:23)."

Tragically, it's not just the Jewish priests or individual Christians who have vitiated their witness by allowing corruption to take root. The church has been responsible for much good, including the improved social status of women, and the building of schools and hospitals around the world; not to mention the joy of salvation she's helped bring to countless lives. However, we've also sown seeds of bigotry, greed and political corruption, in addition to allowing the proclamation of a false 'Gospel', which keeps people in bondage. It may be that you've turned away from the church because of the heartache that's been caused to you, and this is something for which I sincerely apologise. Maybe it will be of some consolation to have seen the degree to which such activities grieve God's heart, too: they sadden Him to the extent that He left His very own house. However, while the church may have failed you, Jesus never will! His love for you is such that He was prepared to leave the glory of heaven to come to earth and redeem your life. Now, isn't that something to be thankful for?

It might be helpful to mull over a few questions, while contemplating what you've read.

i. If you're a Christian, is there any aspect of your life that might be grieving the Holy Spirit?

ii. Is the church you attend somewhere God feels at home? If not, what could you do to change that? (Or maybe you need to change your church!)

iii. If you haven't yet accepted Jesus into your heart, do you believe that He loves you? If so, why not give Him a chance? If you become a Christian, it's a good thing to attend a fellowship, but there will inevitably be times of hurt, because churches are comprised of fallible human beings. That said, Christ Himself will never hurt you: He gave His life so He could know you!

Standing In The Gap

> *"And I sought for a man amongst them, that should make up the hedge, and stand in the gap before me for the land, that I should not destroy it: but I found none (Ezekiel 22:30)."*

Sometimes, the Christian life can be a bit of a mystery! We serve an omnipotent God, Who by definition therefore has the power to do whatever He decrees; yet He chooses to involve us, fallible human beings, in His plan for salvation! I can imagine the angels turning to one another, with wings over their eyes, and saying something along the lines of, "Why did He entrust that task to Benjamin? I'd have done a far better job!" The sad reality is that they're almost certainly right! Nevertheless, God continues to use me, as He does you! Another paradox is the fact that our prayers can apparently make a difference to an immutable God! I appreciate that people of a strict Calvinistic persuasion have a different view, and I'm not looking for a theological argument here, but prayer assuredly must have an impact. It surely wouldn't have been a discipline Jesus practised so assiduously, if this wasn't the case; nor would James have written that, "Ye have not because ye ask not (James 4:2)."

In Genesis 18: 22 - 33, we're given a wonderful picture of intercession, or standing in the gap, as Abraham pleads for Sodom, home to his nephew, Lot. Abraham begins by asking whether God will judge the righteous with the wicked, and requesting that Sodom be spared if fifty righteous men could be found in the city. When God agreed to this request, Abraham almost impudently bid the Lord down to forty-five, then to forty, and finally to ten. He probably stopped there, thinking that Lot and his family, plus a few friends, would surely yield a quorum, but the spiritual environment was such that not even ten just men lived in Sodom. Even then, God evacuated Lot and his family before judgement was pronounced, thereby honouring His commitment to Abraham, that He would not judge the righteous with the wicked.

Following the infamous incident with Aaron and the golden calf, of which we read in Exodus chapter 32, God indicated to Moses that it was His intention to wipe out the nation and start again with him (Exodus 32:10). Given that God is omniscient, and therefore knew in advance that the people would transgress in such a way, this wasn't an angry reaction to rebellion, but a measured, pre-planned response to their sin. Moses' intercession for the nation, including his remarkable offer to forgo his eternal reward on their behalf (Exodus 32:32), resulted in God forestalling judgement. We therefore see that, not only does God reserve judgement for a last resort, but that He will, even then, be persuaded towards clemency, when a sincere intercessor pleads the case of an individual, family, region or country. Ezekiel 22:30 demonstrates that, as bad as things were in Israel at the time, it was still God's heart to show mercy, and He was actively looking for someone to bring the case before Him. When no intercessor could be found, He was honour-bound to pass sentence on a people who had acceded to the curses which would emanate from disobedience (Deuteronomy 27: 11 - 26), defied His Law, then failed to repent.

In many respects, the times in which we live are not entirely dissimilar to the Israel of Ezekiel's day. Even within the church, God's Word isn't always highly esteemed, and we're increasingly seeing good being decried as bad and evil lauded as good, which is a scenario described in Isaiah 5:20. Moreover, statute books around the world are increasingly laden with legislation that dishonours God and exalts everything which is contrary to His nature. As a consequence, many of our nations are ripe for judgement, but there are faithful intercessors, all around the world, who are praying on behalf of the national governments who wish to undermine, or even eradicate, their faith. Could it be that judgement is only being forestalled because these people are praying, thereby making the case for the defence in the heavenly courtroom? God is never constrained by our prayers, but the implication of Ezekiel 22:30 is that our willingness to travail in prayer can give Him the legal basis for commuting sentences that would otherwise be handed down. What a privilege we have to intercede for our families, friends, communities and nations: let it not be said in our day that there was no-one to stand in the gap!

May these questions be a call to action:

i. Do you regularly plead before the Lord for your family, nation and individuals around the world, who do not yet know Jesus?

ii. Were there people who were praying for you, before you were saved? If so, have you thanked them?

iii. Have you read some of the accounts of revival; e.g., Ulster in 1857 - 59 and the Hebrides in 1949, and how they were birthed in prayer? I'd thoroughly recommend doing this: it will provide a tremendous inspiration to pray!

Divine Revelation!

"And at the end of the days I Nebuchadnezzar lifted up mine eyes unto heaven, and mine understanding returned unto me, and I blessed the most High, and I praised and honoured him that liveth forever, whose dominion is an everlasting dominion, and his kingdom is from generation to generation (Daniel 4:34)."

What a remarkable profession of faith from a redoubtable king, born outside of God's covenant relationship with Israel, who previously had a reputation for brutality that few could rival! King Nebuchadnezzar's radical conversion has to be of immense encouragement to anyone who has been called to witness in an environment characterised by absolute rejection of the rule of God. The backdrop to these events also provides an invaluable insight into the role of an evangelist, and the way in which the Holy Spirit impacts a person's heart, during the process of salvation.

When the people of the southern kingdom of Judah persisted in their sin and refused to return to the Lord, He raised up the king of the mighty Babylonian Empire, Nebuchadnezzar, to capture Jerusalem and bring the cream of her citizens back to Babylon. These captives included Daniel, whose Book contains Nebuchadnezzar's amazing declaration, and also Hananiah, Mishael & Azariah, who were later re-named Meshach, Shadrach & Abednego. These four young men remained faithful in their worship of the One, True God, which put them on a collision course with their new ruler, who wished to exalt himself and reign forever! However, they were always respectful in their dealings with the king, which is an essential prerequisite for effective

Christian witness: if we don't treat people with respect, they won't want to hear what we have to say - and why would they?

Reminiscent of Joseph in Egypt, Daniel's wisdom and faithfulness led him to a responsible position in the Babylonian government: he also had a gift for interpreting dreams, again like Joseph, which the Lord used to enable him to build a relationship with the king. When, in Daniel chapter 2, the king dreamt of a polymetallic figure, he sought for an interpretation, which his court astrologers were unable to provide. Being inspired by the God of Heaven, Daniel not only interpreted the dream, but did so without even having been told what it was! In essence, Nebuchadnezzar was the head of gold, but the presence of other metals demonstrated that his kingdom would be finite, which wasn't what he wanted to hear! Railing against this, he constructed a gigantic golden statue, which he ordered everyone present to worship: it was the refusal of Meshach, Shadrach & Abednego to yield to this demand that resulted in the famous incident, where they were condemned to the fiery furnace. Nebuchadnezzar decreed that the furnace be heated to seven times its usual heat, demonstrating his unassuageable anger towards anyone who crossed him: no sign of a softening of the heart so far!

While the quiet witness of Daniel and his companions may not have impacted the king's heart to date, he was about to have an encounter with the God of the Bible! He was clearly outraged by the response of the three faithful Jews, recorded in Daniel 3: 17 & 18, that "Our God whom we serve is able to deliver us from the burning fiery furnace, and he will deliver us out of thine hand, O king. But if not, be it known unto thee, O king, that we will not serve thy gods, nor worship the golden image which thou hast set up." However, he must have reflected on these words when God did indeed deliver them from the fire, walking with them through the trial (Daniel 3: 24 & 25). This led to Nebuchadnezzar's first acknowledgement, recorded in the next verse, that they were "servants of the most high God." Whether this was a true conversion, or an initial emotional response, is hard to tell, but God was definitely at work! This incident emphasises a point made in an earlier reflection: God may sometimes help us plot a course through the test, rather than exempting us from it; either in order to teach us about our character, and His, or to reinforce our witness. When we go through trials, the world is watching. If we pray for deliverance and it doesn't immediately come, it may be that God intends to use our response as a beacon to observers who aren't yet Christians, for whom the genuineness of our lives will speak far louder than any amount of preaching.

Even after such a revelation from above, Nebuchadnezzar fell into pride, but he later repented and made the wonderful declaration of God's majesty, which we read in Daniel 4. Daniel's patient witness certainly opened up a pathway to Nebuchadnezzar's heart, but true salvation can, ultimately, only be a sovereign act of the Holy Spirit. Having said that, this isn't the end of His role; only the beginning! After salvation, we need Him as much as ever but, even then, there will still be occasions when we stumble, or maybe fall. When new Christians err, they might be tempted to think they've 'blown it' and can't return to the Lord, but this is a lie from Satan: the truth is that anyone can repent at any time, and turn back to Him. We will still have to live with the consequences of our sin, but our relationship with God will be restored - albeit that we'll need to commit the time to make it work - and His Holy Spirit will help us navigate the path towards restoration.

King Nebuchadnezzar's proclamation of faith contains some interesting axioms. He observed that his understanding returned to him - referring to his deliverance from a temporary period of insanity, which the Lord sent as a rebuke for his pride - and that only then was he able to praise and worship God. He also recognised that God's Kingdom, and not his own, could uniquely be eternal. It is a sign of true conversion to magnify and honour God: I have no doubt that we'll see Nebuchadnezzar in heaven, and we're privileged to read such a wonderful testimony. Although all glory must go to the Lord, Daniel's role should never be underestimated: he clearly cared for Nebuchadnezzar, even when he was a brutal dictator. We, too, must be careful to remember that the people with whom we share this earth were created in God's own image, and that His Son gave His life for them, in order that they could inherit eternal life. This is not to say that our witness will always be effective! In contrast to Nebuchadnezzar, his grandson, Belshazzar, whose life Daniel also impacted, was "weighed in the balances and found wanting (Daniel 5:27)." As he partied, mocking the living God, his kingdom, and ultimately his life, were dramatically taken from him. Our responsibility is to be faithful in delivering the message, allowing God to take care of the results. Even if spiritual eyes aren't discernibly opening, don't be discouraged: people may not respond immediately, but we're planting a seed, which others will water, for believers further down the line to potentially reap the harvest.

Finally, here are some questions to contemplate:

i. How many people around you, like Belshazzar, do you believe are living for temporary pleasures, oblivious to the eternal implications of their actions?

ii. How faithful are you in witnessing to these individuals, through your love for them, as well as your words? Like Daniel, we must show concern, and not give the impression that we're rejoicing in the coming judgement!

iii. If you don't yet know Jesus as your Saviour, would you like to do so? As Nebuchadnezzar found out, it can be a humbling experience, but that's no bad thing, when humbling leads to repentance, then to eternal life. If a wicked Babylonian king can make this journey, there's no reason why you can't do the same!

Spiritual Warfare!

"Then said he unto me, Fear not, Daniel: for from the first day that thou didst set thine heart to understand, and to chasten thyself before thy God, thy words were heard, and I am come for thy words. But the prince of the kingdom of Persia withstood me one and twenty days: but, lo, Michael, one of the chief princes, came to help me; and I remained there with the kings of Persia (Daniel 10: 12 & 13)."

It must be an awesome experience to see an angel, and quite frightening, too, as exemplified by the fact that they invariably tell the people to whom they're speaking not to be afraid. Prior to the events described in the two verses quoted above, we read, in chapter 9, of Daniel meditating upon Jeremiah's prophecy that the Babylonian captivity would end after seventy years. Rather than adopting a fatalistic approach, Daniel besought the Lord in earnest prayer, confessing the sins of the nation and asking if He'd be so gracious as to forgive them, and him, in order that the prophecy could be fulfilled. This is a beautiful illustration of the heart of the intercessor, as Daniel identified himself with the subjects of his prayer, and pleaded with the Lord as though his life depended on the outcome. This wasn't an attempt to brow-beat God into giving him the answer he wanted - Daniel was far too mature for that - but his attitude was a far cry from the complacency of some believers, who simply wait for prophetic fulfilment to occur, without calling upon the Lord to bring the prophecy to fruition.

Daniel was probably a teenager when he was brought to Babylon, so with seven decades nearly having elapsed, he would have been well into his eighties by the time we're reflecting upon. More than five hundred years later, Paul exhorted his protégé, Timothy, to finish the race well, and he quite possibly had Daniel in mind when doing so. After seventy years of remaining faithful in the epicentre of idolatry, serving multiple kings and thriving in a den of lions, many of us might have been tempted to take things easy, but not Daniel! He wasn't content to offer up a quick, half-hearted prayer, but instead gave every ounce of physical, emotional and spiritual energy, in pleading for the future of his nation. If only we were prepared to do the same, what a difference might we see in the world around us! This level of intercession is undoubtedly costly, but it also yields magnificent rewards, in terms of a close relationship with God, and the joy of seeing apparently impossible circumstances changed by the power of the Holy Spirit. In Daniel's case, he was also given a greater revelation than anyone had received hitherto, regarding the sequence of events leading to the coming of the Messiah, and the Tribulation period, which will precede His return.

The reason for more believers not drawing so deeply from the well of intercession is seen in chapter 10, where the physical impact of this intense spiritual battle is described in detail: "O my Lord, by the vision my sorrows are turned upon me, and I have retained no strength (Daniel 10:16)." Rees Howells, founder of the Bible College of Wales, wasn't a military combatant in World War 2, but many who knew him attested to the physical toll his hours of daily intercession, during those six years, took on his body. Jesus undoubtedly made the ultimate sacrifice when He took our place upon the cross at Calvary, but many saints, up to this day, continue to serve sacrificially, and there'll be a special blessing for them in eternity! Just as a patriot cannot resist the call to serve the nation, prayer warriors are unable to rest until they've given every ounce of energy to defeat the spiritual forces which control our world!

Verses 12 & 13 of Daniel chapter 10 describe the fundamental nature of this conflict. We must never over-estimate Satan's power, but he shouldn't be downplayed, either, because an enemy is never more dangerous than when he's overlooked. Both he, and the demons who serve him, will vigorously fight against our endeavours to shine light into the world, as they strive to keep it shrouded in darkness. However, we are fighting from a position of victory, secured for us by Jesus at Calvary, and there are twice as many angels on our side as there are demons on Satan's (see Revelation 12:4)! Moreover, Satan isn't omnipresent, omniscient or omnipotent: he isn't the direct opposite of God, Who has no equal; if anything, Satan's opposite number is Michael the archangel, of whom we read in Daniel 10:13. Having said all this, we're no match for Satan in our own strength: he has more power and experience than we do, meaning that our spiritual battles have to be fought in the power of the Holy Spirit. We should never speak directly to Satan, either, which is a point we'll consider in a later reflection: even Michael was so cautious as to retort, "The Lord rebuke thee (Jude 1:9)," rather than taking him on directly.

Returning to the verses under consideration, it's encouraging to see, in verse 12, that Daniel's prayers were heard immediately. Nevertheless, it took three weeks for an answer to come! Playing on the words of the old worship song, I wonder how often we give up on the brink of a miracle! The reason for the delay was spiritual opposition from the 'prince of the kingdom of Persia', who was a demonic being, anxious to prevent Daniel's prayers from being answered. Whenever we earnestly intercede for an individual, event or location, we're entering into a spiritual battle, and cannot expect our opponents to give up without a fight. Daniel ultimately prevailed, with the help of Michael, and we'll succeed, too, provided we fight the battle using the Lord's strategy, with the power of the Holy Spirit, and are diligent to equip ourselves with the spiritual armour God provides for us (Ephesians 6: 10 - 18).

SPIRITUAL REFLECTIONS - I

Are you ready for a few questions?

i. How might events have unfolded if Daniel had ceased to intercede, prior to the twenty-first day?

ii. What are the spiritual forces controlling your community - and are you willing to fight for its liberation from them?

iii. Looking back on your Christian life, have you credited Satan with too much power, or too little?

Mercy In Judgement

"And I will sow her unto me in the earth; and I will have mercy upon her that had not obtained mercy; and I will say to them which were not my people, Thou art my people; and they shall say, Thou art my God (Hosea 2:23)."

The prophet Hosea was primarily speaking to the ten tribes comprising the northern kingdom of Israel, prior to the invasion of that land by the Assyrians in 722 BC. In common with many of the prophets, he had a difficult message to deliver, which was essentially that the defiance of the nation, and the wickedness of their kings, had waxed to such an extent that the correcting hand of God's judgement would be necessary. In order to capture people's attention, God frequently instructed His prophets to act out their messages, and Hosea was required to do this in an extraordinary way: by marrying a woman who would be unfaithful to him, and bringing her back home in a spirit of forgiveness. In so doing, Hosea was illustrating God's broken heart for the lost condition of the people He loved, while assuring them that their removal from their homeland wouldn't be permanent. Thus, although Hosea's recorded prophecy opens with a hard message, portending the apparent inevitability of judgement, even if repentance was forthcoming, it is pervaded with an undercurrent of hope.

The verse selected for this reflection exquisitely illustrates God's mercy in judgement: He only ever turns up the heat just enough to bring us back to Him, in order that relationship may be restored and we again enjoy the benefit of His provision. Have you ever noticed that there's a perfect balance in everything God does? We see this in creation, where the earth is sufficiently close to the sun to give us warmth, but not so close that we're incinerated. Similarly, the ratio of water to land on the earth's surface ensures the rainfall which is required to irrigate the land, without it perpetually being inundated. The atmosphere, too, has a perfect balance of nitrogen, oxygen and inert gases to support our lives and the production of the crops we need for survival.

Precisely the same principle applies when God instigates judgement: He doesn't seek to punish His people, but to correct us, in order to protect us from the inevitable harm that we'll do to ourselves if we don't walk in fellowship with Him. Any less of a chastening would confirm us in our sin, making us ripe for destruction by the Enemy; any more would be too much for us to endure, destroying our confidence in His goodness. Satan will always try to persuade us that God doesn't love us, and that He's forgotten about us, or even that the chastening we experience, either individually or corporately, is evidence that He doesn't exist. However, the very opposite is true! It would actually be cruel for God to chastise us any less than He does, just as it would be negligent for a doctor to prescribe less medication than we need, simply because we don't like the taste of it.

The verse we're considering here has a New Testament analogue in 1 Peter 2:10, which reiterates these concepts from a post-Calvary perspective: "[You] in time past were not a people, but are now the people of God: which had not obtained mercy, but now have obtained mercy." The preceding verse contains the wonderful promise that we are a "chosen generation," who have been called to "show forth the praises of him who hath called us out of darkness, into his marvellous light!" We can only do this if we're walking in the light ourselves, and our tendency to wander into shadowy areas from time to time is what creates the need for correction which, as Hosea illustrates, is always mercifully administered.

Mercy doesn't come by God allowing us to sin with impunity, thereby destroying our lives, but by Him correcting us just enough to bring us back on track. Of course, as we've reflected previously, not all the consequences of our sin arise from God's direct judgement. It stands to reason that our actions have emotional, physical and practical consequences, but by turning back to God, preferably sooner rather than later, our lives will again reflect the glory He intends for us to exhibit to the world, pointing people towards the cross of Calvary, from whence their hope of redemption will be found.

Will you show me mercy, if I pose you a few questions?

i. Do your actions reflect God's heart for people, in the way that Hosea's did?

ii. What kind of world would we live in if there were no consequences for our actions, either temporally or eternally?

iii. When you are required to chastise people, whether in your role as a parent or manager, do you seek to be merciful, in order to ensure that you don't "provoke them to wrath (Ephesians 6:4)?"

Have You Ever Seen The Like?

> *"Hear this, ye old men, and give ear, all ye inhabitants of the land. Hath this been in your days, or even in the days of your fathers? Tell ye your children of it, and let your children tell their children, and their children another generation. That which the palmerworm hath left hath the locust eaten; and that which the locust hath left hath the cankerworm eaten; and that which the cankerworm hath left hath the caterpillar eaten (Joel 1: 2 - 4)."*

Did your parents ever use the phrase, "Have you ever seen the like?" If they did, there's a good chance that it wasn't complimentary: perhaps something along the lines of, "Have you ever seen the like of that mess!" Well, in time-honoured fashion, have you ever seen the like of 2020? Earlier in the year, swarms of locusts devoured everything in their path, across vast swathes of Africa, leaving extraordinary devastation in their wake. Then, of course, there were the incessant headlines relaying news of pandemic, death-tolls and ever-changing restrictions. It definitely hasn't been the year most of us might have hoped for, but these events certainly aren't unprecedented; for example, there was the Spanish flu pandemic of 1918 and, three years earlier, a locust swarm in the Middle East precipitated a major famine. Having said this, the locusts of which Joel writes are believed to be figurative, portending successive waves of judgement, either on the kingdom of Judah itself, or on the entire world, during the period known as the Great Tribulation, which is referenced in Matthew 24: 21 & 22, and described in detail in the Book of Revelation.

Frequently, the Old Testament prophets had messages that were applicable to two different time periods (near- and far-application), and this was the case with Joel, who was calling on the inhabitants of the southern kingdom of Judah to repent, at the same time as prophesying of events which are still future in our day, relating to the period immediately preceding the Lord's return. Joel's prescription, for a nation on the verge of calamitous destruction, was for citizens from all walks of life to humble themselves in fasting and repentance. As we observed when the Lord spoke to Ezekiel, lamenting the absence of anyone to stand in the gap, the sincere intercession of a faithful prayer warrior can radically transform the spiritual trajectory of a community. Every generation has the opportunity to decide its fate; either by rejecting God, thus inviting judgement, or by turning back to Him, thereby importuning Him to heal our land (2 Chronicles 7:14).

What of our own generation? Joel's message is particularly relevant to the current age, because it could well be that he was actually writing to us! Chapter 2 of his Book describes a battle in which Israel is miraculously liberated from a northern army, which is quite likely to be the conflict described in Ezekiel 38 & 39. This is the first time in world history when the countries specified as forming an alliance against Israel, including Russia and Iran, have been allies, rather than adversaries. Although we don't know the hour of the Lord's return, we are called to discern the seasons and, if the events of Ezekiel 38 & 39 are close at hand, His return may not be much further in the future! This means that we could be the generation which is caught up in the Rapture (1 Thessalonians 4:15). While such a thought may sound exciting, it would also imply that people we know, who haven't yet accepted Jesus as their Saviour, are on course to endure the Tribulation. Even if this isn't the case, none of us is immortal, and we'll all ultimately appear before the Lord. Provided we've lived for Jesus, we won't be judged for eternal security, but we will still be rewarded - or not - on the basis of our faithfulness with the gifts which have been entrusted to us. If we decide to live for ourselves, we'll be judged on our own merits, which may sound attractive, until we realise that God's standard for entry to heaven is perfection, which we can never achieve by our own efforts! As in Joel's day, and irrespective of whether we're the generation that sees the Lord's return, the choice is very much ours: repent and be saved or continue not to give God a second thought, until it's too late. Which camp will you be in?

To conclude a sobering reflection, here are some questions of potential significance.

i. What is your understanding of eschatology (end-times events)? Is this something addressed by your church?

ii. Does the possibility that the Lord could return during your lifetime influence the way you live?

iii. Has 2020 been a difficult year for you? If so, imagine how much harder the Tribulation would be to endure! Why not make it your mission to fast and pray for the people you care about, who may have to live through the type of calamity described by Joel?

Justice!

> *"Thus saith the Lord; for three transgressions of Israel, and for four, I will not turn away the punishment thereof; because they sold the righteous for silver, and the poor for a pair of shoes (Amos 2:6)."*

Have you ever read the Bible, placing yourself in the position of some of the Book's major characters? For example, how would you have reacted if, like Thomas, you hadn't been present when Jesus first appeared to the ten other faithful apostles? Your name may not actually feature in God's Word, but His Book is written specifically for you, as a revelation of His loving desire to give you the best life you could possibly have, both now and into eternity. The depth of God's love for us is emphasised in the verse we're currently reflecting on, where the prophet Amos reveals the grief He felt when people He cared about were consistently mistreated. Injustice is something God abhors and, while punishment doesn't always follow as quickly as we might like, it will inevitably occur, if repentance and restitution from the wrongdoer aren't forthcoming. God is merciful in giving us the opportunity to amend our ways, but judgement won't be postponed indefinitely!

Amos was from the southern kingdom of Judah, but his proclamation also pertained to the north. Initially, he foretold judgement on Israel's neighbours, many of whom were immensely hostile towards them. However, he also had words of significant rebuke and warning for his own people of Judah; then for the ten northern tribes, collectively known as Ephraim, which was the largest tribe of the ten. Even on this side of Calvary, we are always judged on the basis of the revelation and responsibility that have been given to us: no more and no less. Thus, when God gave Amos words of rebuke for Israel's neighbours, they were being judged for their cruelty and violence towards their fellow human beings, rather than their direct defiance of God. These nations had not been given the Law, so were not judged by it, but there were standards of integrity and decency to which they were expected to adhere. It no doubt pleased the people of Israel to hear that God intended to punish their enemies, and they quite possibly believed that, as a nation set apart for Him, they would be exempt from criticism. However, the very opposite was the case!

Israel enjoyed the privileged position of being a nation set apart by God, and it was against this standard that they were therefore to be assessed. Other nations weren't judged for their unfaithfulness to God, because they didn't have a covenant relationship with Him, in the way that Israel and Judah did. In contrast, the rebuke for God's chosen people was that they had turned their backs on Him and served other so-called deities. Ironically, the gods that they turned to were frequently those of the surrounding lands, which had been unable to deliver those nations in battle against Israel! This idolatry didn't only have an adverse spiritual impact on Israel: it influenced their attitudes towards the most vulnerable people in their society, resulting in a hardness of heart that led to the cruelty described in Amos 2:6. Tragically, we never seem to learn, and have done the same thing today, turning from the God Who mercifully delivered us during World War 2; instead inclining our hearts towards Eastern religions and making gods out of ourselves. The consequence has been exactly the same: we've become a selfish, uncaring society that thinks nothing of performing acts of brutality against our most vulnerable citizens, unborn children, in what should be the safest place of all, the womb of the mother. Heartbreakingly, this is a scenario for which the church must accept a significant share of responsibility: both on account of its inclination to stigmatise women who become pregnant in circumstances of which it doesn't approve, and also due to a dogmatic anti-abortion stance that frequently stops short of offering the constructive alternatives befitting of an organisation that is genuinely pro-life.

We live in what is termed a pluralist society, but there is still only one way to heaven; through the blood and sacrifice of Jesus Christ. While it's important to respect the beliefs of others, we mustn't compromise our own values, in order to conform to their expectations. The standard against which we will be judged, as believers, is our faithfulness to utilise the gifts God has given us. Everyone has a choice in relation to accepting Jesus, but a decision to reject Him results in a progressive hardening of the heart, until such time as the truth is almost completely obscured. The best - indeed only life-giving - decision remains, as in Joshua's day, to determine to "fear (respect) the Lord, and serve him in sincerity and truth (Joshua 24:14)." Other people will make their own decisions, but will you decree, as Joshua did in the very next verse, that "as for me and my house, we will serve the Lord?" It will be the best decision you ever make; not to mention the most important.

These questions don't have the same eternal significance, but they may be worth considering, nonetheless.

i. Are you more anxious for judgement to come when the person in the wrong is someone other than yourself?

ii. Do you believe that Western culture's departure from Biblical teaching has produced a better, more caring society?

iii. If you don't have a Biblical framework for decision making, how do you determine what is right and wrong? If your standard is what you subjectively believe to be right, how do you resolve the conflicts which inevitably arise when other people apply different criteria to the same situations?

Beware Destruction!

> *"The pride of thine heart hath deceived thee, thou that dwellest in the clefts of the rock, whose habitation is high; that saith in his heart, Who shall bring me down to the ground? Though thou exalt thyself as the eagle, and though thou set thy nest among the stars, thence will I bring thee down, saith the Lord (Obadiah 1: 3 & 4)."*

The land of Edom is situated in modern-day Jordan, between the Dead Sea and the Gulf of Aqaba. In contrast to the relatively cordial relationship that currently exists between Israel and Jordan, Edom was a constant snare to her northern neighbour. She perpetrated numerous acts of heartless aggression against God's people, and it may therefore come as something of a surprise to see that it was her pride, and not her overt wickedness, for which she was being judged. What's wrong with pride? After all, we're proud of our children when they score a winning goal or achieve a fantastic test result! In fact, there's nothing wrong with this: it's perfectly natural to exult in one another's successes, encourage others at times of disappointment and, yes, take pride in our families' achievements.

The type of pride Obadiah was referring to was the haughtiness of spirit that seeks to exalt an individual above God, thereby blinding his or her heart to divine revelation. As mentioned previously, God not only imposes constraints on our behaviour for the benefit of others, but also to ensure our own wellbeing; in particular, He's committed to diverting us from attitudes and activities which will ultimately destroy us. The fact that pride is sufficiently dangerous to warrant correction is illustrated by the fact that it is the very sin which led to the fall of a beautiful angel called Lucifer, who henceforth became known as Satan! Lucifer led the worship of God in heaven, but he wasn't satisfied with this privilege, and decided he'd like to elevate himself above God Himself. We read of his self-exaltation, fall from glory and ultimate fate in Isaiah 14, verses 12 - 16.

Anyone who rejects Jesus decides, by default, to follow Satan, and will therefore be destined to endure a similar destiny: as we read in Proverbs, "Pride goeth before destruction, and a haughty spirit before a fall (Proverbs 16:18)." This axiom could be applied to events in our everyday lives, but the fundamental implication is both spiritual and eternal. Because God loves us, He doesn't want us to suffer the same fate as the adversary who's intent on our destruction, and He therefore tries to get our attention in this life, as He did with Nebuchadnezzar, before it's too late. Following his own display of pride, Nebuchadnezzar was inflicted with a severe form of insanity, which ultimately brought him to his spiritual senses. However hard this must have been at the time, his conversion of heart was surely worth it: it's far better to be humbled in this life than in the next one!

As a contrast to pride, it's instructive to consider the attitude of our Saviour, Jesus, Who created the world, yet allowed Himself to be born in humble surroundings, then grow into an Adult Who would serve sacrificially and be a Friend of us sinners! The most significant test we ever take only has the one question, and we have a lifetime to supply the answer. This question is whether or not we'll accept Jesus as our Saviour, and pride is one of the major obstacles to us giving the right response. Frequently, this is manifested in a stubborn reluctance to admit that salvation can't be attained through our own efforts, but instead requires the atoning sacrifice of Jesus on the cross at Calvary. Let's therefore pray for the Holy Spirit to root out all pride, both from our own lives, and the lives of those we love!

SPIRITUAL REFLECTIONS - I

These questions aren't as important as the ultimate one, but they may still be worth running through your mind:

i. Who is the most important person in your life: Jesus, yourself or someone else?

ii. Can you recall an occasion when you began to think too highly of yourself, and suffered the consequences?

iii. What's the best way to prevent yourself from becoming too prideful? I always find that reflecting on Calvary helps: my sin put Jesus on the cross and, without His sacrificial love, I'd have been destined for destruction!

Running From God!

"But Jonah rose up to flee unto Tarshish from the presence of the Lord, and went down to Joppa; and he found a ship going to Tarshish: so he paid the fare thereof, and went down into it, to go with them unto Tarshish from the presence of the Lord (Jonah 1:3)."

Do you remember our reflection taken from Leviticus, in which we addressed the issue of racism? Well, whisper it quietly, because we'll see him in heaven, but it seems that Jonah had racist tendencies of his own! His particular prejudice, of which we read in his Book, was against the people of Nineveh, which was the capital of Assyria, but in this regard Jonah wouldn't have differed from many of his Jewish contemporaries. The Assyrians had a reputation for absolute ruthlessness and were the greatest threat to Israel's security, at the time when Jonah was sent to preach to the Ninevites. Given that Jonah's message was one of judgement, we might think he would have been eagerly anticipating his mission of pronouncing doom on Israel's arch-enemy. However, he knew God too well, and realised that He'd suspend judgement, should they be willing to repent. It seems that, for Jonah, the thought of spending eternity with the Ninevites, even if they reformed, was too much to endure!

Clearly, Jonah wouldn't have agreed with Abraham Lincoln's perspective that, "The best way to destroy an enemy is to make him your friend!" He therefore embarked upon a course of action which never does anyone any good: he began to run from God! Following various dramas, involving a boat, a storm and a great fish, Jonah finally found himself in Nineveh, demonstrating the reassuring truth that God's providence can over-ride our petulance. Jonah's appearance, and doubtless his odour, had been radically changed by the three days he spent in the fish, but his mission - and his imperfect heart - remained the same. After three days traipsing through the streets of Nineveh, proclaiming a message of imminent destruction that didn't even offer any hope of redemption, Jonah's worst fears were confirmed: the people, including the king, repented and God spared them from judgement. Rather than rejoicing over the wonderful spiritual harvest he had helped to reap, Jonah sulked over his personal discomfort and accused God of being too merciful (Jonah 4:2)!

Before we're too quick to criticise Jonah, it's a good idea to search our own hearts: are there any people groups we're perhaps not keen to see saved? Even if that isn't the case, we certainly can't claim to be flawless! Jonah's story demonstrates God's ability, and His willingness, to use imperfect vessels, which is great news for us, because it means that we all have a role to play in the spiritual conflict which is raging around us. In fact, the imperfection of the vessel gives God more glory, due to the results not so easily being attributable to us! In many ways, Jonah provides an example of how not to conduct a mission: his heart and attitude were diametrically opposed to God's, but his reluctant witness was still a success, because God was at the centre of it. Reassuringly, we can't thwart God's plan: if we opt out, He'll find someone else, but He's so gracious that He'll frequently give us another chance, as He did with Jonah. How about you? Do you need a second chance? Maybe you grew up in a Christian home and wandered away from the Lord, or perhaps you made some choices you regret. It's never too late to come back, while you have breath, and God may choose to use you in a wonderful way, if only you'll give Him the opportunity!

Here are a few more questions to ponder; hopefully not while on the run!

i. Have you ever made what seemed to be a complete mess of a divine mission, only for God to turn it into an outstanding success?

ii. Why do you think God continued to use Jonah to preach to the Ninevites, rather than choosing someone else to replace him, after he ran away?

iii. Are you currently running from God? If so, would you like to come back? There's no need to wait for your circumstances to change, which is never a good idea: He'll accept you exactly as you are, if only you'll decide to re-dedicate your life to Him.

Fiends In High Places!

"Thus saith the Lord concerning the prophets that make my people err, that bite with their teeth, and cry, Peace; and he that putteth not into their mouths, they even prepare war against him. Therefore night shall be unto you, that ye shall not have a vision; and it shall be dark unto you, that ye shall not divine; and the sun shall go down over the prophets, and the day shall be dark over them (Micah 3: 5 & 6)."

Harsh words indeed! Rather than speaking to their audience in a monotone voice, many prophets actually sang their prophecies, which led to the accusation that those who came to hear them were frequently more intent on being entertained than on receiving instruction. The poetic language Micah uses suggests that this may well have been his style, too, but the admonitions the Lord gave him to deliver to his fellow seers wouldn't have made for pleasant hearing, whether they were spoken, sung or acted out in a drama, as was the manner of Jeremiah and Ezekiel. Ungodly 'prophets' had been deceiving the people, lulling them into a false sense of security that they wouldn't be judged for their sins, but now it was their turn to be called to account. Effectively, the Lord was telling them that, in return for keeping their hearers in the dark, they'd experience darkness from above, which would be eternal if they refused to repent.

The privilege of leadership confers with it a significant responsibility, and a failure to discharge this in an appropriate manner has serious ramifications, both for the individuals concerned and the people they serve. In many respects, this concept of service is the key: leaders, whether they be political or spiritual, are intended to be servants of the people; not their masters. This attitude of service was graciously demonstrated by our Saviour, Jesus, and anyone who doesn't seek to follow His example is effectively claiming to know better than our Lord, which is a recipe for disaster. Political and spiritual rulers occupy a powerful position, both on earth and in heaven. Although God isn't a respecter of persons (Acts 10:34 & Romans 2:11), a godly leader can have a significant influence in forestalling judgement, as demonstrated by Hezekiah, King of Judah, and also the King of Assyria, who led his nation in repentance, after hearing Jonah's message of imminent destruction.

In the same way that political rulers set the tone for their countries, and have the authority to engage in actions with long-term implications, our spiritual overseers exert power in both the seen and unseen realms. Their influence can be positive, as with Samuel, or negative, which we see in the case of Eli's sons, but they can never absolve themselves from responsibility for the spiritual welfare of their nations. It is extremely powerful when a Christian leader repents on behalf of the inhabitants of their land, in the manner that Daniel did in chapter 9 of his remarkable Book. Their words carry authority in heaven, possibly over and above those of regular citizens, because spiritual forces themselves have hierarchies, which apply both to faithful angels and those who fell from grace, thus becoming demons.

Tragically, it isn't only angels that fall from grace: the countless reports of pastors and ministers who have abused the people's trust have done almost irreparable damage to the institution of the church which, on many occasions, has seemed more intent on protecting itself than on defending the innocent. This has been graphically illustrated in multiple instances of clerical abuse, which defy description and break countless hearts. They certainly break the heart of God, as alluded to in our reflection on the meditation that 'God is good'. Scripture contains an unambiguous warning of the high standard of judgement for spiritual leaders (James 3:1), which means that no-one should aspire to the office of minister without a clear calling and a clean heart. To occasionally fail to live up to the high standards of office is one thing, but to cynically use the church as a cover for despicable crimes is an outrage for which the perpetrators will face severe judgement in eternity, even if they escape censure on earth.

Heads of churches and denominations can do immense harm to the spiritual welfare of a nation, way beyond their own sphere of authority, when they bring God's Name into disrepute. This has been seen time and again throughout the church's history, where various heresies and departures from Biblical doctrine have left people confused and bewildered, causing many to walk away from their faith. Deliberate abuse of power is something that greatly distresses God, and He has harsh words for those who behave in an unjust way, as we see in Proverbs 20:23. The abuse is exacerbated when it relates to matters of faith, because it has the potential to leave individuals in a spiritual limbo, from which they may not necessarily emerge. This is graphically illustrated by Jesus Himself, when He referred to the punishment which awaits anyone who causes children to lose their faith, saying that it would be better for them to have millstones hung around their necks (Matthew 18:6).

For those of us who are not pastors or ministers, we may think we are off the hook, but that's not the case! The first thing to say is that pastoring a church is an extremely challenging vocation, and can only be attempted in the power of the Holy Spirit. Anyone who assays to fulfil such a role without this anointing is in the wrong occupation, and needs to find alternative employment, for the sake of themselves and their congregations. However, those who have responded to a genuine call need our encouragement and support, not to mention our prayers, as they endeavour to balance the practical and emotional demands of their roles with family and other commitments, all while undergoing the intense spiritual attack that comes with the territory of serving the Lord. Moreover, we cannot excuse ourselves from these standards, because we are leaders ourselves! We may not be priests or bishops, at least in the ecclesiastical sense, but Scripture describes us as a royal priesthood (1 Peter 2:9), meaning that we all carry a level of responsibility. It's essential that we discharge this in accordance with God's precepts, because we could be the only Christian some people know, and any dishonesty or breach of integrity on our part has the potential to deter them from seeking to encounter Jesus. Some of us might have additional responsibility afforded to us, as leaders of families, house groups, or Bible studies: such a role is a privilege, not a right, and should be regarded seriously! Those of us who've placed our trust in Jesus will one day rule with Him in eternity (Revelation 5:10), but we should surely start by appropriately using the authority we have here and now!

Do you have enough authority to respond to a few questions?

i. Why is it necessary that "judgement must begin at the house of the Lord (1 Peter 4:17)?"

ii. If you're a Christian, how well are you exercising the authority that has been given to you, as a follower of Jesus Christ?

iii. If you don't yet know Jesus as Lord, are there some pastors you respect more than others? Of the ones you respect, what makes them stand out...and might you be tempted to attend a service or two?

Devastation!

"But Nineveh is of old like a pool of water: yet they shall flee away. Stand, stand, shall they cry; but none shall look back (Nahum 2:8)."

We've been here before, haven't we? Nineveh was the city to which Jonah reluctantly preached, producing a heartfelt repentance on the part of the people that elicited forgiveness from God. Just over a century has now elapsed, and Nahum has been sent to pronounce judgement, which duly followed, when the Assyrian capital was destroyed by the Medes in 612 BC. There's no record in Scripture of what happened in the intervening period, but it must certainly have been that the spirit of penitence didn't pervade the land for long. Isn't that so often the way, even in our own lives, especially when we were younger? We'd do something wrong, get caught, beg forgiveness, then before too much longer we'd be doing the same thing again - or something worse! The same cycle can occur in our Christian walk, especially early on, when we resolve to live a changed life, make a mistake, seek God's forgiveness, then sin again, prompting us to wonder if we're even saved! The good news for us is that our names aren't expunged from the Lamb's Book of Life, simply because we fall short in certain areas, although we certainly ought to repent, in order to restore our relationship with the Lord and avoid grieving His Holy Spirit.

Given the unfailing mercy of our God, there may even have been the possibility of a reprieve for Nineveh, had they genuinely repented in response to Nahum's preaching, as they did in response to Jonah's. However, they remained hard-hearted until the bitter end, with disastrous consequences, and they weren't the only people to travel such a path. In the 700s BC, around a century before Nahum's time, the spiritual condition of both the northern and southern kingdoms of Israel had deteriorated to the extent that God resolved to discipline them. The northern kingdom didn't turn back, precipitating their invasion by Assyria, but Judah had a collective change of heart. The repentant attitude of the southern kingdom ensured that they were spared for a season, but they ultimately returned to their old ways, resulting in their Babylonian captivity.

Similar patterns have been discernible in more recent times, where nations that experienced magnificent revivals, yielding tremendous blessings, have, within a few generations, squandered their spiritual inheritance and forsaken the God Who revived them. Why does this happen? One obvious reason is that we forget the lessons of the past and consider ourselves to be more sophisticated than the generations which went before. This pseudo-sophistication gives us a false perspective relating to matters of faith although, paradoxically, it is often associated with a growth in fascination with non-Christian belief systems, and even the occult. The idolatry we indulge in further blinds us to the truth, producing a misplaced confidence that we can continue in rebellion with impunity. Such an attitude isn't surprising, because the false gods to which we've turned don't respond to our prayers, so we erroneously conclude that the True God won't intervene, either! This is exactly the trap into which the Edomites fell, when their arrogance prompted them to dismissively ask whether anyone could bring them down to the ground (Obadiah 1:3).

The Ninevites appear to have followed a similar path: they had become so accustomed to their Assyrian Army defeating everyone on the battlefield that they forgot the lesson their ancestors had learned from Jonah, which is that everyone, whether they believe in Him or not, will ultimately be answerable to God. In His sovereignty, He determines the manner and timing of our being called to account, but it will inevitably happen for us all, whether in this life or the next. While it may be too late for us to save Nineveh, we still have the opportunity to ensure that our own nations don't follow the same path, by continually serving as watchmen & women, and standing in the gap as intercessors. Let's do so, before it's too late!

Nahum's message for Nineveh may not have been a positive one, but maybe you'll be able to take some positives out of these questions!

i. Has your own city or nation fallen into the same trap as Nineveh, by trusting in military strength or financial resources, and forgetting about God?

ii. The Assyrians were a cruel adversary to God's chosen people of Israel but, in His mercy, He sent two prophets to warn them of His judgement. If you're not yet a believer, does this change your perception of people who warn you of judgement, even if it's not a message you want to hear?

iii. If you *are* a Christian, what are you doing to ensure that your country experiences God's blessing, instead of His judgement?

Would You Believe It?

"Behold ye among the heathen, and regard, and wonder marvellously: for I will work a work in your days, which ye will not believe, though it be told you (Habakkuk 1:5)."

Wouldn't you be wonderfully encouraged if the Lord gave you words similar to these, in response to your prayers? It sounds like a spiritual dream come true, but for Habakkuk it turned into something of a nightmare, although all came good in the end! The prophet was pouring out his heart to the Lord, in relation to the moral decline of Judah, exemplified by the fact that there didn't appear to be any penalty for heartless crimes committed against innocent citizens. God began His response with the verse quoted above, and I'm sure Habakkuk would have been happy if He'd ended there. However, in the very next verse, He elaborated by saying that the Chaldeans were His chosen vehicle for chastising the nation, which certainly wasn't what Habakkuk wanted to hear!

In keeping with all true prophets, Habakkuk loved his country, and it seemed unconscionable to him that the Chaldeans, who had a reputation for inserting hooks in the noses of their captives, amongst other acts of brutality, would be used by God to humble His people. When Habakkuk brought these concerns before the Lord, He graciously responded by showing him that the Chaldean correction was only a part of His plan. Although the Chaldeans were to be used by God to provoke Judah to repentance, Habakkuk saw that they themselves would be judged; at least in part because of their excessive cruelty towards his compatriots. Despite the apparent craziness of our world, God remains in control: we only see part of the picture, and that perhaps hazily, but He sees everything with perfect clarity!

There's a tremendous amount that we can learn from Habakkuk; not least, our need to be prepared for God to act in unexpected ways. When we bring our petitions before the Lord, our primary focus must be on Him, rather than our trials, or even our proposed solutions. Imagine what might have happened if Jesus hadn't prayed for God's will to be done, when He asked in Gethsemane whether it might be possible for the cup to pass from Him (Matthew 26:39). Had the Son not completely yielded Himself to the Father, we might have still been lost in our sins, which demonstrates that we should never dictate to Him a course of action, because He always knows best! Habakkuk eventually realised this, extolling God for His righteous faithfulness, concluding that he would "rejoice in the Lord" and "joy in the God of my salvation," because "the Lord God is my strength" (Habakkuk 3: 18 & 19).

In order to lead a healthy, productive Christian life, we need to reach the same conclusion as Habakkuk: yielding ourselves to God always produces a spirit of praise! That's obviously not to say we shouldn't pray; just that we need the appropriate perspective when we do so! When we bring God the burdens of our hearts, we're well advised to leave the answers in His hands, being prepared for Him to do something we wouldn't believe. Any solutions we come up with are in the halfpenny place, compared to the outcomes God will want to craft from His eternal wisdom, foreknowledge of the future, and profound love for us and the subjects of our prayers! Perhaps, if there's a life-lesson Habakkuk teaches us, it's that we need to pray-se!

If Habakkuk was with us today, I wonder if he might ask similar questions to these:

i. Who are the 'Chaldeans' in your life: people you'd prefer not to have to deal with, but whom God is using for a purpose?

ii. When you pray, and things seem to be getting worse, could it possibly be that God is working His answer, without you seeing it?

iii. Do you come to the Lord in prayer with a menu of possible solutions, or in a spirit of praise, allowing Him to craft the answers?

Joyous Inheritance!

"The Lord thy God in the midst of thee is mighty; he will save, he will rejoice over thee with joy; he will rest in his love, he will joy over thee with singing (Zephaniah 3:17)."

When reading these wonderful words of encouragement, it's hard to believe that Zephaniah's recorded prophecy contains stark warnings of destruction, both for the nation of Israel and the world as a whole. In many respects, the reason for judgement was the same in both instances: rejection of divine revelation, leading to eternal separation from God. Although the people of Israel received unique insights into God's majesty, and were repeatedly delivered from their adversaries in miraculous ways, they lapsed into idolatry on numerous occasions. This unfaithfulness not only impaired their close relationship with God, in the same way that sin tainted the communion Adam and Eve had with Him in Eden, but it also resulted in a steady decline in moral standards. Rather than simply giving a nod to the false gods of pagan nations, many in Israel entered fully into their worship, to the extent that they even sacrificed their children to Molech, which they were specifically instructed not to do. Verse 8 of Psalm 115 warns us that we will ultimately resemble the deities we worship. Thus, if we worship a loving, selfless Saviour, those traits should be evident in us, whereas loyalty to a cruel and tyrannical pseudo-god will have a profoundly negative impact on our character.

Particularly insulting to the One True God is the fact that the people of Israel continued to 'worship' Him alongside these other idols, in a form of religious syncretism designed to enjoy the blessings of Judaism alongside the perceived benefits of alternative religions. Eventually, their rebellion became so serious that it needed to be dealt with, in order to prevent them from doing irreparable harm to themselves and to subsequent generations. Of course, God could have simply wiped out the nation without warning but, in His mercy, He sent numerous prophets to alert them to what would happen if they didn't repent. We even see this in relation to the Flood, where Noah's one-hundred-and-twenty-year project in building the ark was a prophetic act of material significance. His contemporaries chose to mock and ignore the alarm, but that wasn't God's fault, just as a parent can't be blamed if a child disregards wise counsel and burns his or her hand on the stove.

Despite our perceptions, the message of the prophets was essentially a positive one; that forgiveness would emanate from repentance, just as is the case in our own lives. Even in instances where nations had gone too far, making judgement inevitable, there was the promise of restoration, once they had repented and paid the penalty for their collective sins, which is what happened when the nation of Judah returned from their Babylonian captivity after seventy years. The situation in our world today resembles that in idolatrous Israel and, because God is consistent, we are nearing the point where the world will be judged. As in Noah's day, vast swathes of society continue to ridicule people of faith, and the outcome will be the same. Those who heed God's warning will be protected from the judgement to come, while those who don't will perish. This perhaps seems harsh: what about the millions of perfectly good people, who simply choose not to put their faith in Jesus? The reality, however, is that there is no middle ground: like the generation who lived at the time of the Flood, we're either completely in the ark or completely out, where our Ark is Christ Himself. As Jesus said in Matthew 12:30, "He who is not with me is against me." We therefore have to decide whether we wish to attend the Marriage Supper of the Lamb (Revelation 19: 6 - 9) or endure the Great Tribulation (Revelation chapters 6 to 19:5): God sent His Son to spare us from judgement, but He won't over-ride our decision.

We've considered in some depth the consequences of rejecting Jesus but, like Zephaniah, let's conclude with the joy that awaits those who decide to place their trust in Him. Our decision to accept Jesus as our Saviour isn't a one-off act, following which we return to life as normal; neither is it merely a formal legal contract, sparing us from being sentenced to hell. From the moment of salvation onwards, we have a wonderful Counsellor and Advocate, in the form of the Holy Spirit, Who guides our decisions and fills our hearts with His peace. As if this wasn't enough, God views us in the way He views His own Son, to the remarkable extent that He rejoices over us and performs mighty works through our fallible frames. We thereby have the unmissable opportunity to magnify His Name, in return for which we receive the privilege of participating in the fulfilment of His plans for the world.

You may not previously have considered Zephaniah all that much, except perhaps to contemplate his name, but he had an important message, which is as applicable to our generation as it was to his own. We *might* not have prophets in the same sense today, although many of God's servants do have prophetic gifts, but we certainly do have God's Word and the convicting presence of the Holy Spirit. If you doubt the truth of the Bible, or the validity of Zephaniah's message, why not try to prove or disprove it for yourself? There's far too much at stake to simply sit on the fence. After all, you'd almost certainly invest considerable time researching a house that you planned to live in for the next twenty or thirty years, so you surely owe it to yourself to check out Jesus's claims in relation to eternity.

Finally, some questions to ponder:

i. Who do you worship...and who do you resemble?

ii. Do you believe in the 'middle ground' of purgatory? If so, can you find any Scriptures to support your view?

iii. Might you, like many in Zephaniah's day, have a syncretistic faith, that combines aspects of various belief systems? If so, which of the gods that you worship do you believe have the power to deliver you in times of crisis?

Never Give Up!

"Then spake Haggai the Lord's messenger in the Lord's message unto the people, saying, I am with you, saith the Lord. And the Lord stirred up the spirit of Zerubbabel the son of Shealtiel, governor of Judah, and the spirit of Joshua the son of Josedech, the high priest, and the spirit of all the remnant of the people; and they came and did work in the house of the Lord of hosts, their God (Haggai 1: 13 & 14)."

Our reflections taken from the Biblical books of prophecy have contained numerous references to the Babylonian captivity, which came upon the southern kingdom of Judah, as a consequence of their rebellion against God. It can frequently be the case that the anticipation of a transition, and the shaking when it initially occurs, prove to be worse than the reality, once we adapt to our changed circumstances. This very much seems to have been the situation in relation to the Babylonian exile; certainly if the numbers are anything to go by! When, after seventy years, Cyrus issued his decree allowing the people of Judah to return home, only around 5% (just under fifty thousand out of a population of approximately one million) availed of the opportunity. Babylon was a prosperous land and the people had settled there, demonstrating that it only takes a generation or two for a heritage to be lost. Oral histories were extremely popular in the day, and Haggai's contemporaries would have heard all about their ancestral homeland, but they were comfortable where they were, and the upheaval of returning to Judah and starting again didn't seem too appealing.

Even the 50,000 or so who did return didn't appear particularly enthusiastic about rebuilding the Lord's House! Perhaps a combination of competing priorities (their own homes, families, etc.) and the overwhelming size of the project led to them putting this off. In addition, the Temple possibly didn't seem as important as it had been, prior to captivity. Some may have reasoned that, if the presence of the Temple in Jerusalem didn't spare them from invasion, it wasn't worth having! Of course, this implies that the Temple might itself have become an idol in their own eyes, assuming more importance than God Himself. Moreover, they'd been able to worship God from Babylon, if they'd wanted to, so why was there a need for a dedicated House of the Lord in Jerusalem? After all, they could worship from their own homes. Perhaps there are parallels here for us, as we emerge from the restrictions of the pandemic: it's been wonderful to have the opportunity to connect with services on-line, but is there a danger that we might have got too comfortable doing this, to the extent that we may not be completely committed to the idea of returning to corporate fellowship?

Furthermore, there was significant political and religious opposition to the rebuilding of the Temple. The Samaritans had instituted their own tradition of worshipping on Mount Gerizim, and didn't want this to be impacted by the rebuilding of the Temple in Jerusalem. How many of us fall short of what God has planned for us, because of our observance of formal tradition? Doing things a certain way because they've always been done that way isn't a good reason, unless that way is the right way! Throughout history, it's noticeable how frequently the civil and religious powers have united to conspire against God's will. The institution of state religion signalled the virtual death knell of the church in countries such as France and the UK, and no doubt many other nations, too. Reasons for yielding to formal observance and succumbing to reactionary hostility to change can easily be rationalised; for example by saying, "God has a productive use for my life; He wouldn't want me to be excluded from the church." What would have happened to the Gospel if the apostles had thought like that, where the consequences they faced for faithfulness to God's Word were imprisonment and martyrdom? This obviously doesn't mean for us to be foolhardy, suffering unnecessarily as a consequence, but if God has told us to do something, we need to do it, irrespective of what our friends, employers or society might say!

We can often be prone to rationalise our failure to accomplish something we've been called to do (or even for indulging in things we shouldn't be doing!), in an attempt to disguise the fact that we've fallen into the trap of walking by sight instead of faith. Satan may give us the excuses, but we're frequently all too keen to accept them! Moreover, we often have the tendency to spiritualise our inactivity (sins of omission) or inappropriate actions (sins of commission), thereby persuading ourselves, and others, that we haven't really back-slidden. Of course, not everyone will be taken in by our excuses: a faithful friend who is walking closely with the Lord will be prepared to 'call us out', and we need to be willing to take their advice, before our hearts get too hard and our ears too deaf for us to listen. Haggai, Zerubbabel and Joshua played this role for those who returned to Jerusalem, and they had the confidence that they were right, because the Lord promised He was with them (verse 13). They themselves could have rationalised that, "There are only three of us, what can we do; surely the people won't listen to us?" but, instead, they were faithful, and the Temple was rebuilt as a result. How many projects - or lives - lie in ruins because somebody failed to provide a word of encouragement? These three gentlemen, who were respectively the prophet, governor and high priest, saved the Temple and helped the nation to healthily realign her priorities. There can be a powerful impact when people work together to accomplish something for the Lord, especially when they occupy positions of leadership. There is an obvious contrast with the 'fiends in high places' scenario described in our reflection taken from Micah: in Haggai, Zerubbabel and Joshua, the people had *friends* in high places; one letter can make quite a difference to a spiritual destiny!

Have you got time to consider a few questions?

i. Do you or your church observe any traditions that might be stifling the work God is looking to do in your life or fellowship?

ii. Are there any areas in which you're rationalising your disobedience to God's call on your life?

iii. Has the Lord called you to be an encourager? If so, why not ask Him, at the beginning of each day, who you might be able to encourage, and how?

Regret And Redemption

> *"And I will pour upon the house of David, and upon the inhabitants of Jerusalem, the spirit of grace and of supplications: and they shall look upon me whom they have pierced, and they shall mourn for him, as one mourneth for his only son, and shall be in bitterness for him, as one that is in bitterness for his firstborn (Zechariah 12:10)."*

Have you ever done something you've really regretted? Maybe you're living with that regret now and, even as a Christian, you might be having to work through the consequences of your actions, just as King David did three thousand years ago. We're privileged to live in the redemptive power of the cross, but there are still implications for everything we do! Sometimes, it may take a while for the regret to sink in: we make a decision without first seeking the Lord, and everything seems to be going okay, until we realise this wasn't the job He wanted us in, or that we shouldn't have been so hasty in relocating. This period, between the commission of a mistake and the realisation of regret, is precisely where many Jews are living now. Rather than simply moving to the wrong house, or leaving the job they were supposed to be doing, they made the biggest mistake in history, by plotting the crucifixion of their Messiah! As calamitous as this may sound, it was a circumstance used by God to bring salvation to the Gentile (non-Jewish) world. For those of us who aren't Jews, there's no need to be judgemental: it was the Roman civil authorities who sent Jesus to the cross and our own sins, allied to His profound love, which held Him there. Moreover, were we not blinded to the truth for a period of time, prior to the dawning of the realisation that the Jesus we'd previously rejected was in fact our Saviour?

Although Christians can see, taking the Old and New Testaments together, that Jesus was both the Jewish Messiah and the Saviour of the world, not everybody has this insight, because such things are spiritually discerned (1 Corinthians 2:14). Many people, possibly including yourself, have their eyes blinded, either by rejection or religion. These two 'r' words sound a million miles apart, but they're actually even closer together in reality than they are in the dictionary! The impact of consistently rejecting the message of the Gospel - that Jesus died for our sins and rose again to give us eternal life - is that our hearts become increasingly hardened, and our spiritual eyes progressively more dim, making it harder for us to see the truth. As with Pharaoh in Moses's day, God gives us so many chances, but ultimately confirms us in our decision.

Surely religion is different? Not necessarily so! Jesus didn't come to give us religion - the world had enough of that already - but to invite us into a personal relationship with Him. Adherents to a plethora of belief systems are living in spiritual darkness, either because they choose to do so, or because they decide not to seek the truth. I can be confident in saying this, because Jesus is the Truth (John 14:6), and anyone who seeks Him will find Him (Matthew 7: 7 & 8). Just like rejection, religion causes a hardness of heart that was exemplified by the Pharisees who plotted to kill Jesus. But isn't Christianity a religion? Not really; or at least it shouldn't be! Sadly, many people throughout history have attempted to turn our faith into a rules-based belief system, but Jesus came to set us free from mere outward observance and give us a real, vibrant relationship with Him. While religion represents mankind's failed attempt to get close to God, or our perception of Him, Christianity represents God's unique action in coming close to us: literally living amongst us, then giving His Holy Spirit to do the same. That's not to say we should disregard the precepts for Christian conduct: to do so would be to live for ourselves, trampling Jesus's sacrifice underfoot, as the Hebrews were warned against doing (Hebrews 10:29). Once we truly encounter the Saviour Who laid down His life for us on the cross at Calvary, it will be our privilege to live for Him, in order not to cause offence to His Holy Spirit. Living a compromised Christian life is a recipe for misery, leaving us in limbo between material and spiritual worlds, without any possibility of power in our ministry. Worldliness (rejection) and legalism (religion) both leave us searching for something more, which can only be found in the Way of grace and liberty, afforded to us by the cross.

One day, as Zechariah tells us, the veil will be removed from the eyes of the Jews, just as the veil in the Temple was torn in two, when Jesus died at Calvary. This miracle was God's invitation for us to come to Him, via His Son, and that invitation is still there for us today. Is your heart veiled to the truth? If so, why not meet with the real Jesus, as we explore the Gospels together? It may not be your own heart that remains veiled, but that of a friend or family member. Let's pray for those veils, like the one in the Temple, to be torn in two! The weeping of the Jews, who finally realise what they did to their Messiah, will pale into insignificance, compared to the distress of those who reject Jesus until they die. There can be absolutely no regret worse than realising that everything Christians told you about Jesus was true, after it's too late to change your mind. The good news, indeed the best news, is that there's no need whatsoever to live with this regret: why not accept Jesus into your heart today, and move instantly from regret to redemption?

How about three questions for personal consideration?

i. If you're a Christian, how do you avoid lapsing into legalism, while remaining true to your faith?

ii. Do you know any people who, despite not yet being Christians, would actually be quite attracted to Jesus, if they met Him, and saw the difference between His sacrificial love and dead religion?

iii. Do you have any Jewish friends? If so, how do you address the topic of Jesus as Messiah and Saviour, or is this not something you discuss?

Prophecy, Fulfilment And Expectation

"Behold, I will send my messenger, and he shall prepare the way before me: and the Lord, whom ye seek, shall suddenly come to his temple, even the messenger of the covenant, whom ye delight in: behold, he shall come, saith the Lord of hosts (Malachi 3:1)."

What better way to conclude the Old Testament? Malachi's prophecy was written after the people of Judah returned from their Babylonian captivity, at a time when hearts were again turning from God. The opening verses of chapter 2 record God's warning to the unfaithful priests, who were not only profaning the Temple, but corrupting the land, as had been the case prior to exile. This depressing state of affairs may have contributed to the fact that the nation didn't hear from God for approximately four hundred years, following the proclamation of Malachi's scroll. In these circumstances, we could be forgiven for thinking that the Old Testament would end on a negative note, lamenting our failure, as a human race, to learn from our past lessons, and yield to God's will for our lives. Certainly, there are insights into how He must have felt, watching the people He loved reaping the destruction which inevitably emanated from a sequence of selfish decisions. However, we also have this magnificent ray of hope.

It is evident from Scripture that the Holy Spirit loves words and delights in puns, one of which may be seen in the verse we're considering. There is considerable doubt as to whether Malachi was a specific individual, and the name is widely believed to have been derived from a Hebrew word, meaning 'my messenger', indicating that the writer, in common with all the true prophets, was bringing a word from the Lord. The word 'messenger' appears twice in Malachi 3:1, but in neither instance does it refer to the prophet himself! The description of "my messenger," who shall "prepare the way," is a reference to John the Baptist, who heralded Jesus's arrival as Messiah and Saviour. If these words seem familiar, that's because this section of Malachi's prophecy is referenced in three of the four Gospels, Matthew, Mark and Luke, as having been fulfilled by Jesus's cousin. The latter part of Malachi 3:1, along with the subsequent five verses, relate to Jesus Himself! Specifically, however, they refer to His return to earth, known as His second coming, when He Himself will be the Messenger.

When Jesus first came to earth, He was a suffering Servant, teaching by word and example, while providing a personal revelation of God. Those who heard His words at the time, along with everyone who has read them subsequently, had the opportunity to accept or reject the truth of His revelation. Everyone who accepts Him will be spared from the ultimate judgement: the alternative is to be "weighed in the balances and found wanting," as was the case with King Belshazzar. Thus, when Jesus comes again, it will not be to proclaim a message of forgiveness, because that time will have passed. Instead, He will pronounce judgement on those who have rejected Him and failed to honour the nation of Israel. For those of us who have placed our faith in Christ, His return for His Church, in the event known as the Rapture, is our "blessed hope (Titus 2:13)." However, for everyone who chooses to live without Him, there will come a "great and terrible day of the Lord (Joel 2:31)." It might be tempting to defer these uncomfortable thoughts until another time, or even attempt to forget them completely, but today is the day of salvation (2 Corinthians 6:2), and we can't guarantee having a 'tomorrow' in which to make a decision. This may sound morbid, but we never know when our lives might end or, indeed, when the Lord may return; for, as Peter warns us, "the day of the Lord will come as a thief in the night (2 Peter 3:10)." Those who aren't expecting Jesus to come in judgement will get a terrible shock, but they can't say they haven't been warned: He has fulfilled every prophecy Scripture made about Him, and it's only mercy that delays His coming. Who knows, He may just be waiting for you!

Here are a few questions to reflect on, as we conclude our journey through the Old Testament.

i. Have you considered whether you might be a 'messenger' to your school, university, workplace or community?

ii. Are you eagerly anticipating the Lord's return, actively dreading it, or somewhat indifferent?

iii. Have you been surprised to see the way in which the Old Testament not only prefigures Jesus's earthly ministry, but also foretells His second coming?

Let's end in prayer:

> *Heavenly Father, thank You for preserving Your Word for us, throughout the millennia, and also for the confidence its fulfilment gives us, in relation to Your plans for our lives. Thank You, Jesus, for redeeming everyone who puts their trust in You, irrespective of the era in which they lived. Holy Spirit, please open our eyes to the truth, as we reflect upon Scripture, and encounter the Saviour Who made eternal life possible. In Jesus' Name. Amen.*

Now, are you ready to explore the Gospels?

A Special Invitation!

"And Jesus, walking by the sea of Galilee, saw two brethren, Simon called Peter, and Andrew his brother, casting a net into the sea: for they were fishers. And he saith unto them, Follow me, and I will make you fishers of men. And they straightway left their nets, and followed him (Matthew 4: 18 - 20)."

Have you ever met anyone who completely transformed your life? It may have been a teacher who unlocked your academic potential, a sports coach who turned you into an integral member of the team, or the spouse who was the first person to truly love you. For Andrew and Simon, the day when Jesus called them was probably a day like any other, as they woke early and headed out to sea, with the intention of taking their catch to market and preparing their nets for the next day. Isn't it frequently the way that the most transformative moments in our lives occur when we least expect them? How's your day been so far? Maybe, like these two brothers, you've been hard at work, or perhaps you're enjoying a well-deserved day off. It could even be that you're hoping for a new start: if so, you've come to the right place, because that's precisely what Jesus offers! For Simon, just like Abram, that new start was signified by the receipt of a new name, which wasn't the case for Andrew. For both of them, their decision led to leaving a career, although again this is far from always the case. Who knows how your new start will look: wouldn't it be exciting to find out!

When we plan changes in our lives, there's inevitably a significant amount of preparation involved, such as studying for qualifications, researching the place we're moving to or getting to know the person we intend to marry. Obviously, it's a good idea to read the Gospels, if you'd like to know more about Jesus, but unlike these other decisions, no preparation is required: all you need to do is to accept His invitation to follow Him! You may think you need to effect certain changes, or perhaps clean up your life, before you come to Jesus, but that's not the case. If you try this, you'll still be labouring under the same misapprehension, ten or fifteen years from now! In fact, no amount of cleansing can ever make us righteous in God's eyes: the only way we can ever enter into His presence is to come in the Name of Jesus, by accepting His invitation to follow Him. Note that Andrew and Simon decided to follow Jesus immediately: that's how long it takes to become a Christian!

As a consequence of their decision, these two brothers lived amazing lives, witnessed wonderful miracles and spent three and a half years in the company of God Incarnate! We read throughout Scripture of their remarkable exploits, but if they'd declined Jesus's invitation we'd never have heard of them again. We make multiple decisions on a daily basis, but none is as important as whether to accept Jesus into our hearts. In this regard, our lives are continually at a crossroads (literally, a *cross* roads!), until we come to faith. Whereas the invitation afforded to Andrew and Simon was a one-off, we're fortunate to attend services, listen to podcasts and read books, where that invitation is made all the time. In common with these two brothers, though, the choice is ours: are we going to accept His call?

One obvious question for today is what it means to follow Jesus. For Andrew and Peter, it was evidently a case of physical following, with spiritual implications, which they may not initially have fully discerned. For us, it's the other way round! Our decision to follow is a spiritual one, as we overcome our doubts about Jesus's power to change our lives and ask Him to fill our hearts with His Holy Spirit. However, this spiritual decision has very real physical manifestations, as we are moulded into His image, enabling us to fulfil our potential and enter into the rich experience He has prepared for us. Understandably, there may be an element of fear: what happens if I don't like the new life Jesus gives me, or I suffer for my faith? These are perfectly valid questions, but you can have absolute confidence that God's plan is the best plan for your life. He won't lead you any faster than you're able to go, and He'll never fail you, or forsake you (Deuteronomy 31:6). In many instances, a foretaste of what God has prepared for you is provided by your talents and interests. You may not always have believed in Him, but these are attributes the Lord has endowed you with, and He'd delight in giving you His Holy Spirit, to enable you to go even further. In addition to endowing you with new gifts, His Spirit will grant you wisdom and discernment to make the most of your natural abilities, as with Andrew and Simon, who were converted from fishers of fish to fishers of men. However He uses you, I can honestly say that I don't know a single person who has regretted their decision to follow Jesus. For anyone considering postponing that decision, I can also say that I don't know any Christians who wish they'd come to faith later in life; in contrast, I'm aware of plenty who regret not having accepted His invitation sooner!

Of course, our initial acceptance of Christ mustn't be the end of the matter. As Jesus said Himself, regarding those who profess a commitment, "No man, having put his hand to the plough, and looking back, is fit for the kingdom of God (Luke 9:62)." This might sound rather harsh to our ears, but Jesus is expressing the inescapable truth that we can only enter into the abundant life He's prepared for us if we continue in faithful obedience, in the same way that we don't become a famous footballer by attending a solitary training session. Perhaps this is the situation you're in today: your decision to follow Jesus was genuine, but you've been diverted from the path and aren't sure if there's a way back. The Devil will tell you there isn't, but he's wrong! Jesus loves you as much today as when you first gave your life to Him, and He'd love to walk with you through the challenges you face, however insurmountable they may seem: after all, "nothing is too difficult for God (Jeremiah 32:17; see also Luke 1:37)!"

This is not to say that deciding to follow Jesus is any guarantee of an easy life: both Andrew and Simon Peter faced many tests and were ultimately martyred for their faith. However, as radical as it sounds, such an outcome is far better than living mundane lives, dying a natural death and heading to a lost eternity! Let's be bold, follow Peter's later example of stepping out of the boat (Matthew 14:29) and, like Andrew, continually lead people to Jesus.

It might be instructive to consider these questions, as you reflect on Jesus' invitation:

i. If you're not yet a Christian, do you know any trusted believers, who you might ask about the difference following Jesus has made to their lives?

ii. Again, for those of you who don't yet know Jesus, what's your biggest fear, in relation to possibly accepting Him as your Saviour?

iii. For people who are Christians, without being overly 'preachy', are you able to show colleagues or classmates how your life is better with Jesus than it was without Him!

Let's finish our first reflection from the Gospels by coming before the Lord in prayer:

> *Heavenly Father, thank You for Your invitation to encounter You, which is evident from nature, the call upon my heart and, most especially, Your wonderful gift of a Saviour. Lord Jesus, I was late in responding to Your call, and am incredibly grateful to You for Your humility in accepting me, after I claimed to have found You when, in fact, it was the other way round. Holy Spirit, I will always be indebted to You for continuing to point me towards Jesus, even when I believed I knew better. Please do the same for people about whom I care deeply, who do not yet have the joyous privilege of following Jesus, nor the wonderful assurance of eternal life. In Jesus' Name I pray. Amen.*

A Different Side To Jesus!

"And Jesus went into the temple of God, and cast out all them that bought and sold in the temple, and overthrew the tables of the moneychangers, and the seats of them that sold doves, and said unto them, It is written, My house shall be called the house of prayer; but ye have made it a den of thieves (Matthew 21: 12 & 13)."

Have you ever seen a picture of Jesus? I'm quite wary of these things, due to the potential for violating the second commandment, but I can't imagine that you've ever seen a painting depicting Jesus like this! Did Jesus ever get angry? Yes, He did, and what made Him angry was the hypocrisy of the religious classes and the exploitation of poor, marginalised worshippers, for whom He has a special place in His heart. We'll deal with the hypocrisy in the next reflection, but the verses we're looking at here concentrate on exclusion and exploitation.

Although the Temple was ostensibly a Jewish place of worship, it contained a specifically prepared Court of the Gentiles, to which people who weren't Jews could come to worship God. This was particularly important, because God intended the Jews to serve as a witness to the world, in the same way that Christians are intended to be salt and light. The first aspect of these verses which angered Jesus was that the merchandising they describe was taking place in the Gentile Court, thereby preventing anyone who wasn't a Jew from entering into God's presence. Even today, He has harsh words for anyone, such as a false teacher, who attempts to prevent people from coming to faith! This abuse of the Court of the Gentiles was compounded by the nature of the activity that was being undertaken there: it wasn't merely trade, but profiteering. While most sacrifices would be of what we might regard as farm animals, such as lambs and calves, special provision was made for poorer members of society to sacrifice doves, in order to ensure that they weren't precluded from receiving atonement. Such a concept of sacrificing living creatures might seem curious to us today, and even be offensive to vegetarians, but it had a specific historical and prophetic meaning. In particular, it looked back to the sacrifice that was required to make garments of animal skin for Adam and Eve, after they transgressed, and forward to the ultimate sacrifice of the Messiah. In order for an animal to be acceptable for sacrifice, it had to be perfect, or without blemish, in the same way that Jesus needed to be perfect, to be able to atone for our sins. It was possible for doves to be cheaply acquired in the city marketplace, but unscrupulous merchants in the Temple would reject any from external sources which were offered for sacrifice, citing spurious blemishes. This forced the people to purchase alternative doves from the Temple itself, that were no better, but which were sold for a highly inflated price! The moneychangers practised a similar ruse: rather than accepting regular currency for offerings, they stipulated that people purchase a dedicated 'Temple shekel', for which they charged an exorbitant exchange rate.

Jesus is rightly described in Scripture as being meek, but many of those pictures you may have seen confuse 'meekness' with 'weakness'. However, Jesus is anything but weak: He is the strongest Man Who ever lived, and we'll see a full demonstration of His power when He returns to earth in all His glory (Luke 21:27). By exhibiting meekness, Jesus kept His power under control, and His anger was controlled, too. There's nothing wrong with righteous indignation (Psalm 7:11 & Ephesians 4:26), and God would expect us to be displeased about the things that break His heart, such as evil and corruption. Jesus's own heart was clearly broken, and He wouldn't allow the immoral trade to continue. This gives us an insight into the humanity of a Saviour Who, notwithstanding His deity, exhibited all the human traits of tiredness (John 4:6), hunger (Mark 11:12) and grief (John 11:35). While we don't often think of Jesus as being angry, it's probable that we rarely think of Him as weeping, either. The latter verse from John is the shortest in the Bible - "Jesus wept" - but it speaks volumes for His humanity and personality. Jesus was weeping over the body of Lazarus, which is something we can surely relate to, if we've ever lost a loved one. Jesus's grief might seem surprising, if we reflect that He was about to raise Lazarus from the dead, but I picture Him looking back throughout history, and forward into the future, standing in solidarity with everyone who ever had been, and ever would be, bereaved. Of course, there's the spiritual dimension, too, as both physical and spiritual death arose from the curse that emanated from mankind's sin. Unless we're taken up in the Rapture, we won't be able to escape physical death, but rejection of Jesus results in eternal anguish from which His own death was required to save us. It was this prospect of people He loved facing both physical judgement and a lost eternity that led Him to weep over His beloved Jerusalem, in Luke 19: 41 - 44. These verses immediately precede Luke's description of Jesus driving the moneychangers from the Temple, bringing us full circle!

Might you be willing to contemplate a few questions?

i. Do you weep over the things that break God's heart?

ii. Can you find it difficult to control your anger? If so, ask the Holy Spirit to help you!

iii. If you haven't yet accepted Jesus as your Saviour, does the fact that He'd grieve over the implications of your decision give you cause for thought?

Hypocrisy

"Woe unto you, scribes and Pharisees, hypocrites! For ye are like unto whited sepulchres, which indeed appear beautiful outward, but are within full of dead men's bones, and of all uncleanness (Matthew 23:27)."

Following on from our previous reflection, we here see Jesus leaving us in no doubt as to His hatred of hypocrisy and contempt for false teaching. The Jewish Pharisees personified religion, which blinded their hearts to the extent that they failed to recognise their Messiah and plotted to crucify Him, from the time He claimed to be the Son of God. They equated His claim with blasphemy, which would have been an accurate conclusion, had His assertion not been true! Although they knew the Scriptures backwards, the Pharisees couldn't spare the time to establish whether Jesus's claims to be the Messiah might possibly be genuine. In contrast to the perceptions many hold, Jesus was the most anti-religious Person Who ever lived! He showed utter contempt for the hypocrisy of many of the religious leaders, who used their positions to accumulate wealth and achieve power, with little regard for the people they were supposed to be serving. Jesus always had time, however tired He was, for men and women who came to Him with genuine questions, but He ruthlessly exposed the lawyers (experts in the Jewish Law), who valued their own reputations above anything else. Where these traits are found in the church today, Jesus's attitude is certainly the same: He identifies far more readily with an unemployed mechanic, who has legitimate questions about the Bible, than He does with a doctor of theology with a head full of knowledge and a cold heart. If you've been turned off religion, please be assured that you can still find a home with Jesus: He doesn't have a religious bone in His body!

Speaking of bones, what's all this about sepulchres? Jesus here was exposing the Pharisees for looking righteous on the outside, but being desperately wicked internally. Their demonstrations of piety were legendary, including their practice of wrapping their cloaks tightly around them, to avoid coming into contact with anything perceived to be unclean, in the eyes of the Law. This obsession produced perverse results, which Jesus illustrated in the parable of the good Samaritan (Luke 10: 30 - 37), where both a priest and a Levite refused to come to the aid of a stricken traveller, whereas a man from Samaria gave his time, energy and financial resources to ensure the victim's wellbeing. This type of teaching would have enraged the Jewish leaders, who had a long-standing disregard for the Samaritans, owing to their belief that God should be worshipped on Mount Gerizim, rather than in the Temple. Our Lord's intention was to illustrate the difference in heart that motivates people's actions.

Jesus famously urged his listeners to, "Judge not, that ye be not judged (Matthew 7:1)." The concept here isn't to eschew the exercise of discernment, regarding who we associate with, but that we have no right to condemn others, when we ourselves are far from perfect. Displaying typical humour, He described the scenario, a couple of verses later, where someone might point to a speck of dust in his brother's eye, while having a plank of wood in his own. The primary reason that we're not qualified to judge is that we're not God, even though some of us try to help Him out from time to time! However, a significant supplementary reason is that God judges on the basis of motive, whereas we only see outward actions, and are therefore in no position to make an informed evaluation. Jesus illustrates this in Luke 21, verses 1 - 4, where He observes that, while rich men may have contributed liberally to the Temple treasury, their gifts cost them virtually nothing, due to their abundant wealth, whereas a poor widow, who made a contribution of two mites, which were of little intrinsic value, had actually been far more generous, due to her sacrifice in compromising her ability to meet her own needs. Beyond this was a difference in motive: giving to look good, versus a genuine desire to support the Temple. Of course, a third reason for not assuming the role of judge is that there'll inevitably come a time when we ourselves fail, at which point we'll be pleading for clemency; something we're more likely to be afforded if we've previously been forgiving of others. This is the essence of Jesus's statement that follows on from His exhortation not to judge, "For with what judgement ye judge, ye shall be judged: and with what measure ye mete, it shall be measured to you again (Matthew 7:2)."

What about hypocrisy in the church? Yes, it's certainly a problem, but it's important to clarify what hypocrisy really is, which is pretending to be something you're not. For example, a supposed Christian who condemns someone for perceived immorality while themselves being involved in an affair is a hypocrite, because he or she is projecting the image of being beyond reproach, and qualified to judge others, while being more guilty than the person they're judging. Jesus had tremendous fun with such people, when they presented Him with a woman they claimed to have caught in the act of adultery (John 8: 3 - 11). Their hope was that He'd have her stoned, as their interpretation of the Law would have required, thereby invalidating His credentials as a Friend of sinners. Instead, He sent them away with their tails between their legs; quite possibly after publicly drawing their own peccadilloes to their attention! Hypocrisy such as this in the church is profoundly detrimental, but not every Christian who sins is a hypocrite: sinning is a product of being human; it only becomes hypocrisy when compounded by pretence. Whether we're hypocrites, or merely sinners, there's still hope for us, provided we're prepared to allow Jesus to transform our hearts and minds, by the power of His Holy Spirit! I'm constantly amazed by how different my thoughts and attitudes now are, compared to when I first came to the Lord, and know many other believers who would say the same. Why not allow Him to change your life, too? It will be the best decision you ever make!

Now, how about some questions?

i. Have you ever done something that was judged particularly harshly, when you had the best of motives?

ii. Does reflecting on such an occasion help you to see how other people might frequently be due the benefit of the doubt, despite outward appearances?

iii. Is it reassuring to know that God judges on the basis of motives, and not outcomes?

Well Done!

> *"His lord said unto him, Well done, thou good and faithful servant: thou hast been faithful over a few things, I will make thee ruler over many things: enter thou into the joy of thy lord (Matthew 25: 21 & 23)."*

What a contrast to Jesus's words of admonition for the religious classes! These verses are taken from Jesus's famous parable of the talents, where talents represented considerable sums of money. I'm sure you'll be familiar with the story: three servants were respectively entrusted with five talents, two measures and a single talent by their master, prior to his departure for an overseas trip. The first two servants doubled their return, but the third hid his talent in the ground, thereby achieving nothing in his master's absence. Obviously, the businessman was delighted with the servants who traded successfully, to whom he gave the commendation recorded above, but he wasn't so impressed with the third, who he described as "wicked and slothful (Matthew 25:26)!"

Wouldn't it be wonderful to hear those words from Jesus, "Well done, thou good and faithful servant!" Just like the servants in the parable, our Master has gone away, following His ascension to heaven, but He hasn't left us without jobs to do! One day, He'll return for us, and He'll expect us to have done something with the treasures that He's given us: both our natural, God-given abilities, and the gifts endowed to us by the Holy Spirit. Now, clearly, everyone who accepts Jesus as their Lord and Saviour receives the assurance of everlasting life, meaning that we don't need to worry about our eternal destinies. This is the essence of salvation but, as wonderful as that is, it shouldn't obscure the fact that we're saved for a purpose. Do you know what your purpose is? First of all, if you're not yet a Christian, it's to give your life to the Lord, because we can achieve nothing of eternal value until then. After that, we all have an obligation to be 'salt and light' (Matthew 5: 13 & 14), acting as witnesses to those who are in the same position as we were: wandering in darkness, without having Jesus to illuminate the way. In addition, we have the amazing privilege of being part of the global Body of Christ, accomplishing His will on earth, through the power of His Holy Spirit.

The good news is that we all have a role to play: it's not like the school playing fields, where we might have been omitted from the team or only reluctantly selected by a captain who had no other option! As mentioned previously, we are "fearfully and wonderfully made (Psalm 139:14)," and we've been created to fulfil a special function that no-one else can fulfil. There's absolutely nothing wrong with admiring certain individuals, and learning from them, in terms of how they handle difficult situations or interact with other people. However, it's essential that we don't fall into the trap of imitating anyone else: God has made you to be unique, and He wants you to be the authentic you, because no-one else has been created to do what you can do!

This sounds fine in theory, but what is it that we're intended to do? It's important not to overly mystify this, because by excessively dwelling on what our calling might be, we could either become paralysed by fear, in case we miss it, or fail to see the opportunities that are in front of us. Hopefully, if you're a new believer, you'll be able to find a church fellowship with sound teaching and a vibrant prayer meeting. As you notice things that are going on, you'll see opportunities to contribute: perhaps by serving on a prayer team or joining the worship band. In general, the openings that interest you will be consistent with the natural talents God has given you: for example, if you have a heart for people, and a listening ear, Christian counselling might be an avenue to pursue. On the other hand, if you're tone deaf, joining the worship team probably wouldn't be a shrewd move! Obviously, our opportunities to serve the Lord aren't constrained to the church setting: your life itself should become a testimony of God's faithfulness, in addition to which there are likely to be various outreaches and mission-based activities in which you'll be able to participate. Don't be afraid to learn by making mistakes: frequently, trying something that doesn't work out helps redirect us to where our calling lies.

Over and above our innate abilities, believers should receive at least one spiritual gift from the Holy Spirit (see 1 Corinthians 12). Ask the Holy Spirit to overflow you with His presence and bestow upon you whichever gift(s) He chooses, remembering that these are *His* gifts, meaning that it's His prerogative to decide which one(s) He gives you! We're all part of the Body of Christ, and our role might not be glamorous, but it's essential nonetheless. How much thought do you give to your abdominal tract? Yet, think how challenging life would be without it! If you're an encourager, then encourage people: they may achieve great things as a consequence, and part of that achievement will be credited to your account, because you were faithful in bringing the word God gave you. Similarly, if you have a gift for teaching, ask the Holy Spirit to help you bring the Word to life for those around you, inspiring them to serve the amazing God of the Bible, Who is revealed through its pages. It's possible that your calling might seem insignificant compared to someone else's, but it's important that you don't get distracted by what other people are doing. Note that both the servants who were given the five and two talents received exactly the same commendation (verses 21 & 23 of Matthew 25 are virtually identical). The world might have seen an entrepreneur who made a big profit and a small businessman who just got by, but God saw two faithful servants, both of whom achieved a 100% increase! In spiritual terms, you may not consider your calling as a parent to be as significant as being a pastor, but if you invest spiritually in the lives of your children, there's no knowing what they'll become! Our role is to use the gifts God has given us and leave the results to Him!

Jesus's teaching was always balanced: against the promise of heaven there's the warning of hell. This wasn't intended to scare people, but to prepare them, in order to give them the opportunity to make the right decisions, while they had time. Similarly, regarding the rewards of the believer, there's the potential for us to receive the praise recorded in the verses we're reflecting upon, or to be harshly rebuked, like the unfaithful servant, who did nothing with what was given to him. All Christians receive the gift of salvation, but for some, who simply sit back and wait for eternity, there's the prospect of being "saved as though by fire (1 Corinthians 3:15);" either because they didn't achieve anything of value or due to the impurity of their motives. Don't be like the unfaithful servant, making hollow excuses; instead, use the talents that have been given to you: if we all do this, we'll be rulers with Christ in eternity, and won't that be amazing!

Do you have the gifting to consider some questions?

i. What are the areas in your church, where you might be able to serve, if you're not doing so already?

ii. How might you be able to utilise your natural abilities for the glory of God?

iii. What spiritual gift(s) have you been given, and are you maximising its/their potential?

Resurrection!

"And the angel answered and said unto the women, Fear not ye: for I know that ye seek Jesus, which was crucified. He is not here: for he is risen, as he said. Come, see the place where the Lord lay (Matthew 28: 5 & 6)."

What's the most remarkable event of your life? For Mary Magdalene and the other Mary, to whom the angel was speaking in these two verses, these miraculous events came at the end of an excruciating time, during which they had seen the Man in Whom they'd placed all their hopes tried, beaten, crucified and buried. It can be hard to process information at the best of times, but when we're engulfed by grief it becomes almost impossible, as every aspect of our circumstances joins with the world around us to cry out, "There is no hope." In the midst of our torment, it is exceedingly difficult to see the fallacy of this assertion, just as the promises we've previously been given seem hollow in their apparent implausibility.

The depth of our grief is proportional to our love for the person we've lost, so both of these women, whose lives Jesus had transformed, must have been completely devastated. Now they were trying to make sense of everything that had happened, and possibly wondering whether the previous three years had been a dream. They had seen Jesus perform wonderful miracles, most notably the resurrection of Lazarus, and He'd even promised that He would rise from the grave after three days (John 2:19), but on this particular Sunday morning they were coming to anoint His body. It seemed implausible to think that He might have risen from the dead: after all, He often spoke figuratively, and who could possibly raise Him, if He Himself was gone?

SPIRITUAL REFLECTIONS - I

For many of you reading this reflection, your own doubts about the reality of Jesus's resurrection may currently be presenting an apparently insurmountable stumbling-block to coming to faith. Perhaps you've been intrigued by the Old Testament Scriptures, and how they point towards Jesus, and maybe you've grown to like the Teacher we've encountered in Matthew's Gospel, but people don't simply rise from the dead, do they? Well, not usually but, having said that, Jesus wasn't the first Person in history to do so! In 1 Kings 17, we read of Elijah resurrecting a widow's son, while his protégé, Elisha, raised the son of a Shunammite woman, as recorded in 2 Kings 4. We're also familiar with Jesus's three recorded resurrection miracles - not only the raising of Lazarus - which prefigured both His own conquest of death and the hope that we all have, as believers, of being united with our Lord in eternity.

As C.S. Lewis points out, the option of accepting Jesus as merely being a Good Teacher isn't open to us: if He didn't rise from the grave, then He's a hoaxter and a liar, which certainly doesn't qualify Him as being 'Good'! We therefore have to decide if He was a deeply flawed individual or the Son of God. Three days after what appeared to be his greatest victory, Satan met with his most calamitous defeat, when Jesus returned to life, thereby proving all His claims to be true and demonstrating His absolute power over any force that would seek to oppose Him. It is therefore understandable that the Enemy would spend the next two thousand years trying to persuade people that the resurrection didn't happen, because this is the only way he can take them with him to a lost eternity. After all, who wouldn't choose to follow Jesus, if they really believed that He rose from the dead and had the power to give them the same everlasting life!

The question then is whose account is to be believed: Jesus's or Satan's? Historically speaking, there is absolutely no denying that Jesus's tomb was empty, three days after His burial. Both the religious and political leaders were desperate to quell this new 'sect' of Christianity, and the best way for them to counteract the claims that Jesus had risen would have been for them to produce His body, which was something they were unable to do. This point is even conceded by Flavius Josephus, a Jewish historian, who was hostile to Christianity, but nonetheless largely accurate in his writing. If we accept that the grave *was* empty, but wish to refute the resurrection, what are the alternatives? One suggestion is that Jesus didn't actually die on the cross, but revived in the cool of the tomb, so couldn't have been resurrected, because He hadn't previously been dead. An acceptance of this assertion takes far more faith than to believe in the resurrection, because it would have necessitated Jesus to regain the requisite strength to roll back the stone from in front of His tomb! These stones were generally sufficiently heavy to require several men to manoeuvre them and, even if He had surmounted this obstacle, Jesus would then have needed to evade the capture of the sentries guarding His grave.

If you join me in accepting that this theory is completely implausible, then perhaps the most viable alternative is that Jesus's body was stolen by His disciples, in order to validate their claims that He had risen from the dead. Such a contention might initially appear persuasive, but it, too, has substantial flaws. The Roman authorities were aware that such a plot was a distinct possibility, so the soldiers who were appointed to guard the tomb would have been on pain of death. It doesn't seem credible that they would all have simultaneously been asleep sufficiently long for the disciples to move the stone, retrieve Jesus's body and effect their escape, all without waking a single soldier. Moreover, such an act would have taken considerable courage; an attribute that was in short supply when the disciples, except for John, abandoned Jesus during the crucifixion and, in Peter's case, even denied knowing Him! Assuming that they had managed to overcome their fear and circumvent the Roman garrisons, one of the apostles would surely have broken rank when they were arrested and sentenced to their own deaths, due to their consistent proclamation that Jesus had risen from the dead. Not many people believe in a project or vision to the extent that they're willing to die for it, but who on earth would lay down their life for something they knew not to be true? Yet, even secular history attests to the fact that, of the eleven faithful apostles, ten were martyred, while John was exiled to Patmos.

So much for the alternatives, what about the case *for* the resurrection? The first point to make is that the Gospel account doesn't show the disciples in a good light: it's hardly the script you'd write if you were looking to institute a new belief system! First of all, while the male disciples behaved like scared children, the initial witnesses to Jesus's resurrection were women: this wouldn't have been the strategy a spin doctor would have adopted, because the testimony of women was accorded such low esteem in first-century Israel that it generally wasn't admissible in court! Then there is the profound impact on the apostles, who went from being a demoralised, ramshackle bunch to a group who preached with power and confidence, once they were reunited with their Risen Messiah, spent a further forty days in His company, and received the Holy Spirit on the Day of Pentecost. Acts 1:3 speaks of the "many infallible proofs" Jesus provided of His resurrection, in the forty-day period prior to His ascension to be reunited with His Father. Although it may be argued that this isn't an impartial source, neither the Jewish nor Roman authorities were able to refute the assertion that the Jesus they had crucified was alive, walking amongst them, and performing the types of miracles which had characterised His ministry, prior to Calvary.

Perhaps Jesus's ascension solved this problem for them, but it led to what may be the greatest ongoing evidence for His resurrection: the continuing witness of the Holy Spirit, Who empowered the apostles, and subsequent generations of believers, to perform wondrous acts, which continue up to this day, as observed in the powerful ministries of Jarrod Cooper, Jonathan Conrathe, and many others. It is this same Spirit Who is touching the hearts of people all around the world, every day of the year, and awakening them to the reality that the Jesus Who He raised from the dead is the One Who, if invited to do so, will give them the eternal life that He promises in Scripture and currently enjoys in heaven. You might not be completely convinced, but maybe you're not as sceptical as you previously were? If that's so, why not do some research of your own? 'The Case for Christ' by Lee Strobel and 'Evidence that Demands a Verdict' by Josh McDowell are good starting points: both were written by former atheists, who embarked on separate missions to disprove the Gospel, and became believers, as a result of what they found!

Would you be willing to reflect on a few questions?

i. If you don't believe in Jesus's resurrection, what is your biggest barrier to doing so?

ii. Would you give your life for something you didn't believe to be true?

iii. How would you have written the resurrection story, if it hadn't been true, but you were looking to start a new sect?

Finally, it doesn't seem right to move on from such a reflection, without a closing word of prayer:

> *Heavenly Father, I thank You for the fact that all things, including death, are under Your control, and for Your mercy in sending Your Son to give me life. Lord Jesus, I still find it hard to comprehend the depth of Your love for me, and apologise for so infrequently expressing my gratitude for Your sacrifice. Thank You for Your obedience and faithfulness, which purchased the redemption of a rebellious individual, who all too rarely displays these qualities in return. Holy Spirit, thank You for raising Jesus from the grave and also for resurrecting me spiritually, at a time when I needed a Saviour, but didn't realise it. I invite You into every area of my life and implore You to witness to the people I love, who don't yet know Jesus, of the reality of His resurrection and the wonderful future that awaits them, once they accept His offer of eternal life. In Jesus's Incomparable Name I pray. Amen.*

Unstoppable Faith!

"When Jesus saw their faith, he said unto the sick of the palsy, Son, thy sins be forgiven thee (Mark 2:5)."

The opening twelve verses of the second chapter of Mark comprise a remarkable passage of Scripture, exquisitely depicted by Seamus Heaney, in his evocative poem, 'The Skylight'. I'm obviously no Seamus Heaney, but let me try to paint a picture! After calling His disciples, Jesus taught authoritatively in the synagogue in Capernaum (Mark 1:21), where His confident declaration of spiritual truth contrasted starkly with the academic manner of the scribes, who always cited other sources and never taught in their own authority. Powerful teaching is one thing, but Jesus's words were endorsed by compelling actions, which demonstrated the love and compassion of the One in Whose Name He had come. Wherever He found people bound by spiritual attack or diminished by sickness, He respectively delivered or healed them, as He did subsequently in Mark chapter 1, where He healed Simon Peter's mother-in-law of a fever, in addition to working innumerable other miracles. Jesus later travelled throughout Galilee, teaching in the synagogues and performing many more wondrous acts, even healing a man of leprosy, which was unheard of at the time. These miraculous deliverances weren't intended for show, but to reveal God's heart to people whose perception of Him had been distorted by the cold, uncaring religious elite. In complete contrast, we read, in Mark 1:41, that Jesus was "moved with compassion."

Despite the absence of radio, television, or even newspapers, word of mouth would have ensured that Jesus's exploits were earnestly discussed in every home and marketplace throughout the region. Just like today, some believed, others didn't, and many more simply continued with their lives, indifferent to the glory that was being manifest around them. Another similarity to today is that Jesus wouldn't, and still won't, intervene in people's lives, unless they ask Him to! We could only be a prayer away from a miracle, but if we don't ask then we'll never know! Of course, the same principle applies in relation to salvation itself, which requires us to come to Jesus, rather than waiting for Him to come to us. Oftentimes, as we're about to see, we require someone to bring us to Jesus: it may well be that you trace your decision to accept Him as your Saviour to the faithfulness of a friend in inviting you to a service that you weren't particularly enthusiastic about attending!

In first-century Israel, there was no state social security system, as a consequence of which physical disability implied considerable financial deprivation, which is why it was such a common sight for people to be begging outside the Temple in Jerusalem. We can never over-estimate the value of a loyal friend, who will stand by us when times are tough and offer words of encouragement for the journey. For several years, four men from Capernaum had a burden on their hearts for a friend who was completely debilitated by a condition called the palsy (the Bible doesn't say there were four, but this is a reasonable supposition: one to hold each corner of the stretcher). They'd obviously heard about Jesus's teaching in the synagogue and the miracles that were attributed to Him, but while they were processing all this information He moved on, and they must have wondered whether their chance had gone. Whenever we miss an opportunity, we're generally far more committed to taking it next time around so, when the men heard that Jesus had returned to Capernaum, there was no stopping them, as they translated their burden from an emotional one to a physical one! Jesus was teaching and, as you might imagine, the venue was packed. Even for four strong adults, carrying a man on a stretcher over any real distance is an exhausting venture that takes considerable time, meaning that they were late for the meeting. How might we have reacted? Perhaps we'd have been discouraged and trudged disconsolately back home, rationalising to ourselves that we probably wouldn't have got to see Jesus in any case and, as for miracles, well, they're for other people, aren't they? Frequently, the desperation of our circumstances is what provokes us to push for an answer, and this may well have been what happened here: maybe the four men resolved something along the lines of: we've carried our friend all this way, we don't have the energy to carry him home again, and we certainly can't leave him here! Whatever their reasoning, their faith was rewarded!

When the faithful friends realised that they wouldn't be able to make their way through the crowds to get to Jesus, they made a hole in the roof, through which they lowered their stricken companion, bringing us to the verse that we're considering in this reflection. They were no doubt delighted when Jesus began to address their friend, thinking they'd be able to walk home together and regale sceptical acquaintances with their account of a wonderful miracle. However, they were in for a surprise: instead of the words they were hoping to hear, "Get up and walk," their ears resonated to the sound of, "Thy sins be forgiven thee!" We're incredibly fortunate that, while we have an obligation to make the first move in coming to Jesus, He is abundantly gracious in giving us what we need, even when we ask for the wrong thing. This principle is evident in prayer, as illustrated by verses 26 & 27 of Romans chapter 8, which describe the Holy Spirit interceding on our behalf, when we don't know how to pray ourselves. Although neither the man's friends, nor the man himself, may have realised it at the time, absolutely nothing can ever be remotely as important as the forgiveness of sins, which is an essential prerequisite for us receiving our eternal inheritance. The way to receive this forgiveness is the same for us today as it was in Capernaum back then: we need to come to Jesus! We almost certainly won't be making a hole in the roof to do so, but the principle is exactly the same: we can't allow any obstacles to deter us, either from bringing people to Jesus or from coming to Him ourselves. Jesus's miracle enraged the watching scribes, who correctly inferred that only God can forgive sins, and therefore accused Him of blasphemy, which was ultimately the 'crime' for which the religious leaders conspired to have Him crucified. They were obviously correct in their premise, but desperately wrong in their conclusion, demonstrating that accurate doctrine is of no use to us, if it doesn't make the transition from our head to our heart.

While Jesus's pre-eminent concern for us is always our eternal wellbeing, He delights in blessing us during our life on earth, and He was only too glad to give the man with the palsy the healing he and his friends were looking for. In some instances, but by no means all, infirmities we suffer may arise as a consequence of our own sin or disobedience, whereas all illness has its origins in the original sin of Adam and Eve, which brought a curse upon the earth. God will sometimes accede to our requests for healing, whereas on other occasions He won't, but when He does heal us it should always be the case that we give Him the glory, as happened on this occasion, when the observers were "all amazed, and glorified God, saying, We never saw it on this fashion (Mark 2:12)." Even when we don't receive the healing we desire, everyone who accepts Jesus has the wonderful assurance of eternal life, knowing that it's far better to enter into heaven maimed than to be condemned to hell in perfect physical condition (see Matthew 18:8). Let's give thanks for the wonderful, merciful God we have the privilege to serve!

These questions might be worth considering, as you reflect on what you've read:

i. Do you know anyone who needs to be brought to Jesus, perhaps by inviting them to a church service?

ii. What are the obstacles you face in your everyday life, either in coming to Jesus yourself, or in bringing others to Him?

iii. If you don't yet know Jesus as your Saviour, would you like to have your sins forgiven? If so, you can: just pray this prayer, or something like it, and eternal life will be yours!

> *Heavenly Father, thank You for sending Your Son, Jesus, to help me appreciate Your profound love for me. Lord Jesus, thank You for Your love and humility, in coming to bring hope and restoration to a troubled world. I'm genuinely sorry for not having always been the person You intended me to be, and for the things I've thought, said or done, which have caused offence to You,*

and to other people. Today, I want to invite You into my life and accept Your offer of forgiveness for my sins. Holy Spirit, please come to dwell within me, direct my paths and empower me to live the rest of my life for Jesus, in Whose Precious Name I pray. Amen.

If you've prayed this prayer, or something similar, in all sincerity, then you're now a member of God's extended family!

Come Home!

"I will arise and go to my father, and will say unto him, Father, I have sinned against heaven, and before thee, and am no more worthy to be called thy son: make me as one of thy hired servants. And he arose, and came to his father. But when he was yet a great way off, his father saw him, and had compassion, and ran, and fell on his neck, and kissed him (Luke 15: 18 - 20)."

Have you ever tried to run away? I have to confess that I did once: I ended up in Liverpool, but had no idea what to do when I got there, so apologetically came back home! Maybe you've done something similar: perhaps you've even tried running from God, as Jonah did, in a passage of Scripture we were looking at previously. As in Jonah's case, the Lord won't make it easy for you but, if you're sufficiently determined, He *will* let you go, because He respects your freedom of choice, which He'll never over-ride. There's nothing better for our lives than to be fulfilling the purpose for which we were created: serving God and shining His light into the world. However, there's frequently a tension between what we ought to be doing and what we want to do, which can lead to us making wrong decisions that take us away from the loving embrace of our Saviour. When we're in that predicament, it can be tempting to keep on running, because it often seems easier to keep going in the direction we're facing than to stop, turn around, and commence the long journey back. There are so many notional reasons for continuing along the wrong track, especially if it's the path our friends are following: fear of being different, not wanting to acknowledge that 'those Christians' were right and, perhaps, anxiety as to the rebuke we might face if we come back to the Lord. The longer we leave it, the harder it gets, as we become less sensitive to the Spirit's overtures and more entrenched in our perception that we're doing the right thing. However, we need never fear the Lord's response, once we make the decision to return to Him: all we need to do is to take one step in His direction, and He'll take ninety-nine to come and meet us!

You may recognise these verses from Luke's Gospel as having been taken from the parable of the prodigal son. In an immensely patriarchal society, the son had painfully insulted his father by asking for his inheritance before due time, effectively saying that he wished his father was dead, so that he could have enough money to travel abroad and enjoy the pleasures of life. Just like King Solomon, the son soon found that indulging natural instincts eventually leads to misery and despair, as his money ran out and his putative friends abandoned him when he was no longer able to show them a good time. There's only one Person Who will unfailingly stand by us: the Friend Who sticks closer than a brother (Proverbs 18:24)! In due course, the son began to realise this, as he descended into penury, finally ending up feeding swine, contrary to the Jewish Law, and thereby becoming a pariah. He was so hungry that he even craved the husks he was feeding to the pigs, and only when his situation got this desperate did he finally contemplate returning home. His plan was to see if his father would hire him as a servant, but the father wanted so much more!

Although this story is known the world over as the parable of the prodigal son, Pastor Greg Laurie of Harvest Christian Fellowship aptly describes it as "the parable of the loving father." While the son was destroying his life in a foreign land, squandering the money his parents had lovingly saved, the father mourned in his spirit for the loss of a son, who he desperately wanted to see back home, enjoying the loving provision of his family. Can you imagine his delight, when he saw his son appear over the horizon, then went running to meet him? It wouldn't have been dignified for an older man to run in the Israel of Jesus's day, and the description is all the more poignant when we consider that it depicts our Heavenly Father's love for us, which knows no bounds. Have you wandered from the Lord? If so, He is desperate for you to come back to Him, which is the very reason for Him having told this story. It may not happen immediately but if, like the son in the parable, you continue to rebel against God, your road will ultimately lead to misery and heartache. There are at least two reasons for this: the increasingly illogical decisions we make when we're not walking with the Lord, and His attempts to put roadblocks in our way, to prevent us from enduring the torment of destruction. If you're in that position today, I would urge you with all my heart to take the first step towards coming back home. As much as He loves you, God won't take this step for you: in the same way that the son's return voyage began with "coming to himself (Luke 15:17)," allied with a decision to "arise and go (verse 18)," our route back must always begin with repentance (turning from our sin) and a conscious decision to return to the Lord. If we're willing to do this, God will do the rest, unhesitatingly accepting us back into His family, as we escape spiritual death and re-emerge into life (Luke 15:24). Unfortunately, not everyone will be so happy: subsequent verses consider the father's other son, who resented the feast that was arranged to celebrate his brother's homecoming. You may encounter similar attitudes when you come back home to the Lord, but just ignore anyone who expresses them: they'll reap their own judgement one day, whereas you'll be eternally forgiven!

The following questions might be interesting for private thought or discussion in a small group:

i. Do you consistently pray for the prodigals in your own life, continuing to love them, despite the heartache they're causing you?

ii. How does your church respond to men or women who return, after a period of absence, during which they may not have been walking with the Lord?

iii. Are you a prodigal yourself? If so, why not come back home? I can promise you that you won't regret it!

SPIRITUAL REFLECTIONS - I

Thy Will Be Done!

"And he was withdrawn from them about a stone's cast, and kneeled down, and prayed, saying, Father, if thou be willing, remove this cup from me: nevertheless not my will, but thine, be done (Luke 22: 41 & 42)."

It is difficult to find a more moving passage of Scripture than the twenty-second chapter of the Gospel of Luke. Incredibly, the chapter begins with the priests - the people who should have been upholding the Law - and the scribes plotting to kill their Messiah. Despite their preoccupation with keeping every jot and tittle of the Law, their hardness of heart led them to break it in numerous egregious ways in having Jesus condemned to death during the Feast of Passover. Isn't this often the way with religion? Minor points are emphasised, in order to keep people out of the club, while those on the inside are breaking the rules with impunity! Another characteristic of religion is the tendency for individuals to put on a show of piety, in order to advance their personal position, which is precisely what Judas Iscariot had been doing since becoming one of Jesus's apostles. In keeping with many of us, the apostles had considerable difficulty in accepting the pre-eminence of the spiritual over the physical, as a consequence of which their primary focus was upon Jesus overthrowing the Roman Empire and establishing His Kingdom on earth. Their recurring arguments over who was the greatest point to a debate over which of them would occupy the various positions around Jesus's post-revolution cabinet table. Undoubtedly, Judas, who had been the treasurer for the disciples, had his eye on the position of Minister for Finance, but when his expectations weren't being met he took the unconscionable decision to betray Jesus. Although this is something that had to happen, in order for Biblical prophecy to be fulfilled, it doesn't mean Judas can be in any way exonerated. As Jesus said Himself, speaking of this very event, "It is impossible but that offences will come: but woe unto him, through whom they come (Luke 17:1)!" Soberingly, we read in Luke 22:3 that Judas's act of betrayal was not only motivated by Satan, but that Satan actually entered into him. Persistent rejection of Jesus is an extremely dangerous path to follow, and Judas's experience demonstrates just how dangerous it can be.

If you've ever lost someone you love, you'll be all too aware of the importance of saying "goodbye." This is an opportunity that tragic circumstances can deny to us but Jesus, knowing what was to come, was able to enjoy a final meal with His disciples, during the course of which He exhorted them to remember Him, by sharing the bread and wine, which symbolised the sacrifice that He was about to become, with His body literally broken for us, and His blood shed for our sins. It had taken the blood of an animal to cover the sins of Adam and Eve, but that was only a temporary solution: now the sins of everyone who is willing to accept Jesus's offer of forgiveness were being expunged for all of history, prior to Calvary, and for the entire future, from that point on. The lack of spiritual acuity on the part of the apostles is illustrated by the fact that it was at this very point they again began to argue about their comparative greatness (Luke 22:24)! After warning Peter of his imminent act of denial which, unlike the betrayal perpetrated by Judas, led to heartfelt repentance meeting with abundant forgiveness, Jesus took time in Gethsemane to pray. It was from there that He besought His Father with this most moving, impassioned prayer, which is the focus of our reflection. Jesus experienced such excruciating agony of spirit, soul and body at this time that, as we read in Luke 22:44, "His sweat was as it were great drops of blood;" a condition called haematidrosis. Crucifixion was a cruel death for anyone to suffer, and it was generally reserved for the worst criminals of the day. I won't go into too much detail here, as I want this to be a book that can be read by all the family, but victims essentially suffocated, fighting for each increasingly shallow breath, as mind-numbing pain seared through their body. However, it was more than likely another kind of pain that led Jesus to ask if this cup might possibly pass from Him. Never before in history had He been separated from His Father: even while on earth, having voluntarily forsaken the glory of heaven, Jesus was in constant communion with Him, but now this was about to change. In order for God, as a righteous Judge, to be able to accept Jesus's atoning sacrifice for our sins, He literally had to become sin for us, meaning that the Father couldn't look upon Him while He was on the cross. This is surely what led to His impassioned cry, "My God, my God, why hast thou forsaken me (Matthew 27:46)?" Tim Hughes couldn't have expressed our indebtedness any better when he penned the words, "I'll never know how much it cost to see my sin upon that cross," which feature in his classic song, 'Here I Am To Worship'. Our only fitting response must surely be to "Call upon the Lord and be saved," which is the very next refrain in Hillsong's rendering of his magnificent anthem.

There are innumerable lessons we can learn from this compelling passage of Scripture, but I'll conclude our reflection by considering six of them.

1. Serving God is costly: if He didn't spare His Son from suffering, then He won't spare us, where that suffering is required for His purposes to be accomplished.

2. It is necessary for us to pray in accordance with God's will: not getting an affirmative answer doesn't mean He doesn't care or isn't listening. Although Jesus asked for the cup to pass from Him, it was necessary for Him to be made sin for us.

3. We will often receive supernatural assistance when serving the Lord, and in need of additional strength. We see this in verse 43 of Luke 22, where an angel strengthened Jesus.

4. Our greatest victories are frequently preceded by apparent defeats: Jesus provided the ultimate demonstration of this, as He had to be crucified before He could be resurrected.

5. We shouldn't be sleeping, whether spiritually or physically, when we ought to be praying! While Jesus was praying in Gethsemane, the disciples were sleeping, which cost them

SPIRITUAL REFLECTIONS - I

dearly, due to the fact that they failed to take hold of the promises He had given them, and fled in terror at His arrest.

6. Prayer can be defensive, as well as offensive: after finding His disciples sleeping, Jesus urged them to "pray, lest ye enter into temptation (Luke 22:46)."

Prayer precedes victory, whereas praylessness precipitates defeat. Jesus's victory at Calvary, to which we owe our eternal security, was won in Gethsemane, which should surely inspire us to constantly be in a spirit of prayer, as Paul exhorts us to be in 1 Thessalonians 5:17.

Will you be able to stay awake long enough to ponder a few questions?

i. Have you ever considered that, if you don't serve Jesus, you'll ultimately end up serving Satan, as happened to Judas?

ii. How seriously do you reflect upon Jesus's sacrifice, when you take Communion?

iii. Do you pray defensively, as well as offensively, in order that you don't enter into temptation?

The lyrics quoted in this reflection were taken from the song 'Here I Am to Worship', written by Tim Hughes and performed by Hillsong. The copyright for this song is owned by Thankyou Music* and a licence to reproduce these lyrics has been purchased from Integrity Music.

*Adm. By Capitol CMG Publishing worldwide, excl. UK and Europe, admin at IntegrityRights.com.

Saved!

"And one of the malefactors which were hanged railed on him, saying, If thou be Christ, save thyself and us. But the other answering rebuked him, saying, Dost thou not fear God, seeing thou art in the same condemnation? And we indeed justly; for we receive the due reward of our deeds: but this man hath done nothing amiss. And he said unto Jesus, Lord, remember me when thou comest into thy kingdom. And Jesus said unto him, Verily I say unto thee, Today shalt thou be with me in paradise (Luke 23: 39 - 43)."

What an amazing scene! Crucifixion was invented by the Persians, then refined by the Roman authorities to maximise the pain inflicted on the most notorious criminals they wished to execute. Although we often refer to the two individuals crucified alongside Jesus as being 'thieves', the word Luke uses here, malefactor, is more appropriate. It's quite likely that the two men were actually insurrectionists, and that the middle cross, on which Jesus laid down His life for us, had been prepared for Barabbas, whose name, perhaps more than coincidentally, translates as 'son of the father'.

Isn't it remarkable how the same scenario can produce radically different reactions in people we consider to be intrinsically similar? We might invite two friends to a church service, one of whom responds positively to an altar call, while the other dismisses the invitation, preferring to focus on the afternoon's sporting action. This points to the potential for the Gospel to divide, as individuals separate themselves on opposite sides of an invisible line that demarcates our eternal destinies. Conversely, the Gospel also has a breathtaking propensity to unite people from radically different backgrounds, such as Simon the zealot, a Jewish nationalist anxious to overthrow Roman rule, and Matthew, who collected taxes on behalf of Rome, and would therefore have been perceived as a turncoat. If the two malefactors crucified with Jesus were Barabbas's accomplices, then it's quite conceivable that they would have known Simon, and observed the transformation in his character, after he became a disciple. Even if this wasn't the case, they both now found themselves on the verge of death, facing into eternity as bit-part players in the greatest drama that the world has ever seen. Except, that was the strange part: despite the massive crowds who had come to see Jesus - some to support Him, others baying for His blood, and many simply inspired by curiosity - the world didn't see a great deal, because it was shrouded in darkness (Luke 23:44).

This supernatural phenomenon must have contributed a considerable sense of foreboding to an emotionally charged day, when the angelic powers of heaven collided with the demonic forces of hell in a spiritual precursor to Armageddon. Even at the best of times, human beings have a tendency to focus on themselves, so the reaction of the first malefactor is somewhat understandable. He was in extreme pain and on the brink of death, so it's only natural that he would clutch at straws, hoping that, if Jesus really was the Messiah, He might use His supernatural power to end their torment. However, in common with many people who come close to Jesus, without actually accepting Him, he was looking entirely through natural eyes, and therefore missed the point. Certainly, Jesus had the power to bring Himself, and the other men, down from the hill of Calvary but, had He done so, He wouldn't have been able to save anyone, in an eternal sense, because our salvation is predicated upon Jesus having died for our sins and risen from the grave.

We can't know for sure what impacted the heart of the other malefactor, but he must surely have been moved by the compassion and authority Jesus demonstrated during a time of immense suffering, as He pleaded with His Father to forgive the men who were crucifying Him (Luke 23:34). Like his fellow criminal, he knew he would imminently die, but he had sufficient faith to call out to Jesus. He might not have completely understood the implications of what he was saying, but as we've reflected recently, when we come to God in all sincerity, He'll respond to our prayers, even if we don't know what we should be praying! It may even be that Pontius Pilate played a role in this man's salvation, due to the sign he placed over Jesus's head, proclaiming Him to be the King of the Jews. There's no limit to the instruments God can use, even if they're attempting to sign His death warrant!

We might think that we don't have anything in common with the malefactors either side of Jesus, but our predicament is actually very similar. Our death hopefully isn't quite so imminent, but one day it will come, and where we spend eternity will be determined by whether or not we cry out to Jesus. We, too, have the offer of forgiveness, should we choose to repent, right up until the time we take our final breath - but not beyond. Back then, in 32 AD, one malefactor mocked, while the other repented. It's the same for us today: some of our colleagues will mock Jesus and reject Him, but the life-determining question, as it always has been, is whether we will have the courage to call out to Him for salvation. Ultimately, we have no other option, because, just like the malefactors on the cross, we can't save ourselves.

Please take time to consider three important questions:

i. Are you being swayed by other people's opinions in the decision you're making about Jesus or, like the wise malefactor, are you willing to go against the grain?

ii. Do you think Jesus would have allowed Himself to suffer as He did, if His death hadn't been necessary for our salvation?

iii. Have you learned enough about Jesus, during our Gospel reflections so far, to at least begin to consider entrusting Him with your life?

SPIRITUAL REFLECTIONS - I

Overcoming Tradition

> *"There was a man of the Pharisees, named Nicodemus: a ruler of the Jews: the same came to Jesus by night, and said unto him, Rabbi, we know that thou art a teacher come from God: for no man can do these miracles that thou doest, except God be with him. Jesus answered and said unto him, Verily, verily, I say unto thee, Except a man be born again he cannot see the kingdom of God (John 3: 1 - 3)."*

Please don't get me wrong: I have a genuine regard for tradition and, as you may have noticed, the verses I've selected for these reflections have been taken from the King James version of the Bible. However, it's imperative that our traditions don't become meaningless rituals or, even worse, idols which are elevated above God Himself. Taking Bible translations as an example, it's far better for someone to be reading the authentic Word of God in their favourite translation than to leave another version sitting on the shelf, gathering dust! Just like religion, tradition can present a significant barrier to people coming to faith, because in both cases perceived loyalty to a particular form of observance provokes feelings of resistance and guilt, when the invitation comes to look at things from a different perspective.

Some of our reflections have carried exceedingly harsh words for the Pharisees, who had amongst their number an extreme sect of hypocritical Jewish leaders, who plotted to kill Jesus. As with any group, however, they weren't completely homogeneous, and there were some good people amongst them! In fact, we'll meet some former Pharisees in heaven, albeit as a consequence of their decision to accept Jesus as Saviour; not their Pharisaic tradition. Nicodemus clearly saw something in Jesus that led him to the conclusion that He had been sent by God. This was the motivation for Jesus's miracles: while He delighted, and still delights, in bringing healing and restoration to a hurting world, His primary focus was on bringing glory to His Father in heaven (John 17: 1 - 3). At this stage, Nicodemus probably didn't recognise Jesus as being the Messiah, but he had seen enough to be compelled to meet Him and find out more. Faith isn't about making an irrational decision to trust in something and hope it might be true: it should be based on a firm foundation, built upon the evidence we see all around us. That evidence is provided by a number of sources, including creation, God's Word and the ongoing witness of the Holy Spirit. To ignore these things, or to attempt to suppress them, leads to the spiritual dullness and hardness of heart which characterised many of the Pharisees, whereas to consider them for oneself is a sign of intelligence. Unquestioningly accepting Jesus's claims doesn't necessarily represent genuine faith or, at best, it only produces a shallow faith that's easily shaken. Jesus would expect us to consider His claims seriously, as the Bereans did with Paul (Acts 17: 10 - 12). When we do this, we'll come to a deep understanding of the truth which produces strong roots, ensuring that our faith withstands the storms.

The first step in our journey of faith is always coming to Jesus, which is exactly what Nicodemus did. As a Jewish leader, he probably didn't want to come during the day, prompting questions as to why he needed guidance from another Teacher, but it doesn't matter how or when we come, as long as we come! Jesus's response certainly surprised him, but it's the same response He'd give us today. Most people understandably celebrate their physical birthdays, marking a milestone in their journey through life. However, that milestone is a tragic one if the individual concerned doesn't yet know Jesus, because it signifies another step towards an eternity without Him. By far the most significant day in our lives - a day when the heavenly realm celebrates alongside us - is when we are 'born again' into a new relationship with Jesus as our Lord and Saviour. From that point on, we become dual citizens: residents of earth, with a passport to heaven! This is what Jesus meant when He said to Nicodemus, "That whosoever believeth in Him should not perish, but have eternal life (John 3:15)." All human beings are created with an eternal spirit, but the decision we make in relation to Jesus determines where that eternity will be spent. Even though we all have an eternal future, a future without Christ couldn't be called 'life'.

Jesus actually taught far more on hell than He did on heaven (see Luke 16: 19 - 31, for an example): not to frighten people, but to prevent them from going there. When we love someone, we'll warn them of the dangers that a certain course of action might present to them, which is precisely what Jesus was doing. Jesus doesn't condemn us: we condemn ourselves by refusing to follow Him to eternal safety, which is the essence of His words to Nicodemus in John 3:17, "For God sent not his Son into the world to condemn the world; but that the world through him might be saved." This is the backdrop to perhaps the most famous passage of Scripture, which a minister I know and respect perceptively describes as the Gospel in miniature: "For God so loved the world, that he gave his only begotten Son, that whosoever believeth in him should not perish, but have everlasting life (John 3:16)."

Happily, Nicodemus not only got the message, but accepted it. In John 7:50, we see him contending with his fellow Pharisees, reminding them that it was unlawful to judge a Person, let alone condemn Him to death, without first hearing His evidence. Then, in John 19:39, he, along with Joseph of Arimathea, anointed Jesus's body, prior to His burial. This was an act of worship, far more than it was a ritual of mourning: Nicodemus had made the transition from tradition to faith, and my prayer is that you, too, will do the same!

Nicodemus asked plenty of questions, and here are a few of my own:

i. Are there any traditions you observe, which might prevent you from coming to Jesus?

ii. If you're a Christian, do your actions, and not merely your words, point people to Jesus?

iii. Have you been born into a new relationship with Jesus as Lord and Saviour? If you haven't done so yet, why not read the Gospel of John in full, to meet Him for yourself? I'm sure you'll like Him!

Abundant Life!

"The thief cometh not, but for to steal, and to kill, and to destroy: I am come that they might have life, and that they might have it more abundantly (John 10:10)."

The verse we're considering in this reflection concludes with a full stop, but it supplies an exclamation point for our Christian faith! While the third chapter of John's Gospel leaves us in no doubt as to our need to be born again ("Ye *must* be born again" - John 3:7 - emphasis added), and how that re-birth is accomplished (entering into a saving relationship with Jesus), the tenth chapter reveals the glory of what we're born into. Tragically, many people have completely the wrong idea about the Christian faith, and much of the fault for that lies at our own door. Yes, there are media outlets which are hostile to our cause, who seek to divert people from the Truth, but could anything be more off-putting than a curmudgeonly, judgemental, joyless Christian?

I understand that everyone faces valleys in their lives, which can be tortuous and grief-ridden at times, and that Christians aren't exempt from these trials. However, if the persona we generally project to the world is of someone without hope, then why would anyone be interested in what we believe? This is not to say we should be putting on an act, which is the whole point of John chapter 10: the life we have in Christ should be so abundantly productive that His joy spontaneously flows out of us! Such spontaneity is what Jesus referenced in John 7:38, where He described the "rivers of living water" which would emanate from believers. John added his own commentary in the very next verse, aided by the benefit of experience, explaining that this abundant life, or living water, would flow from our relationship with the Holy Spirit. Our fellowship with the Spirit is intended to be so pervasive that we can't but help manifest life to our communities, irrigating spiritually arid environments with the hope of the Gospel. This isn't something we should need to strive to do: it should be as natural as water flowing through a ravine!

The life which Jesus describes in John 10:10 contrasts starkly with the joyless existence produced by religion, where people live in fear of the repercussions that will follow if they fail to appease their 'god'. Those thieves, to which He referred, were the false teachers, whose doctrines literally led to His own death and figuratively enslaved the population at large. There's perhaps no better illustration of this enslavement than the Sabbath, which was turned from a beautiful opportunity for rest and fellowship into a joyless burden, requiring the observance of multiple volumes of arcane rules. The perversity of this interpretation was graphically illustrated by Jesus, Whose Sabbath day healings enraged the religious classes, to whom following the letter of the Law was far more important than the potential for healing and restoration. However, it isn't only Judaism that places such a burden on people: all other religions do, too, and even Christianity very often falls into this trap, especially when little or no consideration is given to the Holy Spirit.

As mentioned in our reflection which looked at the similarities between religion and the rejection of Jesus, idolatry (putting anything above God in our lives) will ultimately enslave us in much the same way. Anyone who views their primary purpose in life as anything other than serving God will ultimately come under the control of whatever it is they're serving, whether it be a person, career or passion. This will inevitably result in us becoming "heavy laden (Matthew 11:28)," whereas, in contrast, Jesus promises His followers that, "My yoke is easy, and my burden is light (Matthew 11:30)." Some of the language surrounding the Christian faith can sound quite negative: especially the concepts of 'giving our lives to Christ' and 'dying to self', but what we're given far outweighs the value of what we give! The beautiful imagery of John chapter 10 is of Jesus as a faithful Shepherd, Who willingly laid down His life for us, His sheep. If we give Him our sin, guilt and shame, He'll give us eternal life in return! By no longer living for ourselves, we cease to be dominated by concerns of what people think of us, or whether we 'come up to scratch', and instead become sons and daughters of the Living God, with all the resources of heaven at our disposal! Let's use these resources - the natural talents God has given us, allied to the gifts we receive from the Holy Spirit - to live abundant lives for Christ and point people to Him!

I'll conclude our reflection with a few questions:

i. Does your church fellowship exhibit abundant life? If not, could it be that, corporately, you're not according the Holy Spirit the honour He deserves?

ii. Is your Christian walk inspired by the Holy Spirit? If this isn't the case, might it be that you haven't fully invited Him into your life (see Luke 11:13)?

iii. If you're not yet a Christian, have you been put off by the concept of 'giving your life to Christ'? If so, might the assurance of receiving *abundant* life in return prompt you to reconsider your decision?

One Way!

"Thomas saith unto him, Lord, we know not whither thou goest; and how can we know the way? Jesus saith unto him, I am the way, the truth and the life: no man cometh unto the Father, but by me (John 14: 5 & 6)."

Controversial words! To many people, the teaching that there is only one way to heaven is offensive, but it was taught by Jesus, Who Himself is "the Truth," and so it's something we can confidently assert to be true. Many of our contemporaries respect Jesus, and accept Christianity as *a* way, but Jesus here confirms that He is *the* Way. Any other interpretation is offensive to God Himself, because He wouldn't have allowed His Son to suffer so intensely, if Calvary provided only one way of many to eternal security. As a race, humanity became separated from God by our sin, but Jesus is the Way back, and it's only our arrogance, pride and perversity that prompts us to seek an alternative. Imagine if you were faced with a debt you couldn't meet and someone with limitless resources offered to pay it for you: surely you wouldn't cast around for someone else who might possibly be able to help, because your solution has already been found! Just as an individual who insulted your son would be unlikely to be welcomed into your home, people who insult God, by rejecting His Son's sacrifice, won't gain entry to heaven. Indeed, their very act of rejection is a statement that they don't want to go!

It's absolutely imperative to note that the exclusive nature of our path to heaven doesn't, by any means, imply exclusion: the invitation is open to everyone! The way of salvation is one of absolute equality, because no-one can qualify for redemption on the basis of their own merits, meaning that we all have to come through Jesus, Who is "the door (John 10:7)." If salvation could be earned, it would be possible for those who didn't make it to blame impoverishment, upbringing, genetics, or a myriad of other factors but, as it is, those things can frequently motivate us to come to faith. If you rationalise your disability as being a reason for not seeking Jesus, then consider Nick Vujicic, who was born without arms or legs, endured horrendous bullying and experienced deep depression, yet surrendered his life to the Lord, married a wonderful wife and now leads a thriving international ministry. It may be that you cite poverty as a reason for not coming to faith, yet Jesus Himself only owned his clothes and, perhaps, a few simple possessions; in contrast, He famously warned that, "It is easier for a camel to go through the eye of a needle, than for a rich man to enter the Kingdom of God (Matthew 19:24)!" Should you believe that your upbringing is a reason for rejecting Christ, then reflect on the life of Nicky Cruz, whose amazing book, 'Run Baby Run', is a testimony of his deliverance from murderous gang life in New York, after an encounter with the remarkable David Wilkerson and the infinitely more remarkable Jesus Christ. Even religion isn't an insurmountable barrier: as we reflected recently, Pharisaic Nicodemus came to the same Jesus Who today is appearing to Muslims in dreams and visions, testifying to them of the One Way to Heaven. Jesus will send His witnesses, whether they be human or angelic, to anyone with ears to hear: the question, as ever, is whether we're prepared to listen. Christianity may be a 'one-way' belief system, but that Way is open to all!

No doubt this message will be controversial but, if we only focus on the controversy, we'll miss out on the richness of the promises contained in John chapter 14. Following Jesus not only leads to salvation, but to the promise of participating in a Body that will do greater works than Him (John 14:12). This may perhaps relate to magnitude, but can certainly be applied to geographical reach, because the reality of the Holy Spirit living in every believer enables the glory of God to be manifest throughout the world; not merely in a specific location, as was the case during Jesus's earthly ministry. We're also promised wonderful answers to prayer (verses 13 & 14), which are predicated on our relationship with Him. It is this relationship that should motivate our desire to keep His commandments, because we demonstrate our love by our faithfulness, rather than by adhering to hollow obligation. All of this can only be possible if the Holy Spirit lives within us (verses 16 - 18). The tremendous peace that He gives us is His seal, proving the authenticity of our fellowship with Him. We know all these promises to be true, because they were made by the One Who is "the way, the truth and the life." Why look for any other way?

I hope you'll find these questions thought-provoking!

i. Have you ever heard or read the testimonies of Nick Vujicic or Nicky Cruz? I'd thoroughly recommend checking them out on-line, if you haven't already done so!

ii. Is your Christian life characterised by peace? If not, is it possible that you might not have completely surrendered your life to the Lord?

iii. Are you currently following a 'way' other than Jesus? If you are, how confident are you that it will lead to your intended destination?

The Eternal Question

> *"Pilate therefore said unto him, Art thou a king then? Jesus answered, Thou sayest that I am a king. To this end was I born, and for this cause came I into the world, that I should bear witness unto the truth. Every one that is of the truth heareth my voice. Pilate saith unto him, What is truth? And when he had said this, he went out again unto the Jews, and saith unto them, I find in him no fault at all (John 18: 37 & 38)."*

Anyone with even a passing knowledge of the Easter story will have heard the name Pontius Pilate, but considerably fewer will know a great deal about him. Therefore, before we consider his own question, an appropriate starting point might be to ask, who was he? Pilate was the proconsul, or governor, appointed by Rome to that outpost of their Empire known as Judaea. His origins were in modern-day Spain and we can glean from historical records that he was a weak ruler, who relied upon his wife to secure him the governorship. It was Pilate's wife who warned him, following a dream, not to crucify Jesus (Matthew 27:19), and there's credible evidence that she herself became a believer, demonstrating that her response to Pilate's eternal question might have differed to his own! Pilate was appointed to Judaea in 26 AD, and remained in post for a decade, meaning that he presided during the entirety of Christ's earthly ministry and, most notably, His crucifixion and resurrection.

Pilate's role was crucial in the Jewish plot to crucify Jesus, because they didn't themselves possess the right to administer capital punishment, which was solely a prerogative of the Roman authorities. Having faced three sham trials in front of the Jews, and after enduring two more before the Romans, Jesus finally came before Pilate. In human terms, Pilate would decide Jesus's fate but, as our Lord pointed out, power ultimately resided with God (John 19:11). The necessity of our Saviour's crucifixion doesn't exonerate Pilate from blame, in the same way that it didn't for Judas, although the same verse shows that Jesus saw the one who betrayed Him as carrying the greater burden upon entering judgement.

Both Scripture and other sources, such as the writings of Jewish historian Josephus, indicate that Pilate was mightily impressed by Jesus, Who he wished to release. There are many reasons for this, including our Saviour's wisdom, authority and refusal to yield to harsh interrogation. Then, of course, there was Pilate's wife's dream! As we read at the end of John 18:38, Pilate didn't consider Jesus to be guilty of the acts of sedition for which He was being tried. (These charges were required because the Jewish accusations of blasphemy would have been irrelevant to Roman minds, who were accustomed to worshipping multiple gods.) However, both life and justice are seldom that straightforward, and Pilate also had other matters on his mind, such as the potential for a Jewish revolt if Jesus was released. Such an uprising, the like of which had occurred previously during his tenure, would almost certainly have signalled his removal from office. We may think it cynical for Pilate to put career and personal popularity ahead of truth and justice, but how many people today do the same? Perhaps more pertinently, how many of us allow our careers or personal ambitions to prevent us from making the right decision in relation to Jesus? It's a fatal fallacy to postpone coming to faith until our circumstances change, because Satan will always find an excuse to prevent us from escaping his grasp!

These conflicting emotions, allied with the hostility of the crowd, obviously caused Pilate some discomfort, and he ultimately decided to literally wash his hands of Jesus (Matthew 27:24), as if to exculpate himself from his actions. The confusion and, perhaps, exasperation he was feeling may have been what prompted his famous question, "What is truth?" This is a particularly relevant question today, for a society that grapples with debates relating to the objectivity versus subjectivity of truth. Increasingly, we're being asked to accept that truth is subjective, but does this assertion stand up to scrutiny? I may be as entitled to my perception of the facts as you are, but what happens if our opinions differ? In some areas of life, this doesn't present a problem: I could have one political perspective, with which you might disagree, and we can both vote for our preferred parties when an election is called. However, in other scenarios, a common understanding of the facts is required, such as if I wanted to build an extension that would reduce the quality of daylight entering your home. It's quite possible that we would both have conflicting interpretations of the planning laws, meaning that an independent arbiter would be required to determine the truth. So, what of matters of faith: can we not all simply 'coexist'? The answer, of which you may disapprove, is both 'yes' and 'no'! Everybody should be free to exercise 'freedom of religion' (hence the 'yes'), but we still have the responsibility to warn people that there is only one way to heaven, as considered in our previous reflection; hence the 'no'.

This brings us to the most important question we all grapple with; namely, what's the truth in relation to Jesus? Our response carries infinitely more significance than a dispute over the vagaries of planning legislation, because our eternal future depends on our answer. Pilate may have attempted to do so, but we definitely can't sit on the fence: we have to make a decision one way or another, and any failure on our part to come to a conclusion will itself constitute a decision. Obviously, a court of law would require evidence, but what more evidence could we need? Jesus's miracles, death and resurrection all point to the fact that He is the Son of God, and I suspect Pilate may have begun to think so, too. What do you believe?

The following questions will hopefully be helpful in crystallising your own thoughts:

i. Do you believe truth to be objective or subjective, and what's the reason for your conclusion?

ii. Are you facing a dilemma, whereby accepting Jesus as your Saviour could have implications for your friendships or career?

iii. Do you think Pilate is likely to have regretted his decision in relation to Jesus?

Mission Accomplished!

"After this, Jesus knowing that all things were now accomplished, that the scripture might be fulfilled, saith, I thirst. Now there was set a vessel full of vinegar: and they filled a sponge with vinegar, and put it on hyssop, and put it to his mouth. When Jesus therefore had received the vinegar, he said, It is finished: and he bowed his head, and gave up the ghost (John 19: 28 - 30)."

In Biblical numerics, the number seven signifies completion, so it probably isn't coincidental that Jesus made seven statements from the cross at Calvary, on which He laid down His life for you and for me. Despite their brevity, which was necessitated by the excruciating pain that seared through His body, these statements provide a compelling insight into the heart and nature of our Saviour. If we accept that moments of crisis in our lives reveal what we're made of, then the words of Jesus from the cross serve as a summary of His love, humanity, authority and deity. Would you like to take a look at them with me?

Statement 1: **"Father, forgive them; for they know not what they do** (Luke 23:34)." Jesus came to bring humanity forgiveness, but we collectively rejected Him, condemning Him to humiliation, scourging and the most horrendous of deaths, as, in fulfilment of prophecy, He was numbered with the transgressors (Isaiah 53:12). Rather than turning His horrifically beaten back on us, as He would have been entitled to do, He extended His nail-pierced hands and implored God the Father to forgive even the people who perpetrated His crucifixion, not knowing that they were conspiring against the Saviour of the world. We may not personally have crucified Jesus, but His death was necessary to atone for our sins (we're all sinners; who amongst us is perfect?). His eternal gift of forgiveness is still ours today, but only if we're prepared to accept it, by acknowledging Him as our Lord and Saviour.

Statement 2: "**Verily I say unto thee, Today shalt thou be with me in paradise** (Luke 23:43)." This is the wonderful promise made to the malefactor who was crucified alongside Jesus and, unlike his fellow wrongdoer, humbled himself to acknowledge the majesty of the Son of God. This man began the day without hope, resigned to a certain death, and he ended it in eternal glory, all because of the decision he made in relation to Jesus. We don't know when our final day on earth will be, but we have the same choice as the criminals who were crucified alongside Jesus. If we cry out to Him, He'll be faithful to commend us to His Father, meaning that our last day on earth will be our first day in heaven. Alternatively, we can rail against Him or passively ignore His sacrifice, meaning that the sin which separated us from God during this life will continue to do so eternally.

Statement 3: "**Woman, behold thy son!...Behold thy mother** (John 19: 26 & 27)!" These instructions, respectively given to His mother, Mary, and John the apostle, reveal the tender heart of a Son towards His mother, who had stood by Him all His life. Simeon had prophetically prepared Mary for the fact that, "This child is set for the fall and rising again of many in Israel; and for a sign which shall be spoken against; yea, a sword shall pierce thy own soul also (Luke 2:34)." Now, at this moment of desolation and heartache, Mary was consoled by her Son, Who entrusted her into the care of the apostle who He knew would live the longest.

Statement 4: "**Eli, Eli, lama sabachthani**?," translating as, "**My God, my God, why hast thou forsaken me** (Matthew 27:46)?" As we've previously reflected, God cannot look upon sin, meaning that the constant communion between Jesus and His Father was broken for the duration of His time on the cross. This separation hurt Him more than the beatings and the nails, but He endured all of these experiences willingly on our behalf, in order that we could enjoy the same communion with God. Our relationship with our Creator, which had been destroyed in Eden, was now being restored, but at what cost!

Statement 5: "**I thirst** (John 19:28)." This acknowledgement demonstrates the humanity of Jesus, Who felt every lash of the whip across His back and convulsed in pain as nails were driven through His wrists and feet. People may try to minimise the extent of Jesus's suffering, but we must never do so. Next time you're tempted to sin, reflect upon the price Jesus paid to purchase your forgiveness.

Statement 6: "**Tetelestai**," which translates as "**It is finished** (John 19:30)." This is a word that Jesus would have used many times during His days as a carpenter, because it was written across receipts, signifying that a bill was paid in full. In this instance, the bill which was being paid was one that we could never afford, as Jesus completed the greatest transaction in history; taking our sin upon Himself and, in return, providing us with the offer of eternal life. In common with any transaction, it's one that we have to willingly enter into: we cannot be saved by osmosis, simply because Jesus died for us: His sacrifice on our behalf only becomes valid when we decide to accept it, just as a cheque remains a mere piece of paper, until it has been cashed.

Jesus was effectively saying that His mission had been accomplished: He'd lived a perfect life until the end, qualifying Him to serve as the ultimate Sacrifice for our sins. An insight into what He was thinking, as He made this statement, is provided by the opening four verses of John 17, where, communing with His Father, Jesus reflected upon having finished the work He had been given to do; that of glorifying God.

Statement 7: "**Father, into thy hands I commend my spirit** (Luke 23:46)." Jesus's final act prior to His death demonstrates that He had, and still has, complete authority over every power, dominion, circumstance and entity, including Satan. Nobody was able to take His life from Him, meaning that His death could only be accomplished by Him dismissing His own Spirit. By extension, He also had the authority to take His Spirit back again, which is the essence of the resurrection. As Jesus prophesied Himself, in John 10, verses 17 & 18, "I lay down my life, that I might take it again. No man taketh it from me, but I lay it down of myself. I have power to lay it down, and I have power to take it again."

As powerful as Jesus's sacrifice is, it was only given eternal effect by His resurrection, which defeated death and enabled everyone who believes in Him to enter into eternal life. This is a point we always need to remember when talking to people about Jesus: yes, He died for them, but He didn't remain dead, and He now lives to intercede for them, on the right hand of the Father (Romans 8:34). What an amazing Saviour we have!

How about a few questions, to conclude our reflections on the Gospels?

i. Do you believe that a mere human being, who wasn't also God, would have been able to display the love, compassion and power that Jesus did from the cross?

ii. Having met Jesus, during our fourteen reflections taken from the Gospels, what is your honest opinion of Him?

iii. If Jesus's love for you, as revealed by His sacrifice at Calvary, isn't enough to prompt you to commit your life to Him, what do you think it would take, before you were willing to make such a decision?

SPIRITUAL REFLECTIONS - I

The Comforter!

"And he said unto them, It is not for you to know the times or the seasons, which the Father hath put in his own power. But ye shall receive power, after that the Holy Ghost (Spirit) is come upon you: and ye shall be witnesses unto me both in Jerusalem, and in all Judaea, and in Samaria, and unto the uttermost part of the earth (Acts 1: 7 & 8)."

We could be forgiven for thinking that, despite being a part of the team, Jesus's disciples struggled to understand the purpose of His earthly ministry! That said, before we give them too hard a time, let's remember that they'd grown up in a conservative Jewish culture which was turned on its head by the Messiah they loved and followed, but Who constantly amazed them with His teaching and persona. Some of His words seemed incredibly harsh, and yet He always had time for people, and performed miracles which left His followers in no doubt that He was the Son of God. At the point where they were anticipating the establishment of His Kingdom, He was betrayed, arrested and crucified, leaving their hopes and dreams in disarray. Then there was the talk of His resurrection, which initially seemed surreal, until He verified it by meeting with them and showing them the nail prints in His hands (John 20:20). In the spiritual realm, Jesus's death and resurrection had defeated Satan and redeemed lost humanity, but such things aren't discerned with natural sight. In common with people we know, who aren't yet Christians, the disciples didn't, at this stage, have the Holy Spirit living within them. When we next get frustrated by the fact that not all our friends and family members can see the truth about Jesus, we'd do well to remember that, before they received the Holy Spirit, the disciples who walked with Him for three and a half years didn't fully understand these things, either! The limitations of their understanding are evident from their perception that everything was back to normal, illustrated by their question of Acts 1:6, as to whether Jesus was about to overthrow Roman rule and restore the kingdom to Israel.

Jesus responded with the verses we're considering in this reflection, which are His final recorded words prior to His ascension into heaven. In essence, He was confirming that His Kingdom would be established, albeit not in the way His disciples expected, prior to commissioning them for the work they were to do in His absence. The astute ones amongst them might have subsequently reflected on the parable of the talents: their Master was gone, but now there was work to be done! One obvious question the disciples might have had is why Jesus didn't simply establish His earthly dominion, there and then: amazingly, this is a question to which *we* are the answer! During the Old Testament, or Old Covenant, period, God worked through the nation of Israel to reveal His love, power and glory to the world. However, His love is for *all* people, and His plan was for both Jew and Gentile to have the opportunity of salvation. This doesn't mean that God has forgotten about Israel - far from it - but we have the privilege of living in a period called the 'church age', between Jesus's resurrection and His return to earth. The purpose of this age, as Jesus described, is for everyone who believes in Him to share the Good News of the Gospel with anyone who doesn't yet know Him as their Saviour. If you don't yet know Jesus, the church age provides you with the chance to get to know Him; if you're already a believer, this is your time to spread the word! For every one of us, our means of being witnesses for Jesus will look slightly different, but it's a duty we cannot shirk. It may be that you're called to speak out for Jesus in the classroom, participate in a city mission, lead a church, serve overseas, or extol His Name in some other way. However, if the context of our service is different for each of us, the power source is always the same: His Holy Spirit.

Understandably, the disciples wanted to have Jesus with them forever: He fed them, calmed storms, healed their relatives and taught them to perform miracles, so they could be forgiven for being apprehensive about the prospect of life without Him. What they couldn't fully appreciate was that, while Jesus was on earth, He was constrained, albeit voluntarily, by the physical limitations attendant with life in a Human body. In John 16:7, He prepared them for the fact that, "It is expedient for you that I go away: for if I go not away, the Comforter will not come unto you; but if I depart, I will send Him unto you." The "Comforter" Jesus referenced is His Holy Spirit, Who takes up residence in every believer, as soon as we place our faith in Him. The primary role of the Holy Spirit is to lead people to a saving faith in Jesus. If you're a Christian, you may recall a time when you began to feel dissatisfied with your life and started to crave a relationship with God. This 'feeling' was the Holy Spirit's prompting to consider matters of eternal significance, while you had the opportunity to do so. Now that you are a believer, the same Holy Spirit lives within you, empowering you when you pray (Romans 8:26) and testify about Jesus (John 15:26). He is also our Guide (John 16:13), meaning that those subtle promptings we receive to travel a different route home from work, thereby avoiding an accident, are loving nudges from the Holy Spirit. Although some people try to mystify the Spirit, He is a Person, Who can be grieved (Ephesians 4:30), and we must be careful not to do this.

One of the Holy Spirit's roles is to convict us of sin (John 16:8). In a legal context, this doesn't sound too auspicious: when we're convicted, we're found guilty! However, the Spirit convicts us in order that we can confess our sins in prayer, bringing them under the Blood of Christ, in order that they no longer have any power over us. This act of confession, for which Jesus Himself is our Mediator, rather than a minister or priest, restores our relationship with Him. Our failure to confess our sins doesn't mean that we're no longer Christians, but it does impair our relationship with God, just as a human friendship is damaged when we offend somebody without saying sorry. Such a state of affairs results in the absence of peace, which is the Spirit's seal upon us (Galatians 5:22). If you're not yet a Christian, you may currently be feeling a sense of unease about your eternal destiny, wondering what the future has in store. This sensation is evidence that the Holy Spirit is witnessing to you about the reality of Jesus's love for you and the need you have to enter into a saving relationship with Him. You can respond in one of two ways: either by praying to accept Jesus into your heart, or by ignoring the 'feeling' (Spirit) and hoping 'it' (He) goes away. If you ignore Him for long enough, He will eventually leave you to your own devices, but this is a dangerous situation to be in, because you can never be sure when, or even if, you will have another chance. In general, these promptings of the Spirit become less frequent as we get older, due to the proclivity for us to become inured to His exhortation.

In keeping with all of Jesus's promises, His pledge to the disciples, regarding the Holy Spirit, was gloriously fulfilled! In Acts chapter 2, we read of the Day of Pentecost, when He descended upon them like a mighty rushing wind, and empowered them to perform miracles which left bystanders glorifying God. It is always the Spirit's role to point people to Jesus, so if we observe individuals exalting themselves we know they're not operating under the anointing of the Holy Spirit. Some of the excesses mistakenly associated with the Spirit have led people to be wary of Him, but He is your Friend, Comforter and Counsellor, so should be welcomed with open arms – and hearts! For evidence of what the Holy Spirit can achieve in and through us, just look at the apostles. Prior to Pentecost, they were scared, confused and bewildered, whereas subsequently they did as Jesus promised, and took the Gospel throughout the known world, in the face of extraordinary persecution!

I know this has been a long reflection, but would you still consider a few questions?

SPIRITUAL REFLECTIONS - I

i. Do you place the same value on all members of the Trinity, or do you perceive them as forming a hierarchy?

ii. Have you got a sense of peace? If you're not yet a Christian, then you shouldn't have! If you are a Christian, but don't have peace, ask the Holy Spirit to show you if there's anything you need to confess.

iii. Do you always invite the Holy Spirit into every new day and situation? One way I try to do this is to pray 'Trinitarian prayers', which involve the Father, Son and Holy Spirit: we serve one God in three Persons, and it would be insulting to leave one of them out!

Responding To The Spirit

"Therefore let all the house of Israel know assuredly, that God hath made that same Jesus, whom ye have crucified, both Lord and Christ. Now when they heard this, they were pricked in their heart, and said unto Peter and the rest of the apostles, Men and brethren, what shall we do? Then Peter said unto them, Repent, and be baptised every one of you in the name of Jesus Christ for the remission of sins, and ye shall receive the gift of the Holy Ghost (Spirit) (Acts 2: 36 - 38)."

The first quarter of the Book of Acts contains two remarkable sermons which produced radically different outcomes, proving that it's the condition of the hearer's heart that determines his or her response to the Gospel message, far more than the quality of the preaching. Peter was a completely different character to the fearful denier of Jesus that he'd been seven weeks previously, by the time he preached to a crowd of several thousand Jews and international visitors on the Day of Pentecost. In the meantime, he had been graciously restored by Jesus and then dramatically filled with the Holy Spirit, along with the other disciples, as his Saviour promised would happen. The Jewish feast of Pentecost, which occurred fifty days after Passover, had just been given new meaning by the dramatic arrival of the Holy Spirit, but it was also a traditional Jewish holiday, meaning there were thousands of visitors to Jerusalem. The Holy Spirit never misses an opportunity to magnify Jesus, and He inspired Peter to powerfully articulate the way in which the Man Who they'd crucified seven weeks previously was in fact the Jewish Messiah.

In a beautifully crafted exposition, Peter showed how Old Testament prophecies had their fulfilment in Christ, and demonstrated the superiority of Jesus to their revered King David, by the fact that Jesus's tomb was empty, whereas David's remained occupied. Peter cited Jesus's miracles as evidence of His Messiahship, but I can imagine there must have been gasps when he proceeded to directly tell them that they had crucified the Son of God! It's not surprising to read that Peter's audience were "pricked in their heart," and passive observers must have anticipated a riot. However, this pricking of the heart, which was the conviction of the Holy Spirit, instead prompted them to ask what they could, or should, do. While it was too late for his hearers to reverse the consequences of their original rejection of Christ, he gave them the good news that it wasn't too late for them to repent (turn back to God), be baptised and receive the gift of the Holy Spirit. This is tremendously encouraging for anyone who believes they've gone too far to be acceptable to God: we have Peter, who denied Jesus, preaching to a mob which precipitated His crucifixion, with the glorious outcome that three thousand men received salvation (verse 41)!

The Holy Spirit didn't only give the apostles power in preaching: He enabled them to perform miracles, too, confirming what Jesus had said about the works His followers would perform after He was gone. It wasn't just the original disciples who received the Holy Spirit: many new believers also did, as revealed in Acts 2:38, and in Acts chapter 6 we read of a fearless man called Stephen, who, "full of faith and power did great wonders and miracles among the people (Acts 6:8)." In addition to peace and power, another hallmark of the Holy Spirit is wisdom, which Stephen possessed in abundance (Acts 6:10), enabling him to outmanoeuvre the religious leaders, in the manner that Jesus always did. When Stephen's opponents couldn't get the better of him, they bribed people to bring false accusations of blasphemy, as had happened to the One Whose Spirit now lived within him. When the time came for his trial, Stephen mounted his own defence, in the form of a masterful sermon, expounding Israel's history from the time of Abraham, up until the point where they crucified their Messiah. His conclusion, that they had "slain them which showed before of the coming of the Just One; of whom ye have now been the betrayers and murderers (Acts 7:52)," wasn't too dissimilar to Peter's assertion of Acts 2:36. The initial conviction was also similar, in that Stephen's audience were "cut to the heart," but their reaction was completely different to that of Peter's hearers, as they stoned him to death.

Rejection of Jesus can prompt people to behave in a barbaric way, especially when this rejection comes in the face of a powerful conviction. Secular history records the Roman Emperor Nero as having been a relatively level-headed ruler until he rejected Paul's witness of the risen Christ, subsequent to which he became a murderous tyrant. Paul himself was present at Stephen's trial and embarked upon a campaign to eliminate Christianity, having been convicted by the witness of a faithful martyr who, emulating his Saviour, pleaded for God not to lay his killers' sin to their charge (Acts 7:60). Fortunately for the world, God gave Paul a second chance, but it took a remarkable encounter to reach him, indicating that each act of rejection takes us progressively further from God, necessitating an even greater revelation of the truth.

I'll conclude with three questions and a prayer:

i. When you witness to people about Jesus, do you begin where they are, as Peter did, relating Jesus to his audience's Jewish tradition?

ii. Does the example of a courageous martyr like Stephen inspire you to resolve to withstand persecution, should it come your way?

iii. Which group would you prefer to be in, when it comes to eternity: those who invited Jesus into their hearts, after hearing Peter's message, or the mob that murdered Stephen?

> *Heavenly Father, thank You for the courageous people You send into the mission field to proclaim the Good News of Jesus in hostile environments. Thank You, too, for those who serve closer to home, witnessing in schools, universities and local communities. Lord Jesus, I'm not sure I'll ever be able to comprehend the price*

You paid for my sin, and I ask that You'll endue me with the strength to honour You, to the best of my ability. Holy Spirit, thank You for convicting me of my rebellion and enabling me to see that I needed a Saviour. Please do the same for my friends and family members who don't yet know Jesus, opening their eyes to the truth and softening their hearts, as You did mine. In Jesus' Name. Amen.

Religion Or Revival?

"And Saul, yet breathing out threatenings and slaughter against the disciples of the Lord, went into the high priest, and desired of him letters to Damascus to the synagogues, that if he found any of this way, whether they were men or women, he might bring them bound unto Jerusalem. And as he journeyed, he came near Damascus: and suddenly there shone around him a light from heaven: and he fell to the earth, and heard a voice saying unto him, Saul, Saul, why persecutest thou me? And he said, Who art thou, Lord? And the Lord said, I am Jesus whom thou persecutest: it is hard for thee to kick against the goads. And he trembling and astonished said, Lord, what wilt thou have me to do? And the Lord said unto him, Arise, and go into the city, and it shall be told thee what thou must do (Acts 9: 1 - 6)."

What a remarkable passage of Scripture! In these six verses we see the beginning of the transformation of an intolerant religious zealot into the vessel God would use to take the Gospel, whose followers he'd been persecuting, into the outer reaches of the known world! Saul had been a student of the legendary rabbi Gamaliel and his Jewish heritage meant everything to him, as a consequence of which he was greatly distressed to see people abandoning the faith to follow Jesus. Although Jesus was the Jewish Messiah, the Jews' rejection of Him resulted in His followers diverging from Judaism and becoming adherents of 'The Way', prior to the term 'Christian' being coined in Antioch. Saul therefore determined to do everything in his power to extinguish this new sect, as he saw it, but he soon came to the realisation that there's only ever one

Winner, when we choose to fight against the Living God! As we've reflected previously, God could have simply wiped Saul out, had He wished to do so but, in His majestic grace, He had a far greater plan, which we see worked out in the remainder of the Book of Acts, not to mention Paul's many epistles.

Although much of the focus when we consider this passage is understandably on Paul, it provides an invaluable insight into how God both sees and feels persecution. When Christians are attacked, the persecutors are attacking Christ Himself, because we are all part of the one Body, in a way that has far greater significance than we perhaps realise. A goad is a long rod with a sharp metal point, which farmers used to prod animals, so what Jesus seems to be saying is that Paul's rebellion was as futile as repeatedly kicking such an implement and expecting to blunt it, when the reality was that he would only destroy himself. This revelation came directly from heaven, hence the dazzling light, demonstrating the depth of God's desire to reach him, and the extraordinary lengths that are required to penetrate a deeply religious heart. It is hard to imagine Paul having responded in any other manner than he did, in surrendering as Peter's hearers had done on the Day of Pentecost, and asking what he needed to do. Jesus's response demonstrates our need to be consistently faithful: God doesn't simply supply a roadmap for our lives and leave us to our own devices! His Spirit continually guides us, but generally only one step at a time. Once we've been faithful in the first step, the next one will be revealed to us, but not until then. If God immediately showed us our destination, we'd go rushing off in our own strength, leaving Him out of our lives, and missing out on everything He wanted us to do along the way! The starting point of our journey is always to accept Jesus into our heart; once we've done this, a wonderful adventure awaits us, as He refines us from within and uses us to make a difference to our world!

The experience of Saul of Tarsus, later Paul the apostle, brings us to consideration of the doctrine of election. The first thing to say here, most categorically, is that God does not pre-determine that anyone would go to hell. It's not His will that any be lost (2 Peter 3:9), but that whosoever comes to Him receives everlasting life

(John 3:16). He therefore certainly doesn't elect anyone to judgement, which would be an action completely inconsistent with His nature of love and justice. Hell is a domain that was created for Satan and his demons, and the only way we can end up there is to consistently reject the witness of the Holy Spirit, calling us to Jesus. Having said this, God is sovereign, and it would be unrealistic to think of Him enjoying lesser privileges in heaven than we enjoy here on earth. Therefore, just as we have the right to choose our own friends, there appear to be occasions when, in another clumsy anthropomorphism, God 'goes out of His way' to impact an individual's heart and bring them to Him. This could be for any number of reasons, but it frequently seems that He has a special role for such people, and this was certainly the case for the murderous Saul of Tarsus, who was transformed into an arch-evangelist and writer of inspirational epistles. The Holy Spirit has been described as the "Hound of Heaven," Who pursues us until the veil of deception is lifted from our eyes. However, the final decision is always ours: not only do we have the choice between acceptance and rejection, but we don't need to wait until things are sufficiently desperate for us to require a dramatic rescue!

It can be tempting to consider people God mightily uses as somehow being super-human, but they had to travel the same route we did: responding to the conviction of the Holy Spirit, confessing their sin and allowing their lives to be transformed by that very Spirit. The Spirit Who resides within them is the same as He Who lives in us, so perhaps the only difference is the desperation with which we seek Him! Paul's life, in terms of his miracles and missionary journeys, exemplifies what we've been saved for, which is not merely to attend church once a week! We should be so grateful for our salvation that it inspires us to play our part in the fulfilment of the Great Commission (Matthew 28: 18 - 20), allowing the Holy Spirit to work through us, in whichever way He desires. Many Christians live joyless lives, primarily because they focus too much on themselves and not enough on the One Who saved them. When our eyes are upon Jesus, we won't be able to help but serve Him with a willing and joyful heart; not to obtain salvation, which is a gift, but because we have the privilege of doing so.

Let's consider a few questions:

i. Do you know anyone who is extremely hostile towards Jesus and Christianity? If so, why not pray for them: they may be closer to salvation than you realise!

ii. Are you faithful in remembering, before the Lord, those who are bound for their faith, as though you were bound with them (Hebrews 13:3)?

iii. Is it possible that you might be kicking against the goads today...and are you ready to be transformed?

Almost Persuaded?

"Then Agrippa said unto Paul, Almost thou persuadest me to be a Christian (Acts 26:28)."

Isn't this one of the most tragic statements in Scripture? Imagine being on the verge of the exciting new adventure represented by life with Christ, then turning back and facing into a lost eternity. For those of you who are currently Christians, have you ever wondered how things might have turned out, if you didn't have Jesus as your Friend and the Holy Spirit as your Comforter? Conversely, if you're not yet a Christian, is there a possibility that Jesus might have spared you from considerable heartache, had you given Him the keys to your life? It could be that, like Agrippa, you were once 'almost persuaded', perhaps after hearing a compelling sermon or listening to a moving testimony, before something prompted you to hang back. That 'something' was a constraint from our spiritual adversary, Satan, who doesn't want us to inherit all the promises God has for us. Whether we like it or not, we're all at the centre of a spiritual battle and, like Judas, we ultimately have to decide whether we're going to come under the authority of Jesus or Satan: there is no middle ground.

There may be some reading this who consider serving Satan not to be all that bad: after all, life is fun and hell is where my friends are! I'm hoping that you'll have read enough in this book to have been convinced of Jesus's truthfulness. Remember, this is the Man Who accurately predicted His own death and resurrection, which no-one else has ever done, so He's surely worth listening to! Rather than taking my word for it, I was therefore wondering if you'd be willing to hear what Jesus has to say, in relation to topics we don't like to dwell on, but certainly need to address.

With regard to the notion that we can simply plot a middle course, without making a decision one way or the other, Jesus had the following words of warning for the Pharisees, which are recorded in Matthew 12, verses 30 & 31:

"He that is not with me is against me; and he that gathereth not with me scattereth abroad. Wherefore I say unto you, All manner of sin and blasphemy shall be forgiven unto men: but the blasphemy against the Holy Ghost (Spirit) shall not be forgiven unto men."

Jesus's statement carries as much validity for us today as it did for His audience two millennia ago: we are either for Jesus or against Him, and to be against Him necessarily means siding with Satan. If we manage to live our entire lives without accepting Jesus's offer of salvation, we won't be able to enter into heaven, meaning that the only other place for us to go will be hell. People don't go to hell because of the wrong things they've done, per se, but because of their rejection of Jesus. As mentioned previously, the role of the Holy Spirit is to convict us of our sin and point us to Jesus. If we refuse to respond, we're effectively calling Him a liar, which is the unpardonable sin of blaspheming the Holy Spirit, referred to by Jesus in Matthew 12:31.

But maybe Satan isn't that bad...or perhaps he doesn't even exist? Let's see what Jesus had to say!

In John 8:44, Jesus said of Satan that, "He was a murderer from the beginning, and abode not in the truth, because there is no truth in him. When he speaketh a lie, he speaketh of his own, for he is a liar, and the father of it."

Jesus here is speaking both physically and spiritually. He is clearly teaching the existence of a literal Devil, who is described elsewhere in Scripture as a destroyer (John 10:10 and 1 Peter 5:8). This destruction can be physical, as demonstrated by the curse that sin unleashed upon the earth, which includes the death of our natural bodies. However, Satan's preoccupation is with people's spiritual destruction, which can ultimately only become a reality when physical death occurs in an individual who has not accepted Jesus as Saviour. Perhaps the greatest lie Satan has been able to perpetuate is that he doesn't exist, because we're never more vulnerable than when we're oblivious to the threat we're facing. His primary objective is to prevent you from believing in Jesus as your personal Saviour, and he'll always use deception to do this, because he completely opposes Jesus's character. Jesus is "the way, the truth and the life (John 14:6)," whereas Satan is a highway to destruction and father of lies, who is intent on causing death. Satan has a hook for everyone: if you have financial insecurities, he'll tell you God will impoverish you; if your fear is being alone, he'll try to persuade you that becoming a Christian will prompt your friends to abandon you; if you like to be in control, he'll sow thoughts of God as a Dictator, Who will dominate your life. However, it's Satan who seeks to dominate, because he loves to see us bound, whereas Jesus came to set us free (Galatians 5:1). In the end, it's a question of who you're willing to believe: the God of the Bible or 'the god of this world'.

Perhaps the thought of following Satan doesn't sound so enticing, but could hell possibly still have its attractions? Shall we see what Jesus has to say?

In Matthew 25:30, Jesus described hell as a place of "outer darkness," characterised by "weeping and gnashing of teeth." This doesn't sound very enticing, does it? The absolute darkness to be encountered there results from the absence of God, Who is the essence of light. This means that we won't be able to see anything or anyone, while the weeping and gnashing of teeth are likely to emanate from the profoundly uncomfortable physical environment, compounded by the intense, unyielding regret of not having accepted Jesus's offer of salvation. Jesus's teachings on hell were intended to emphasise its physical reality and alert people to the binary decision they face during their lifetime on earth. As we previously discussed, accepting Jesus as a Good Teacher (and He is far more than that) implies that He must be both truthful and accurate, meaning we need to accept His teaching in relation to the reality of the eternal judgement from which He came to set us free. The choice is always ours, but I'd implore you not to be 'almost persuaded'!

We'll end our reflections from Acts with three questions:

i. If the potential for eternal judgement wasn't a reality, why would it have been necessary for Jesus to die for our sins?

ii. Whose version of spiritual reality are you more inclined to believe: Jesus's or Satan's?

iii. Do you know anyone who is *almost* persuaded to be a Christian? If so, pray for the Holy Spirit to provide the revelation they need to be able to take that vital, final step!

One Step To Heaven!

"But now the righteousness of God without the law is manifested, being witnessed by the law and the prophets; even the righteousness of God which is by faith of Jesus Christ unto all and upon all them that believe: for there is no difference: for all have sinned, and come short of the glory of God; being justified freely by his grace through the redemption that is in Christ Jesus: Whom God hath set forth to be a propitiation through faith in his blood, to declare his righteousness for the remission of sins that are past, through the forbearance of God; to declare, I say, at this time his righteousness: that he might be just, and the justifier of him which believeth in Jesus (Romans 3: 21 - 26)."

I'm sure you'll be familiar with Neil Armstrong's statement, when he became the first human being to walk on the moon, that his successful mission represented, "One small step for (a) man; one giant leap for mankind." Approximately one thousand nine hundred years previously, the apostle Paul wrote a letter to a group of Christian believers in Rome, in which he emphasised the one step that was required for us to enter into a destiny far more glorious even than exploration of the moon: eternal salvation! Having taken his readers on a depressing tour of the failed practices and philosophies that lead only to disappointment and despair, Paul provides this sudden, welcome injection of hope. Religion (keeping the Law) won't save us, neither will education (the pursuit of knowledge), or being good (all have sinned), but faith in Christ will! In contrast to our attempts to seek fulfilment in academics, sporting achievements or our careers, our new life as a follower of Jesus is only one step away.

Praying to accept Jesus as our Saviour only takes an instant, as demonstrated by the malefactor on the cross, but our spiritual foe will always try to persuade us that we don't have time, or that consideration of becoming a Christian should be deferred until later in life. If we're tempted to wait until our careers have been made, or our families are grown up, we'll then be inclined to wait until we've retired...and who knows whether we'll make it that far! Yes, Jesus will accept everyone who comes to Him, at any stage of life, but every day we delay will be a day we regret, as we lose out on God's blessings for us in this life and forgo His rewards in the next. Anyone who's tempted to wait for a 'deathbed conversion' needs to be aware of at least three things: i) they may not get the opportunity; ii) they'll miss out on the glorious privilege of serving Jesus during their time on earth; iii) if we don't consider Jesus to be worth living for, there's a danger that any profession we make as we die may not be genuine. This is not to say that eleventh hour conversions can't happen - they gloriously do - but there's no guarantee that it will happen to you!

Paul's letter to the Romans is frequently regarded as being the 'fifth Gospel', and the verses quoted above, which comprise a single sentence, form a succinct expression of the Gospel message, from someone who was living evidence of the power Jesus has to redeem even the most desperate of lives. The essence of the human condition is summarised, in that all have sinned, but that salvation is available to everyone who believes in Jesus Christ. This belief isn't a mere formal acknowledgement that Jesus lived, or even that He died and rose again, but a conscious decision to accept His sacrifice as payment for our sins. Paul emphasises the Blood of Christ, which has tremendous power, and it's little wonder that ministers who shy away from references to Jesus's sacrifice lead churches which are dying before our eyes.

Once we take this step of accepting Jesus into our hearts, we receive a multiplicity of wonderful blessings, not least of which are 'righteousness' and 'justification'. Almost incredibly, our Heavenly Father regards anyone who trusts in His Son for salvation in the same way as He regards His Son Himself, which is what it means to be righteous before God. The only standard of righteousness

SPIRITUAL REFLECTIONS - I

God knows is absolute perfection, which isn't something we could come anywhere near to achieving. However, Jesus both could, and did, and He died on the cross in order that we would be able to experience the same relationship with God that He does. How amazing is that! This links in with justification, which is a legal declaration of righteousness which becomes ours, at the moment we accept Jesus as Lord and Saviour. This is only possible because the blood Jesus shed on our behalf is full and complete propitiation, or atonement, for our sins. If heaven is considered as a courtroom, then we might imagine Satan making the case for the prosecution, at which point Jesus may be envisioned as stretching forth His nail-pierced hands to His Father, and declaring words to the effect that, "[   ] is mine, having placed her/his trust in Me." All charges will then be dropped, and we'll be set free to enjoy our eternal reward.

Can you put your name in place of the square brackets? Have you accepted Jesus's payment for your sins? When we briefly discussed the doctrine of election, I confidently asserted that no-one had been pre-destined for hell. There are several reasons I could be so confident, including the just nature of God and the teaching of Jesus, but Paul provides another reason later in Romans, "For whosoever shall call upon the name of the Lord shall be saved (Romans 10:13)." Are you a *whosoever*? If anyone could have been forgiven for thinking that he was disqualified from coming before Jesus it was the feared persecutor of Christians known as Saul of Tarsus. If God will accept him, He'll certainly accept you, but you have to come through His Son first!

How about a few questions?

i. Have you ever tried to attain God's standard of righteousness on the basis of your own efforts? If so, how did you do?

ii. Do you still have doubts about the power of the Holy Spirit to transform a life? A couple of reflections ago, we were considering Saul of Tarsus, who was breathing threats against the church and kicking against the goads. Can you really imagine he'd have written words such as those we've just been contemplating, if the Spirit hadn't been inspiring him?

iii. Have you been putting off your decision to come to Jesus? If so, why not pray to accept Him into your heart today?

> *Heavenly Father, I want to apologise for having tried to do things my own way, and for the pain I've caused as a consequence, both to Yourself and to others. Lord Jesus, I'm sorry for having delayed coming to You for this long: thank You so much for Your patience with me, and for Your amazing sacrifice on the cross at Calvary. I come before You today to ask that You'll forgive me for my sins and send Your Holy Spirit to inspire my new life of faith. Holy Spirit, I invite You into my heart, home, workplace and community: please empower me and use me to transform this world for Jesus, in Whose Enduring Name I pray. Amen.*

No Condemnation!

"There is therefore now no condemnation to them which are in Christ Jesus, who walk not after the flesh, but after the Spirit (Romans 8:1)."

Isn't it always great to hear good news? There's so much negativity around at the moment that it's refreshing to hear something positive but, even then, we can begin to doubt it! Whether because of ingrained cynicism or the number of times we've been let down in the past, we can take some convincing of the veracity of the promises that are made to us. However, Paul here makes a pledge that comes with a lifetime guarantee: once you become a Christian, you are no longer under condemnation, because Jesus has set you free! Having lost the battle for your soul, Satan will inevitably attempt to remind you of mistakes you made before you were a believer, but these were all covered by the blood of Jesus at the very moment you put your faith in Him. It's not necessary to continually repent of these things, because they're completely forgiven, and God can't even remember them (Isaiah 43:25 & Hebrews 8:12)!

Our mistakes clearly aren't limited to the period of our lives before we came to know Christ, but God operates outside of time as we know it. This means that the sins we commit after coming to faith are forgiven in advance, when we enter into a saving relationship with Jesus, on the basis of His sacrifice for us at Calvary. This obviously doesn't imply that we have a licence to sin with impunity: such an attitude on the part of a professed believer would, at the very least, cast doubt on the authenticity of his or her relationship with God. Moreover, just as we would apologise to a friend who we offended, we should always turn from our sins and bring them before the Lord, in a spirit of humble repentance. As the apostle John says, "If we confess our sins, He is faithful and just to forgive us our sins, and to cleanse us from all unrighteousness (1 John 1:9)."

The Holy Spirit does something that sounds similar to condemnation, but is in fact the polar opposite: He *convicts* us of sin: not to make us feel guilty, but to prompt us to bring these things before the Lord, in order that we can leave them at the foot of the cross and be set free from guilt! Satan condemns to enslave, whereas the Holy Spirit convicts to set us free. As mentioned in our reflections upon the Book of Acts, the Spirit seeks to convict people who don't yet know Jesus, in order to draw them into a relationship with Him. However, He also convicts Christians, to prevent them from becoming so entrenched in their sin that they damage their witness and impair their relationship with God. In both scenarios, all three Persons of the Trinity are at work, although we also have a role: the Holy Spirit convicts, we repent, and God the Father forgives, all because of Jesus's sacrifice.

Sometimes, it isn't all that easy to tell the difference between conviction and condemnation, because there's frequently an element of truth in what Satan says. He also knows his Bible better than many Christians, as was demonstrated when he used it in his wilderness temptation of our Lord. It is therefore imperative that we know the Word and have a firm understanding of our inheritance as believers in Christ. I've previously mentioned the dangers of entering into conversations with Satan, but we shouldn't be a sitting target, either. As Jesus promised in Matthew 18:18, "Whatsoever ye shall bind on earth shall be bound in heaven: and whatsoever ye loose on earth shall be loosed in heaven." This isn't a book designed to instruct readers in spiritual warfare, but it's fair to say that we have tremendous authority as believers, which we seldom seem to realise. Luke 9:1 records that, "He (Jesus) called his disciples together, and gave them power and authority over all devils, and to cure diseases." Considering that He's entrusted us with the same Commission as He gave them, do you really think He'd give us any less authority? That doesn't necessarily mean waging all out attack when we don't feel equipped to do so: we still have the option of following Hezekiah's example and taking the Enemy's threats to the Lord (2 Kings 19:14).

Whenever we're in doubt as to our standing with God, Romans chapter 8 is an ideal place to turn for encouragement. If you're a Christian, the following promises belong to you, in addition to no longer being under condemnation: the Spirit that raised Jesus from the dead lives in you (verse 11), you're a son or daughter of God (verse 14), you don't have a spirit of bondage to fear, but of adoption (into the family of God; verse 15), you're a joint-heir with Christ (verse 17), glory will be revealed in you (verse 18), you have glorious liberty (verse 21), the Holy Spirit prays for you (verses 26 & 27) and, famously, all things work together for good for you (verse 28). If this isn't enough, you're also justified and glorified (verse 30), God is for you (verse 31), nothing can separate you from the love of Christ (verse 35), you're more than a conqueror (verse 37) and nothing at all can separate you from God (verses 38 & 39)! Of course, there will be trials (verse 18 references the sufferings of the present time), but these are trials which, with the Lord by our side, and His Spirit living within us, we can overcome. After all, isn't that what people do when they're more than conquerors? If conquerors defeat their enemies, then we have the power to completely rout ours!

It's time now for a few questions!

i. Have you allowed Satan to rob your joy, as a believer, by paying heed to his condemnation, or do you live as though you've inherited all of the promises contained in Romans 8?

ii. Do people in your circle who are not yet Christians know that you love them and don't condemn them?

iii. If you're not yet a Christian, would you like to inherit the promises outlined in Romans 8? If so, you know what to do!

Take Heed!

"Wherefore let him that thinketh he standeth take heed lest he fall (1 Corinthians 10:12)."

Do you sometimes find that there can be a danger of overreacting against an undesirable trait or quality? Jesus was severely critical of the legalistic Pharisees, whose controlling attitude took the joy out of feasts, imposed unnecessary fasts and bound Jews with a harsh interpretation of the Law which nobody could possibly keep. In contrast to this heavy burden, Jesus promised a light yoke (Matthew 11:30), but He also instructed His followers that, "If you love me, keep my commandments (John 14:15)." On an initial reading, Jesus's requirements were even harsher than those of the Pharisees, because He taught that we would be judged on the basis of thought as well as deed (Matthew 5:28). Moreover, He didn't come to dismiss the Law, but to fulfil it and, by doing so, He enabled everyone who trusted in Him to be considered righteous by God the Father.

We mustn't ever doubt that salvation comes by placing our trust in Jesus as our Saviour, but neither should we reduce our spiritual regeneration to a once-and-done formality. Jesus came to give us a new life, and this flows out of an eternal relationship with Him. If we love someone, it should only be natural for us to want to honour them, and live our lives in a way which pleases them. It therefore shouldn't come as any surprise that Jesus interprets the depth of our love for Him as being the extent to which we endeavour to keep His commandments. We might say that it is just as unrealistic to believe we inherit eternal life by uttering a prayer of repentance and continuing with life as it was before, as to suppose we could take our wedding vows, then live as though we were still single. While the Pharisees devised 613 Laws from the Ten Commandments given to Moses, Jesus gives us just two: "Thou shalt love the Lord thy God with all thy heart, and with all thy soul, and with all thy mind (Matthew 22:37)" and "Thou shalt love thy neighbour as thyself (Matthew 22:39)." Both of these instructions are relational: Jesus sends His Holy Spirit to enable us to live this way, but a completely unchanged life is an indication that our conversion may not be genuine, because "Whosoever is born of God doth not commit sin (1 John 3:9)." This doesn't mean that we're expected to be perfect, because none of us can be: John is referring to persistent, unconfessed sin which exhibits a consistent disregard for Jesus's sacrifice at Calvary. If we continue to live in this way, impervious to the Spirit's attempts to convict us, then questions surely have to be asked regarding our commitment to Him.

Corinth was a city renowned for its worldly culture, and it is evident from Paul's letter that the culture was impacting the church there to a far greater extent than the church was influencing the culture. Jesus exhorts believers to be in this world but not of it (John 15:19), meaning that we're to maintain relationships with our school friends and colleagues who don't yet know Jesus, without being caught up in the things they are doing, which bring dishonour to His Name. The Corinthian church actually rejoiced in its liberality, citing extreme examples as evidence that it had resisted the dangers of legalism. However, Paul admonished them, because they had missed the point: Jesus died to set us free *from* sin; not to give us freedom *to* sin. He would say precisely the same to us today, and there are at least six reasons for this.

1. If we love God, we should want to honour Him, rather than cheapening Jesus's sacrifice by using it as a spiritual 'get out of

jail free card'. Sin impairs our relationship with Him and grieves His Holy Spirit.

2. Once we yield to sin in a particular area of our lives, it begins to control us, making it harder for us to escape its snare.

3. Christians who live compromised lives can never be truly happy.

4. The world is watching us, so if we claim to be Christians, yet live exactly as non-believers do, our witness will be completely ineffective.

5. Unconfessed sin is a barrier to our prayers being heard (Isaiah 59:2).

6. Sin isn't good for us! God is omniscient, so He knows what's best for our lives far better than we do. He considers sin to be so abhorrent that He sent His Son to die for it, so it's a serious matter, and certainly not something to be joked about.

Although God hates sin, He demonstrated His love by sending His Son to die for us, while we were yet sinners (Romans 5:8) and, when we confess our sins before Him, in all sincerity, He's faithful to forgive us (1 John 1:9). Thus, it's not a question of legalism or liberalism, but of the authenticity of our relationship with our Saviour. If we're not prepared to live for Him now, then we're unlikely to be prepared to die for Him, if and when persecution comes. Stephen and many others throughout history have demonstrated this to be the ultimate test of our love for the One Who gave everything for us, and we should be prepared to do the same.

There's quite a lot to reflect on here, and you may like to contemplate these three questions, as you do so.

i. Is there a 'besetting sin' in your life that you need to confess before the Lord?

ii. Does your own church fellowship strike the right balance between forgiveness and accountability?

iii. When you fall short in an area of your life, do you consider the impact of your failure on your relationship with the Father, Son and Holy Spirit?

Grace And Endurance

> "And lest I should be exalted above measure through the abundance of the revelations, there was given to me a thorn in the flesh, the messenger of Satan to buffet me, lest I should be exalted above measure. For this thing I besought the Lord thrice, that it might depart from me. And he said unto me, My grace is sufficient for thee: for my strength is made perfect in weakness. Most gladly therefore will I rather glory in my infirmities, that the power of Christ may rest upon me (2 Corinthians 2: 7 - 9)."

In the same way that Isaiah 53 poses a considerable challenge for Jewish rabbis, the verses we're about to reflect upon cause significant difficulties for modern health and prosperity preachers. Whenever our dogma becomes more important than our faith in Christ, we'll resort to extraordinary measures to defend it, frequently at great cost to our credibility. The ultimate demonstration of this was the attitude of the chief priests, who sought to kill Lazarus, after Jesus had resurrected him, in order to destroy the evidence, and prevent people from defecting from Judaism to follow Jesus (John 12: 9 - 11). As in that extreme example, our obsession with proving ourselves to be right, even when we may be wrong, often causes intense pain to those around us, who are either kept in ignorance or persuaded that they are somehow 'lesser Christians' than they ought to be.

In these verses from 2 Corinthians 2, Paul was recounting an occasion, fourteen years previously, when he had caught a glimpse of heaven, which most likely relates to the time when he was stoned and left for dead in Lystra (Acts 14:19). Paul took the revelation he received so seriously that he scarcely spoke about it, and an obvious concern he had was that he might become arrogant, if people were to esteem him more highly because of his experiences. Any true servant of the Lord seeks to extol God, rather than elevating themselves, and Paul appears to have interpreted the unspecified malady that afflicted him as serving a valuable purpose, in keeping him grounded.

The first difficulty the 'name it and claim it' preachers encounter with Paul's text is that he "besought the Lord thrice," belying the assertion that it demonstrates imperfect faith to bring a request before the Lord more than once. Our Lord Himself taught us to be persistent in prayer, and we've previously noted the faithfulness of Daniel in continuing to intercede for three weeks, while the messenger despatched to respond to him was detained by a spiritual adversary. Our prayers must always be contingent on God's will being done, but there's absolutely nothing wrong with bringing our petitions before Him until we receive an answer, whatever that may be. Our reaction when the answer isn't affirmative could be considered to be a yardstick of our maturity as believers: we should always accept, as Paul did, that God's will is best for us!

While the preceding paragraph outlines one difficulty some preachers encounter with this text, a far greater problem for them lies in the fact that Paul wasn't healed. They try to explain this away by saying that it wasn't a physical malady at all, but this appears to be a distortion of the plain meaning of the text. Moreover, even if we were to accept their contention on this point, the fact remains that Paul was subjected to an unwanted affliction, from which he unsuccessfully besought release. When our vain philosophies come up short, our temptation is usually to blame other people for their failure, which is why preachers of a certain persuasion tend to level an accusation of insufficient faith against members of their congregations who aren't healed. This literally adds insult to injury, causing people to question their faith at a time when, by definition, they are at their most vulnerable. If the faith of the subject was a prerequisite for healing, then surely Lazarus could never have been raised from the dead! It's a wonderful thing to have faith for God to work in and through our lives, which He can and will do, but, ultimately, He is Sovereign, and can never be beholden to His subjects.

There are several reasons why God might choose to allow trials in our lives, without granting us the alleviation we request. I've noted some of these below, with particular emphasis on the areas of illness and physical disability, but this list is by no means exhaustive.

1. He may be able to teach us more during the trial, as He walks with us through it, than He would by instantly delivering us.
2. Our patience and endurance have the potential to provide a powerful testimony to doctors, nurses and fellow patients, not to mention our own families.
3. As with Paul, an infirmity might keep us grounded in our faith, preventing us from becoming proud.
4. If our hearts aren't quite right with God, physical illness may be a constraint He lovingly allows in our lives, to reduce the potential for us to fall into damaging sin, and instead lead us into a closer relationship with Him.
5. There may be things He wants us to accomplish which we wouldn't have the time or capacity to do, if it wasn't for our injury or illness. Such was the case with Amy Carmichael, whose inspirational books wouldn't have been written, had she continued with the physically demanding lifestyle that didn't give her a spare moment, prior to her accident.
6. God may intend to use our situation for His glory: as the Lord said to Paul, His strength is made perfect in weakness. We see this demonstrated in the remarkable ministries of saints such as Nick Vujicic and Joni Eareckson-Tada.

Remember that *all* things (including injury and illness) work together for good for those who love God and are called according to His purpose! This doesn't mean to say that these things *are* inherently good in themselves, but there's certainly no reason why the Lord can't use them, as He crafts us into the people He intends for us to be.

Finally, a personal question: when you're going through a trial, do you tend to hide it from others? This is a perfectly natural thing to do, and it's wise not to share our circumstances with all and sundry, but there can be merit on occasions in allowing those around us to see what we're experiencing. I've articulated three possible reasons below, in place of the usual questions.

i. Sharing the trials we go through provides a powerful testimony, as our acquaintances see, in real-time, how God leads us to the other side. Retrospective testimonies are good, but there's always the tendency for people to think that things might have worked out alright in the end, even if God hadn't been in the equation!

ii. It makes it easier for associates who aren't yet Christians to relate to us, when they see that our faith doesn't mean we simply breeze through life without a care in the world.

iii. Fellow believers will be reassured that we're not some kind of 'super saint', who never comes under attack. This will make it far easier for them to seek our advice in the future, because we're always more inclined to turn to acquaintances who have experienced trials similar to the one we're currently enduring.

These concepts can obviously be applied to other areas of our lives, and I hope you might find them useful, as you seek to turn your tests into testimonies. If you're not yet a Christian, my desire is that what you've read might help to explain, however imperfectly, some of the reasons why people you know who *are* believers continue to experience challenges in their lives: it certainly isn't because God has abandoned them! My ultimate prayer is for you to enter into the fullness of the joy that awaits you, as a follower of Jesus Christ: this is a joy which isn't dependent on circumstances, but upon the love He has for us, and the nature of our relationship with Him. Of course, God loves everybody, but it's only those of us who accept Jesus into our hearts who He regards as His children (Galatians 3:26). While we are all subject to the imperfections of living in a fallen world, everybody who places their trust in Jesus is immediately redeemed, with the promise of a glorious future, in which there'll be no more pain; something we'll anticipate at the very end of this book!

Beware Heretics!

"O foolish Galatians, who hath bewitched you, that ye should not obey the truth, before whose eyes Jesus Christ hath been evidently set forth, crucified among you (Galatians 3:1)?"

These seem like harsh words; I mean, who wants to be called a fool? However, rather than being condemnatory, they formed the basis of an impassioned plea from Paul, who was desperate for believers in Galatia not to be led astray by heretical doctrine. The primary challenge they faced in this regard came from a group called the Judaisers, who were discouraged by the numbers of people deserting Judaism for Christianity. They found it impossible to argue against the wisdom of Jesus' teaching, or the power of His death and resurrection, so they cleverly attempted to muddy the waters by trying to persuade new Christians that, while believing in Jesus was all well and good, they still needed to observe the Jewish Law. In essence, their recipe for salvation was faith in Jesus plus observance of the Law! This kind of philosophy persists today, albeit in a different guise: anyone who says that Jesus alone isn't sufficient for salvation is a heretic, and should be ignored. Such false teachers are generally motivated by a desire to control people, and the control is achieved by the 'plus something' that their adherents are expected to do; for example, 'believe in Jesus and donate a proportion of your salary to my ministry' or 'trust in Jesus and distribute a certain number of tracts each year'. On the other side of the coin, we have, as previously noted, individuals who falsely claim that Jesus is only one possible way to heaven. This is intended to ensure that their ministry or system doesn't come into direct conflict with Christianity, by superficially accepting Jesus's teaching, while tempting followers onto a 'broad road' which encompasses a range of other belief systems. While this may appear attractive in a culture where we are encouraged to embrace pluralism, it is a reversion to the type of syncretism that proved so disastrous for the nation of Israel in the era of the judges. It would be even more deplorable for us to fall into such a trap today, because we have the revelation of Calvary and the empty tomb, which is exactly the proposition Paul was making to believers in Galatia. The essential point is that faith in Jesus is both necessary *and* sufficient for us to inherit eternal life!

While the Judaisers could be compared to ultra-legalists, who sought to bring others under their control, there was another group that endeavoured to ensnare Christians in the formative years of the church. These were antinomian Gnostics, who were the liberals of their day, teaching that the body was inherently sinful, meaning that it didn't really matter what it was used for! This fallacy introduced all sorts of debauchery into the church, of the sort Paul warned the Corinthians against. While the term 'Gnostic' may not have recently come across your radar, the concepts they espoused are extremely common today, in the form of liberal theologians, who assert that we can do whatever we want, because Jesus has already paid the bill. Viewing Calvary as a blank cheque to sin, rather than a redemptive purchase which cost God everything, is both an insult to our Saviour and a demonstration that we've ignored the conviction of the Holy Spirit to a dangerous degree. Congregational leaders who teach such heresy will be judged extremely severely, should they fail to repent, but they also pose a risk to their hearers, and it is beholden upon all of us to recognise false doctrine, whenever and wherever we encounter it.

So, how do we avoid being deceived? The first thing we need to do is to seriously study the Word of God, because having the truth contained in our hearts and minds causes spiritual alarm bells to sound every time we hear something that isn't genuine. This doesn't mean simply reading the Bible in the way that a patient might take medicine, but meditating upon what we read, discussing Scripture with other believers and attending Bible studies, whether corporately or on-line. It's essential that we study the whole canon of Scripture, to avoid being deceived by 'ministers' who use selective passages in an attempt to prove a certain point. As Donald A. Carson famously said, quoting his father, "A text without a context is a pretext for a proof text!" However, we'll only be able to recognise the pretext, in order to defend ourselves and warn others, if we're aware of the context, and that comes by knowing the whole Word of God. Knowledge, therefore, is an invaluable weapon in our battle against deception, but it's far more effective when accompanied by a discerning spirit, which we acquire by walking closely with none other than the Holy Spirit Himself. The more we yield ourselves to Him, the more sensitive we'll become, both to the thoughts and actions in our own lives, which might grieve Him, and the attempts of others to mislead us. Paradoxically, the hardening of our hearts, which follows our resistance of the Spirit's attempts to convict us, softens us up for the acceptance of false teaching, which then takes us even further away from God. Just as our first step towards eternity is taken by heeding the Spirit's conviction, our initial step to destruction emanates from ignoring Him!

Please don't ever believe something to be true, simply because someone behind a pulpit has said it, or you read it in a book - even this one! As mentioned previously, everything we read or hear should be checked against the authenticated Word of God, as was the habit of the Bereans in Acts 17:11. This warning is particularly important in an era when people receive much of their instruction on-line, and therefore don't necessarily have the opportunity to discuss their concerns with a trusted minister or other experienced believers. As with all walks of life, and aside from Jesus's offer to exchange our guilt for His glory, things which seem too good to be true are generally precisely that! Doctrines which sound new and enticing are designed to lead you astray and, if you dig deep enough, you'll usually find that they're recycled versions of discredited theories from yesteryear.

With these warnings taken on board, how about some questions?

i. Do you carefully consider everything you hear at church, or on Christian radio, or do you uncritically accept it?

ii. If you're a mature Christian, do you take time to make sure that new believers in your acquaintance are receiving a solid foundation in their faith? This is something we have a particular responsibility for doing when we pray with someone to accept Jesus, because they need to be discipled, just as we did.

iii. Do you know God's Word sufficiently well to be able to guard yourself against being misled, and to ensure you can disciple new believers? Even if we consider this to be the case, we should never be complacent!

— SPIRITUAL REFLECTIONS - I —

Suit Up!

"Put on the whole armour of God, that ye may be able to stand against the wiles of the devil. For we wrestle not against flesh and blood, but against principalities, against powers, against the rulers of the darkness of this world, against spiritual wickedness in high places. Wherefore take unto you the whole armour of God, that ye may be able to withstand in the evil day, and having done all, to stand (Ephesians 6: 11 - 13)."

Once we place our faith in Jesus, we're immediately saved, but God doesn't instantly take us to heaven! He leaves us here for a reason, which is primarily to work with the Holy Spirit in bringing people to a saving knowledge of Jesus, in order that they can enjoy the same inheritance we do. This clearly isn't something that Satan and his demons are going to be too impressed about. Their initial intention, because they hate us, is to prevent us from coming to Jesus, in order that they can take us with them to a lost eternity. Once this objective can no longer be met, they'll still be reasonably satisfied if we're miserable, unproductive Christians, who are simply waiting to die and go to heaven. While we're in this condition, Satan will probably leave us alone, because we're no threat to him, but where's the joy in that? Not only will we lead completely miserable lives, but our communities will miss out on the transformative potential of our prayers and outreach, while we ourselves will lose eternal rewards: not related to salvation, but the blessings that believers step into after receiving their Lord's commendation of, "Well done, good and faithful servant."

It's utterly amazing to come to the realisation that God has put us on the earth for a purpose, and one of the most exciting things about becoming a Christian is beginning to discover what this purpose actually is. The military terminology may seem off-putting, but despite his defeat at Calvary, Satan continues in his attempt to control our world. Our duty, as Christians, is to do whatever we can to release our friends, colleagues and family members, as well as people further afield, from the deception which keeps them in darkness. Because this darkness isn't physical, but spiritual, our battle is also spiritual, waged through prayer, intercession and proclamation of the truth. This might sound rather daunting if we forget that Jesus is fighting alongside us, and has sent His Holy Spirit to dwell within us! However, those reassuring truths don't mean we can simply sit back and wait for victory to come our way: we need to fight for the liberation of the captives who burden our hearts and, like any proficient soldier, it is incumbent upon us to make sure we're equipped with the armour God has provided for us. Paul describes this armour in Ephesians chapter 6, and every Christian should study his analysis carefully, to ensure that he or she is properly prepared for battle.

Wherever we find a promise in the Bible, there is also an implicit warning. The most notable example of this comes in relation to salvation: given that we're saved by accepting Jesus as Lord and Saviour, there is an obvious implication of any rejection of Him. Thus, when Paul writes that equipping ourselves with our spiritual armour will enable us to stand, the inference is that our failure to do so may lead to us falling on the spiritual battlefield. By ensuring that our lives are rooted in the Gospel, we have the foundation we need, not only to stand our ground, but to strategically advance, using our weapons of prayer and God's Word. Satan always seeks to attack the head, whether of a family, church or nation, so we need to be confident of our salvation, which also protects us from the emotional onslaught he'll unleash against us. Our faith in Jesus is our ultimate defence and, while He is our righteousness, unconfessed sin can create chinks in our armour, due to the temporary alignment of our will with the one we're fighting against, instead of the One we're fighting for!

It's particularly instructive to note that, along with Philippians, Colossians and Philemon, Paul wrote his epistle to the Ephesian believers while detained as a prisoner of the Roman Empire. Even though our circumstances may physically constrain us from time to time, they can never change our identity in Christ, as sons and daughters of the Living God! Satan will endeavour to win the battle for our minds, by attempting to persuade us that all is lost, but we enjoy the ultimate protection, in the helmet of salvation, which represents our living, continuing relationship with Jesus Christ. We have a vital, ongoing role here on earth, but we must also look to heaven, aware of the fact that there are only two possibilities for us as believers, so far as our circumstances are concerned: i) they're God's will for us at the time, in which case we must pray for Him to show us how to respond and magnify His Name; or ii) they're not God's will, in which case we have the authority to change them, through the power of prayer! Therefore, whatever our circumstances may be, we need to pray, which is precisely where Paul turns his attention, after describing the spiritual armour God gives us. We don't wear this armour simply to look good, or even purely to defend ourselves, though that's important, but to inflict irreparable damage on the strongholds of the Enemy, as we intercede for fellow combatants, and the prisoners of war whose release from captivity may only be a prayer away!

Are you sufficiently well equipped to handle a few questions?

i. Are you aware of being in a spiritual battle, or is this something you try to ignore?

ii. Do you continually pray for the protection of your family and the people you love?

iii. What is your strategy in interceding for people who do not yet know Jesus? Do you pray for the Holy Spirit to remove the veil from their eyes and shine the light of the Gospel into their hearts?

Peace And Strength!

"Be careful for nothing; but in every thing by prayer and supplication with thanksgiving let your requests be known unto God. And the peace of God, which passeth all understanding, shall keep your hearts and minds through Christ Jesus (Philippians 4: 6 & 7)."

These are two of the most uplifting verses in Scripture; yet they've frequently been used to lay a guilt trip upon Christians, much in the same way as we observed in relation to health and healing. The second word of Paul's instruction is often translated as 'anxious', diverting well-meaning believers along the tangent of suggesting that we should never have any anxieties; almost as if we're expected not to have a care in the world! However, it's inevitable that we'll face circumstances which worry and even alarm us: the question is always how we address them! Think of a manager watching his team on All-Ireland Final day, as they're being over-run in midfield. Do you suspect he'd have a level of anxiety? Almost certainly so! What would you expect him to do next? Clearly, if he prowls the touchline, continuing to feel anxious, without doing anything to address the situation, there's no prospect of his team emerging victorious. Alternatively, should he consult with his selectors, effect the appropriate positional switches and, perhaps, make a change in personnel, there's every possibility that momentum will shift, leading to a triumphant outcome. It might be a clumsy analogy, but we face similar situations in our lives as believers: we may hear unwelcome news about a family member, or receive an adverse medical diagnosis and, initially, we will be worried. Unlike the hurling or football manager (unless he's a Christian!), our response will be both physical and spiritual. In the case of the medical diagnosis, once we've processed the initial shock, we don't simply sit around the house worrying, but seek the appropriate expert treatment. As Christians, we also bring the situation before the Lord in prayer, knowing that no element of our circumstances ever comes as a surprise to God, Who both knew about them, and devised the solution, long in advance. It is the importance of prayer that Paul is emphasising here, as opposed to a trite philosophy of "don't worry, be happy!" Rather than dwelling on them, and allowing them to gnaw away at us, we have the privilege of taking our cares to the Creator of the universe, for Whom nothing is impossible.

How we pray is an important, yet frequently overlooked, element of bringing our petitions to the Lord, which is Paul's reason for emphasising that we need to come before Him with thanksgiving. We may not always feel like praising God in the midst of a storm, but our problems seldom seem as overwhelming when we see them in the context of the awesome, majestic God Who has delivered us in the past, and Who will never leave us nor forsake us. The psalmists provide a tremendous example in this regard: their circumstances frequently seemed dire, but they nevertheless prefaced their petitions with praise and thanksgiving, and Paul would tell us, as he instructed believers in Philippi, that we need to do the same. In fact, we have even more reason than the psalmists to be thankful, with the additional perspective that Calvary gives us: we not only have a Father Who loves us, but also a Saviour Who died for us and the guiding hand of the Holy Spirit to lead us every step of the way, as we negotiate our path through our trials. When we reflect on everything Jesus has done for us, and invite the Holy Spirit into the challenges we're facing, our hearts and minds will be flooded with peace, which is the hallmark of the Holy Spirit upon everyone who trusts in Him. Our failure to do this means facing the challenge on our own, attempting to engineer our own solutions, and forgoing the peace of knowing we're walking through the storm with the Saviour Who calmed the seas. He's simply waiting for us to call on Him, but He won't force His way into our circumstances, meaning that He'll allow us to negotiate our challenges on our own, should we choose to do so.

When we bring our concerns to the Lord in prayer, He gives us the strength we require to stand firm and overcome our trials, rather than becoming a victim of them. The extent of this strength is revealed to us later in Philippians chapter 4, in verse 13, where Paul encourages his readers, ourselves included, that we can do *all things* through Christ Who strengthens us! As ever with these promises, we need to yield to God's will for our lives but, either way, the promise of strength remains valid. If the circumstances we're facing aren't consistent with God's plan for us, He'll give us the physical, emotional and spiritual strength to change the situation, through the power of His Holy Spirit. Alternatively, if the scenario we're encountering is something He's purposed, He'll grant us the capacity we require to work through it for His glory; learning the lessons He intends, knowing that all things work together for good, as we continue to praise Him with thanksgiving. This obviously doesn't mean that we're expected to be thankful *for* the trial, but we can still be thankful *in* it, knowing that the loving God Who has carried us this far through life will never drop us into a gulley.

If you still had any doubt regarding the ability of the Holy Spirit to transform a life, it will hopefully have been dispelled by our consideration of Philippians chapter 4. Here we have Paul, formerly Saul of Tarsus, and previous persecutor of Christians, now imprisoned for his faith in Jesus and proclaiming that all his strength comes from Christ! The wonderful news for us today is that this reality doesn't only apply to Paul, or a special category of 'super-Christians', but to everyone who chooses to place their trust in the Lord. While the journey may sometimes be painful, there's nothing that God and ourselves can't do together, provided we are working towards the accomplishment of His plan for our lives. I suspect Paul's question for us today would be whether we are living as though that were the case!

Now, do you have sufficient strength to contemplate some additional questions?

i. Do you make it your practice to take your cares and anxieties to the Lord, before they develop into fears?

ii. Does your confidence in God to provide for you outweigh your anxiety as to what might go wrong?

iii. What's the worst situation you've encountered as a Christian, and how did God lead you to the other side? Hopefully, reflecting on God's faithfulness to you in this scenario will strengthen your faith in His ability to see you through your current trial, and the next one!

Walk Worthy!

"For this cause we also, since the day we heard it, do not cease to pray for you, and to desire that ye might be filled with the knowledge of his will in all wisdom and spiritual understanding; that ye might walk worthy of the Lord unto all pleasing, being fruitful in every good work, and increasing in the knowledge of God (Colossians 1: 9 & 10)."

I actually cheated a little bit by putting a full stop at the end of verse 10, because the sentence Paul commenced at the beginning of verse 9 doesn't actually end until the conclusion of verse 17! I'd definitely recommend taking a look at the whole chapter: not only to discover the remainder of this epic sentence, but also to see the full context of the verses we're reflecting upon. As was the case in Galatia, false teachers were endeavouring to undermine the faith of believers in Colossae and divert them from the truth. When we, or our ministries, come under sustained attack, it's important that we're able to turn to experienced Christians for help, advice and guidance. The church in Colossae were blessed to have one of the greatest evangelists and Bible expositors of all time, to whom they could turn; not only for advice, but also for prayer!

Remarkably, in a letter written from prison, Paul was encouraging believers elsewhere in the world, demonstrating the heart of a true shepherd, in contrast to the 'hirelings' of whom Jesus spoke in John 10:12. Whereas pedlars of false doctrine will seek to exalt themselves, a genuine pastor will point their flock towards the Gospel of Jesus Christ, which is what we see Paul doing in

Colossians 1:23, where he urges his readers to continue in the faith and not be moved away from the Gospel. It's always exciting to be on the move for Christ, attacking the Enemy, breaking down strongholds and praying with people as they accept Jesus into their hearts. However, there are also times when it's necessary to defend, in order to ensure that we don't lose ground. When we see people who are questioning their faith, or who are vulnerable to potentially being led astray, it's essential that we stand with them: esteeming one believer above another results in those who we perceive as expendable being picked off by the Enemy, leaving the Body of Christ wounded and depleted.

Whereas false doctrine brings discouragement and confusion, sound Biblical teaching builds up believers, helping them to grow in "all wisdom and spiritual understanding." However, the intention isn't that we merely hoard knowledge, in order that we can quote obscure verses and win Bible quizzes! For our faith to be meaningful, it has to be practical, which means actively doing something for the Lord. In over-emphasising the fact that we're saved by grace and not by works, some denominations have devalued works to the extent that it's almost an anathema to suggest that we ought to be doing anything for Christ. A reasonable response would be to ask why God would have endued us with the power of His Holy Spirit, if He didn't intend for us to do anything! The selfless sacrifice of our Saviour at Calvary should motivate us to want to do something in return, just as the condition of people we love, who don't yet know Jesus, must surely provoke us to action. When Paul urges us to "walk worthy of the Lord," it is an invitation for us to get up and participate in the fulfilment of God's plan for our lives: we only walk when we're active, and we won't get very far if we remain seated! Having said that, he's not talking about working for the sake of working, but the type of work which produces fruit. This fruit emanates from our lives as a natural consequence of us having healthy roots in the

Word of God and constantly abiding in the Vine (see John 15: 1 - 5).

In recent years, there has been a welcome realisation that the artificial division between sacred and secular work is dangerous and unhelpful. For reasons that are both financial and historical, many people found their way into ordained ministry despite not having a genuine calling or, perhaps, even being saved. As detrimental as this was to the church, the damage done may even have been surpassed by the contention that, in order to achieve anything of lasting value for Christ, individuals would have to resign from their employment and seek ordination! Not only did this fail to recognise that not everyone with a desire to serve has been called to ordained ministry, but it also left key professions devoid of effective Christian witness. I frequently hear Christians lamenting the political condition of their nations, but many of the same people claim believers should not be involved in politics! Now, certainly, we shouldn't politicise the church, and neither should we fall into the trap of believing that God's Kingdom can be ushered in by political means. However, if believers vacate the political field en masse, they can hardly be surprised when legislation is enacted which is contrary to Christian values. Similar comments apply in relation to education, journalism and all of the other fundamental pillars of culture. The question therefore isn't so much what we do, provided it's not inconsistent with God's Word, but how and why we do it. Our careers can be fruit-bearing ministries, and our families certainly can: it's simply a matter of doing all things "as to the Lord," which is the essence of what Paul went on to advise the Colossians in verse 23 of the third chapter of his letter to them.

Would you consider it too much like hard work if I invited you to consider a few questions?

i. Do you have a trusted believer to whom you can turn for advice, and are you that person for someone else?

ii. Are the things you're doing for the Lord producing as much fruit as you'd like?

iii. Have you considered how you can turn your job into a blessing, by doing it "as to the Lord?"

Our Glorious Hope!

"For the Lord himself shall descend from heaven with a shout, with the voice of the archangel, and with the trump of God: and the dead in Christ shall rise first: then we which are alive and remain shall be caught up together with them in the clouds, to meet the Lord in the air: and so shall we ever be with the Lord (1 Thessalonians 4: 16 & 17)."

Now, here's something to look forward to: the day when the Lord returns for His Church, resurrects believers who have lived before us and takes us all to heaven with Him! The nature and timing of end-times events can frequently be controversial, but the Holy Spirit didn't inspire Paul to write these words to the Thessalonian church for any other reason than to encourage them with the wonderful truth that Jesus will, one day, come back for His global Church! There can frequently be a tendency for us to explain away things we don't fully understand, while unscrupulous false prophets endeavour to exploit our misunderstanding by peddling arcane theories or claiming that they have a special revelation of the truth, which we'll only receive by entering into their inner sanctum. Even well-meaning believers can fall into traps relating to end-times events, with some dividing over matters of sequencing and timing, and others claiming that these things are hidden from us. This outlook promotes an ignorance of essential passages of Scripture, including, in some quarters, a refusal to study the Book of Revelation. If God didn't want us to have this Revelation, He wouldn't have given it to us: it's Satan who tries to suppress God's Word, and we should never be guilty of doing his job for him!

It's interesting to note that Paul's first letter to believers in Thessalonica was, chronologically speaking, one of the earliest Books in the New Testament, written around 50 AD. This tells us that the doctrine of the Rapture, or 'catching away', of the church featured prominently in early teaching and wasn't, as some claim, a heretical addition centuries later. Moreover, Paul was going over ground he'd previously covered with the church, having founded their fellowship and taught them for a period of three weeks (Acts 17:2). Observers who claim that we need to be mature in the faith before we can be trusted with these truths might be surprised to see that, over this short period, Thessalonian Christians received instruction relating to eschatological events which many modern believers consider too complex to contemplate! Paul was writing to them because they had become discouraged by seeing some of their members die before the Lord had returned, so he was seeking to reassure them that, while we may die before Jesus comes back, we will all one day be reunited, and his words will hopefully be of encouragement to us, too!

As ever with church doctrines, a balance has to be achieved between rejoicing in the encouragement that's been given to us and becoming overly complacent; sitting back and awaiting the Lord's return, without living our lives and fulfilling the purpose He has for us! While the Rapture of the Church may represent the end of this age, our contemplation of it doesn't represent the end of our lives! Therefore, Paul's letter doesn't end at chapter 4, but proceeds to teach us how we ought to respond to the glorious hope (Paul, in his letter to Titus, calls it our "blessed hope" - Titus 2:13) of being united with our Saviour. This response, which is articulated in 1 Thessalonians chapter 5, is particularly pertinent for believers in our current era, as we see the chess pieces moving in such a way as to suggest that our Lord's return may be close at hand.

The first thing to note is that we shouldn't be wasting time by speculating over the chronology of the events we've been reflecting upon: we know that they will happen, but it's God's prerogative to determine the manner and timing of their occurrence. If we're experiencing trying circumstances, it's only natural that we would joyfully anticipate the glory which awaits us, but it's also beholden upon us to work while it's still light, gathering in the harvest while we remain able to do so. There will inevitably be intense opposition to our efforts to awaken people to their need for a Saviour, and Paul emphasises the fact that we're in a battle by reiterating our need to put on "the breastplate of faith and love; and for a helmet, the hope of salvation (1 Thessalonians 5:8)." I've previously mentioned Paul's penchant for long sentences, but towards the end of his initial letter to the church in Thessalonica, he gave them seven succinct instructions, which are our marching orders for the time we have available to us, before we're either caught up in glory or taken home to be with the Lord. I've listed these below, with brief comments of my own:

1. "Rejoice evermore (verse 16)." We have a wonderful inheritance in our Lord Jesus Christ, so let's not be miserable Christians!

2. "Pray without ceasing (verse 17)." A close relationship with the Lord should promote a continual attitude of prayer, as we constantly bring people and their circumstances before Him, as agents of change.

3. "In every thing give thanks: for this is the will of God in Christ Jesus concerning you (verse 18)." We will inevitably encounter circumstances for which we are not thankful, but we must continue to live in an attitude of gratitude towards the One Who died, in order that we may have eternal life.

4. "Quench not the Spirit (verse 19)." Anything of eternal value that we accomplish can only be done in the power of the Holy Spirit, but if we grieve Him, by sinning and ignoring His loving conviction, then He will naturally be offended, and our relationship will be impaired.

5. "Despise not prophesyings (verse 20)." God's Word, which points to Jesus's sacrifice, and His exact fulfilment of scores of prophecies, in a way that could never have been achieved coincidentally, gives us complete assurance that we can trust

His claims to be our Lord and Saviour. People may have stoned the prophets and crucified our Lord, but we must keep His promises close to our hearts.

6. "Prove all things; hold fast that which is good (verse 21)." Many false prophets will arise in the last days, and we need to be discerning; ensuring that we're not deceived by erroneous doctrine, and enabling those in our acquaintance to walk in the light of the truth.

7. "Abstain from all appearance of evil (verse 22)." The world around us is far more likely to read our lives than to read their Bibles. If we, as believers, engage in activity that looks in any way dubious, it will discredit our witness towards those who don't yet know Jesus, and discourage Christians who look to us for an example.

And now for some questions!

i. If you were to score yourself out of seven, based on Paul's instructions listed above, how would you do?

ii. Are you able to live peaceably with believers whose interpretation of end-times events differs from your own, knowing that our views on the timing of the Rapture don't directly impact our salvation?

iii. Are you sufficiently wary of individuals who claim they have their own private revelation, as to when the Lord will return?

Receive The Truth!

"And then shall that Wicked be revealed, whom the Lord shall consume with the spirit of his mouth, and shall destroy with the brightness of his coming: even him, whose coming is after the working of Satan with all power and signs and lying wonders, and with all deceiveableness of unrighteousness in them that perish; because they received not the love of the truth, that they might be saved (2 Thessalonians 2: 8 - 10)."

These are sobering verses for anyone who believes that God somehow changed His character during the inter-testamental period, transmuting from a 'God of vengeance' to a 'God of love'. Not only is He inherently immutable, but He is never vengeful and always loving: even His chastisement is designed for the good of ourselves and the people whose lives we have the capacity to influence. Jonah can testify, at his own expense, to the mercy of God under the Old Covenant, while Paul's second letter to the Thessalonians dispels any supposition that judgement is limited to an era prior to Calvary. His first epistle to them, which elucidated the joyous expectation believers have of being united with the Lord, and each other, for all eternity, was followed by this correspondence addressing the seven-year period known as the Tribulation, during which those who remain on earth will be judged for their rejection of God. This warning was not given to frighten believers, because our sanctuary is found in Christ, but to motivate us to intercede for everyone who does not yet know Jesus, in order that the veil of deception may be removed from their eyes.

The verses we're considering deal with subject matters we may not wish to dwell on, but it's imperative that we're fully aware of why it's so vitally important for us to maximise the opportunity we have of bringing people to Jesus. Acceptance of the Gospel isn't merely an optional extra, but an essential prerequisite for entry to heaven, and those who are alive at the time in question, having rejected Jesus, will have to grapple with the realities articulated by Paul in his second letter to the Thessalonians. Our confident expectation of being resurrected to eternal life, or caught up in the Rapture, is only given to people who place their faith in Jesus as Lord. Everyone else faces the prospect of either being resurrected to judgement or enduring the Great Tribulation, which will be the time of the Antichrist (the Wicked, referred to above) and deception. Such a stark reality surely has to concentrate our minds as believers, providing our compelling motivation for reaching those who don't yet know Jesus, which is presumably Satan's rationale for seeking to discourage contemplation of these Scriptures.

If the uncertainty, racial tension and pandemic of 2020 were difficult to endure, then think how bad the Tribulation will be! If you don't yet know the Lord, and consider this to be a hollow warning, then it might be worth contemplating what you've read so far, as we've reflected upon passages from Genesis to Second Thessalonians. Throughout the Old Testament, God alerted His people to imminent judgement: He was faithful to spare those who turned to Him, but everyone who refused to heed His warnings reaped the harvest of their disobedience. The same Old Testament pointed repeatedly to Jesus, Who fulfilled every prophecy that was made about Him, and died on the cross at Calvary, so you could be forgiven for everything that could possibly separate you from God. Jesus's deity and power were proven beyond doubt on the first Easter morning, when He rose from the grave, as a foretaste of the eternal life that He is offering to you. All you need to do, in order to receive your glorious inheritance, is to accept His offer of salvation. Judgement isn't something God relishes, but it would be negligent not to prepare you for the fact that it's something He has to impose, to be consistent with His righteous character, in instances where people refuse to accept the provision He's made for their sin.

For us, as believers, it's reassuring to see that there's absolutely no doubt as to Who has the victory: Jesus won't need to fight against the Antichrist, but will destroy him simply by the brightness of His coming! However, if you're not yet a believer in Jesus, you may be surprised to learn that you're perhaps not in control to the extent that you might think you are. If we reject Him for long enough, it appears that God will place blinkers on our eyes, inhibiting our ability to see the truth. This may be because He is confirming us in our decision, as He did with Pharaoh, or because, as an act of mercy, He is limiting the exposure to the truth of individuals He knows will not believe, due to us being judged on the basis of the revelation we receive. Ultimately, people reject Jesus because they love the darkness more than the light, as He said Himself (John 3:19), and Paul addresses these matters in the verses immediately following the ones we're reflecting upon. It may be that you say you're waiting for a sign, other than what you have in the Bible, before believing in the Lord. If so, this is extremely dangerous, as you run the risk of being deceived: the more resistant we become to the truth, the more susceptible we become to believing a lie. Satan and his demons can perform counterfeit miracles, but there is only one Lord, and our focus needs to be on Him, in order that we're not led astray by impostors.

Do you want to be on the winning team? We may think we're in control, but if we resist the Lord for long enough, we'll ultimately come under the control of something or someone else. We can yield to God's will on earth and enjoy glorious freedom, both now and in eternity, or we can try to be masters of our own destinies, attempting to suppress the overtures of the Holy Spirit, which we know are there, and ultimately bow our knee on the Day of Judgement. The Lord is gracious to defer judgement for as long as possible, but no-one will be able to stand against Him when we're finally called to account. Satan, his demons and the Antichrist will all ultimately bow before Him, so what makes us think we will be any different?

As an alternative to the usual trio of questions, I would urge everyone who doesn't yet know Jesus as their Saviour to give serious thought to the questions at either end of the preceding paragraph: you owe it to yourself to make a decision before it's too late.

Pray!

"I exhort therefore, that, first of all, supplications, prayers, intercessions, and giving of thanks be made for all men; for kings, and for all that are in authority; that we may lead a quiet and peaceable life in all godliness and honesty (1 Timothy 2: 1 & 2)."

In his first epistle to the Thessalonians, Paul instructed them to "pray without ceasing (1 Thessalonians 5: 17)." In case we wondered what we should be praying about, he gives us some ideas, in his initial letter to Timothy! It's interesting to see that four different types of prayer are listed, all of which may be combined on any occasion, when we come before the Lord. Our supplications are requests we make, whether for ourselves or others, while prayer is our general act of communing with God. Intercession is a term which is frequently used interchangeably with prayer, but it goes somewhat deeper, representing our pleading on behalf of an individual or group, for a breakthrough in relation to their circumstances. Daniel's plea for the Lord to be merciful to the Jewish people is a wonderful example of intercession, as is Abraham's petition on behalf of Sodom. When we intercede for someone, we identify completely with them, meaning that we feel, in our spirit, as though the absence of a breakthrough would be as devastating for us as it would be for them. This is exactly how Jesus feels about us, as He intercedes for us on the right hand of His Father (Romans 8:34)! The concept of the giving of thanks is twofold: not only should we thank the Lord for the people in respect of whom we're coming before Him, but we should also be praying in a spirit of thankfulness, knowing that it's only possible for us to enter into the presence of God, in this way, because of Jesus's inestimable sacrifice. Prayer is a tremendous privilege which we must never take for granted, and should certainly never overlook. In the words of S.D. Gordon, "You can do more than pray after you have prayed, but you cannot do more than pray until you have prayed!"

Extending this concept of thankfulness, we mustn't be negligent in thanking God for answers to prayer, even when those answers don't resemble the ones we had in mind, when we first brought our requests to Him! During the earthly ministry of our Saviour, there was a physical cost to Him for the miracles He performed, as illustrated by His observation that power left Him when the lady with the issue of blood touched the hem of His garment (Mark 5:30). The miracles we receive today, and even the interventions we don't necessarily regard as miraculous, are only possible because of Calvary, which cost Jesus everything. I'm sure we'd be offended if we went to extreme lengths to rescue someone and they didn't even deign to thank us; how much more so the Saviour of our souls! However, it's so often the case, in the spiritual world as well as the natural, that eaten bread is soon forgotten: a reality that Jesus commented upon in Luke 17, verses 11 - 19, where He healed ten lepers, of whom only one returned to give thanks. Might this also be the case today? Do we only thank the Lord for one answer to prayer in every ten? Human nature doesn't tend to change a great deal, meaning that may quite possibly be the reality.

This brings us onto the question of who we should be praying for, to which the answer is: everyone! In emphasising the importance of praying for those in authority, which is highlighted in this passage, we frequently overlook the fact that we are instructed to pray for "all men;" a term that can be translated as "all humankind." This isn't intended to be a generic prayer, but the type of supplication and intercession mentioned previously, with particular reference to those in our circle of acquaintances. Timothy was a prominent pastor at the time Paul wrote to him, so was a man in authority himself, but he was nevertheless encouraged to pray for everyone he knew, and we are expected to do the same, albeit that the Lord will, from time to time, give us particular burdens for certain individuals. In Timothy's context this was likely to mean interceding for members of his church and the wider community in Ephesus, many of whom either did not know about Jesus, or hadn't yet accepted Him as their Saviour. For us, Paul's instruction has a practical application in praying for schoolmates, colleagues and neighbours, even if we don't get along with them! In fact, it's a good practice to specifically pray for the people we're in disagreement with, and then praise the Lord as their hearts are softened over time!

A similar comment applies with regard to the importance of praying for our leaders, which is something we're commanded to do, irrespective of whether we agree with their policies. If we're tempted to make exceptions, it's worth considering that Paul wrote his two letters to Timothy from the Mamertine Prison in Rome, while he awaited execution, as decreed by the Roman Emperor, Caesar Nero. It can be tempting to restrict our perception of authority figures to our political leaders, but the description also extends to our parents, teachers, managers and pastors. We're not in a position to complain about the condition of our nations, homes, offices and churches, if we deny those who lead them the prayer we're commanded to give them. Even a brief experience of being in authority, whether as a prefect or acting manager, should be sufficient to confirm that it's no easy task. Our leaders may not be believers, but God can still use them, as He did Cyrus and Ahasuerus, also known as Artaxerxes. If we don't pray for them, we leave them to their own devices, making them susceptible to Satanic deception, in the manner that we considered in our previous reflection. Prayer for our leaders invites God into their lives and decision making; not only for their own benefit, but for the good of those under their authority. Ultimately, this means that we're praying for ourselves, because wise leaders receiving godly counsel will be to the benefit of all of us!

How about three questions?

i. Are you faithful in thanking God for His answers to your prayers, and those others pray for you?

ii. Do you ever contact your political leaders, to let them know that you're praying for them, and ask if they have any prayer requests? It's amazing how many avenues this opens up!

iii. Are you, yourself, a person in authority? If so, do you ask people to pray for you? This isn't selfish: we can't lead in our own strength, and the people we're leading will suffer if no-one is praying for us.

Finally, it seemed appropriate to conclude this reflection with a word of prayer.

> *Heavenly Father, thank You for being our ultimate Authority; for Your faithfulness to us and for supplying the resources we require to live. I wish to bring before You today everyone who has authority over me: may they be Your instruments in accomplishing Your will in the world that You created. Lord Jesus, thank You for the concern You have for all men and women, irrespective of their rank or position. We're indebted to You for Your perfect example of sacrificial leadership, and I ask that You'll strengthen the faith of everyone who has placed their trust in You. Holy Spirit, please remove the scales from the eyes of all who don't yet know Jesus, and endue those in authority, in whatever context, with the wisdom to make decisions that bring honour to Jesus, in Whose Name I pray. Amen.*

The Reliability Of Scripture

"All scripture is given by inspiration of God, and is profitable for doctrine, for reproof, for correction, for instruction in righteousness (2 Timothy 3:16)."

Paul here makes what, if they weren't true, would be audacious claims on behalf of the Book we know today as the Bible. At the time Paul wrote to Timothy, he'd only have had the Old Testament, in addition to certain scrolls, primarily containing the Gospels and his own writings which, along with any letters written subsequently, and the Revelation given to John, ultimately formed the canon of Scripture that now informs our Christian walk. Clearly, the assertions that Paul makes in writing to Timothy are utterly dependent on the reliability of the Bible, which is a topic that has occupied theologians and critics for centuries, and will no doubt fill innumerable books and social media posts into the future. Wherever we stand in relation to matters of faith, one fundamental question we all face is the degree of confidence we can place in the Bible: is it really the Word of God, or is it, as some would suggest, merely a collection of myths and fantasies, based loosely around people and places from a bygone era? If the Bible is found to be authentic, then this realisation must give serious cause for thought to people who don't yet accept Jesus as their Saviour, because we could then be sure that His offer of salvation is the only pathway to eternal life. On the other hand, if the Bible isn't genuinely the Word of God, it may be that Christians have misplaced their trust in Jesus, and invested their lives in a fantasy leading to an eternal cul-de-sac. So, how sure can we be that Paul's claims regarding our Scriptures are actually true?

As a Christian, I find the most compelling argument for the veracity of God's Word to be the fact that all of Scripture points to Jesus: the Old Testament anticipates the coming of the Messiah, Who would lay down His life for His sheep, while the New Testament reflects upon His sacrifice, borne out of love, which carries eternal significance. The very first verse of John's Gospel equates God with His Word, saying that, "In the beginning was the Word, and the Word was with God, and the Word was God (John 1:1)." Jesus both claimed ultimate authorship of the Word of God, and testified to its enduring nature, by confirming that, "Heaven and earth shall pass away, but my words shall not pass away (Matthew 24:35)." Thus, if we believe in Jesus, and trust Him as our Saviour, we should accept His Word unreservedly. Any churches which don't honour the Word of God are not worthy of the name 'church', and should be avoided, because they're not honouring the God of the Word.

Taking a step back, however, why should someone who isn't yet a Christian pay any attention to the Bible? If trust in the Bible is predicated upon belief in Jesus, and someone doesn't yet believe in Jesus, then surely he or she can disregard His Book! The logic of such a position might seem attractive to somebody who doesn't yet accept the Bible as being God's Word, but we need to go deeper than this, because something doesn't cease to be true, simply because we choose not to believe it. During the course of our reflection on Jesus's resurrection, we considered evidence, which I believe to be compelling, for the reality of His victory over death. These evidences included corroboration by secular history, the subsequent empowering of His disciples by the Holy Spirit, and their willingness to die for a cause that they wouldn't have given their lives for, had it been a hoax. Even excluding the rest of Scripture, the events of those three days at Calvary, which changed the world to the extent that we began to measure time from the estimated year of Jesus's birth, point conclusively to the deity of Christ. Moreover, if Jesus truly is the Son of God, as He claims to be, we must be able to trust Him in every matter, including His assertions in relation to Scripture.

One of the most persuasive arguments for the veracity of Scripture is the unerring fulfilment of Biblical prophecies, some of which we've considered in our reflections: the deportation of Judah to Babylon and their release after seventy years, the decision of Cyrus to grant authority for the Jews to return to Jerusalem, and God's promise to Abraham that he would become a father of many nations. Then, of course, there are the prophecies relating to Jesus Himself: that He would be born in Bethlehem, be crucified despite His innocence and rise again from the dead, to cite just three. Perhaps we might wonder whether these apparent prophecies were written in retrospect, especially where those events, such as the Babylonian captivity, are confirmed by secular history, making it impossible to argue against the fact that they actually occurred?

This was the approach adopted by many Bible critics prior to 1947 when, not for the first time, the course of history was changed by a shepherd boy in Israel. It was actually a year before the nation of Israel was formally reconstituted, when the boy in question threw a stone into a cave in Qumran, following which he heard the sound of pottery breaking. Investigation revealed a veritable treasure trove of Hebrew manuscripts that secular, Jewish and Christian archaeologists have confirmed as dating back to around 125 BC. These manuscripts have given us considerable confidence in the accuracy of the Biblical text, because they exhibit only minor differences to the Word we know today. Furthermore, the fact that they pre-date Christ's time on earth dispels any notion that the prophecies He subsequently fulfilled were written retrospectively. These prophecies are so specific that it is utterly inconceivable that they could have been realised by chance, and Jesus didn't, from a natural perspective, have control over many of the circumstances being foretold, such as where He was born (prophesied in Micah 5:2; fulfilled in Matthew 2:1), the decision of His executioners not to break any of His bones (foretold in Psalm 34:20; realised in John 19:33), and their decision to cast lots for His garments (anticipated in Psalm 22:18 and occurring in Matthew 27:35; also John 19:24). We can certainly be confident that the Roman authorities weren't seeking to contrive the fulfilment of Jewish Scripture, while the Jews obviously wouldn't have intentionally done anything that pointed to Jesus being their Messiah, having 'convicted' Him of blasphemy, for making this very claim!

In the decades since the Qumran discovery, numerous other archaeological finds have been made, none of which contradict the Bible. Indeed, many of them add weight to the veracity of Scripture, including the Nazareth stone, which has all the hallmarks of being the reaction of the emperor, Claudius, to the disciples' assertion that Jesus had risen from the dead. Obscure places mentioned in Scripture are continually being unearthed, including the Pool of Siloam, where Jesus is recorded, in John chapter 9, as having healed a man who was blind from birth. This site was discovered in 2004, but discoveries were being made even prior to Qumran, including in Corinth, where Paul's co-labourer Erastus (see Romans 16:23) has been confirmed to have been treasurer, by artefacts disinterred during archaeological digs. It's therefore not only Biblical locations that are continuing to emerge: personalities are being rediscovered, too; another example being a stone unearthed in 1961, which testifies to Pilate having been prefect of Judaea, at the time of Jesus's crucifixion. Many observers obviously have their reservations about these discoveries, but if we're prepared to lay our biases and prejudices aside, allowing ourselves to be led by the evidence, then there's more external support for the credibility of the Bible than we might have supposed.

Outside of archaeology, corroboration for the Bible can be found in many authenticated external writings, meaning that we're not reduced to a circular argument of claiming the authenticity of Scripture from accounts written within its pages. Some of the early church fathers, such as Ignatius and Polycarp, were active while the apostle John was still alive, and he surely would have refuted their writings, some of which are preserved to this day, had they not been accurate. We may contend that, due to being fellow believers, these men were part of a conspiracy, but the same couldn't be said of first century historians, such as Tacitus and Josephus. The former was Roman, the latter was Jewish, and neither were beholden to the Christian faith, but both substantiated numerous passages of Scripture in their bodies of work.

For all of this, however, it is the ongoing capacity of the Bible to change people's lives that is the most compelling argument for its authenticity. When someone such as Nicky Cruz meets the God of the Bible and is transformed from dispassionate gangster to dedicated evangelist, it demonstrates a power that simply can't be found in other sacred writings, none of which contain the prophetic substance we find in the Bible. Ongoing miracles of healing and restoration confirm the power of the Holy Spirit to transform lives, as He points people towards Jesus. It may be that you know someone who was once a fractious, anxious individual, but who is now completely at peace after accepting Jesus into their heart. If so, they serve as living evidence of the faithfulness of Scripture, not to mention the Holy Spirit Who inspired it, the Saviour Who is the Hero of the Book and the Father, Whose love it reveals. The God Who transformed Nicky Cruz's life, that of your friend, and my own, is waiting to do the same for you today, if only you'd give Him the chance!

Would you be willing to consider a few questions about the Bible?

i. Do you subject the Bible to a higher standard of scrutiny than you do any other book and, if so, why is this? Is it because you want to be absolutely sure, or are you looking for an excuse not to believe?

ii. If you don't yet believe the Bible to be the Word of God, have you taken the time to check out any of the external sources, such as the ones mentioned above, some of which might allay your fears?

iii. A question now for Christians: are you confident in your ability to answer genuine queries that people who aren't yet Christians have in relation to God's Word? Even if you don't know the answer to a question someone asks you, take the time to research it, or ask a trusted believer: your actions will help to build a bridge which may ultimately lead that person to faith!

Enough Is Enough!

"But avoid foolish questions, and genealogies, and contentions, and strivings about the law; for they are unprofitable and vain. A man that is a heretic after the first and second admonition reject; knowing that he that is such is subverted, and sinneth, being condemned of himself (Titus 3: 9 - 11)."

We have the wonderful privilege, as servants of the Risen Christ, of sharing our faith with people and inviting them to enter into a saving relationship with Jesus! However, there comes a time when certain individuals exhibit such hardness of heart that it's evident they have no intention of accepting the Gospel. In his letter to Titus, who he had earlier led to the faith, Paul advised this young minister that the best thing we can do in such circumstances is to walk away. This may sound harsh, but it's completely Scriptural: going all the way back to the earliest days of the earth as we know it, God warned a rebellious generation that, "My spirit shall not always strive with man (Genesis 6:3)."

Titus was serving in a difficult environment, on the island of Crete, where there was intense resistance to the Gospel and few, if any, other church leaders, to whom he could turn for advice and encouragement. The purpose of Paul's letter was to provide him with a framework for administering the church on the island, and also to give advice on a topic with which we all have experience: dealing with people who have no apparent desire to be saved! In everything we do, we're expected to follow the example of our Saviour, and we know that Jesus always had time for men and women who came to Him with honest questions. This is an undoubted virtue He demonstrated by revealing to Nicodemus the treasures of Scripture, relating to our spiritual re-birth and the

'Gospel in miniature', which are recorded for us in John chapter 3. Nevertheless, He immediately saw through anyone whose intention was merely to catch Him out, and He frequently sent the Pharisees away with a flea in their collective ear, when they endeavoured to ensnare Him.

A famous example of this is provided in Matthew 22: 15 - 22, where a trap was set regarding whether taxes should be paid to Caesar. Either way, it seemed that Jesus couldn't win: if He'd said that taxes should be paid, He'd have incurred the wrath of the Jews; had He contended that they should be withheld, His opponents would have reported Him to the Roman authorities for insurrection! Rather than engaging in meaningless debate, Jesus confounded them with His wisdom (verse 21), following which they left Him alone for a while, as Satan had done in the wilderness. That particular Pharisaical trap was intended to cause political difficulty for Jesus, but on other occasions opponents sought to ensnare Him in matters of doctrine. Unlike the Pharisees, the Sadducees, who were the liberals of their day, did not believe in the possibility of bodily resurrection. In the very next section of Matthew 22 (verses 23 - 33), we read that they publicly sought to undermine Jesus's teaching on this point, provoking His terse and incisive response that, "Ye do err, not knowing the scriptures, nor the power of God (verse 29)." No-one had ever put the religious leaders in their place like that and, understandably, those who observed these events were "astonished at his doctrine (verse 33)." Even then, the religious lawyers sought to engage Jesus, regarding the identity of the Messiah (verses 41 - 45), but He turned the tables to the extent that they desisted from asking any more questions (verse 46)!

Jesus loves people with a compassion never seen before nor since, and relishes the opportunity to manifest the glory of God in their lives, as when He raised Jairus's daughter from her premature death (Luke 8: 41 - 56). However, He always resisted overtures to perform miracles merely for show, and illustrated His contempt for such an invitation when thus responding to Herod, in Luke 13:32, "Go ye, and tell that fox, Behold, I cast out devils, and I do cures today and tomorrow, and the third day I shall be perfected." In other words, the miracles Jesus had performed to date testified to Him being the Son of God, His resurrection would dispel all doubt, and anyone claiming to need further proof of His deity doesn't have any intention of believing. While we're urged to lead people onto the path of salvation, should they be willing to respond positively to the conviction of the Holy Spirit, we shouldn't waste time, effort and energy by arguing with them indefinitely. Some individuals have no intention of accepting Christ, but will seek to embroil us in futile debate, in order to deflect us from accomplishing the work God has called us to do. In the same way that a footballer needs to retain his composure, when an opponent is endeavouring to rile him, in order to get him sent off, we must remain sensitive to the Spirit and not get drawn into incessant debates. Once it becomes evident that an individual has no desire to meaningfully engage, our best course of action is to walk away, assuring him or her that our door remains open, should his or her mind itself be opened to the possibility of receiving the truth. If the person who's refusing to engage with us is not only deceived, but a heretical false teacher, we should also seek to warn their followers of the heresy to which they're being exposed, using the Scriptures as the basis of our instruction. Similarly, however, if they refuse to listen, we shouldn't provoke an unsavoury argument, but should instead pray for the Holy Spirit to reveal the truth to them!

Perhaps you're that person who seeks to engage Christians in endless debate, without having any intention of accepting Jesus as Saviour! If so, be aware that it's a dangerous thing to do, because any Scripturally-based answers you receive to your questions represent additional revelation, for which you'll ultimately be held accountable, should you persist in your rebellion until the day you die. Moreover, your heart will be hardened by such encounters, reducing your spiritual receptivity, making it ever harder for you to see the light, if and when you decide to seek an escape from the darkness. Having said all of this, Christians shouldn't use Paul's admonition to Titus as an excuse for not witnessing to that difficult co-worker, who we can't envisage ever accepting Christ! We owe everybody an encounter with the Living God: it's only when people seek to drag us down a hermeneutical blind alley that we should desist, in order to spare ourselves from grief and potentially save the individual concerned from even greater condemnation, as they come closer to that unpardonable sin of blaspheming the Holy Spirit.

This reflection may have raised a few questions, but would you mind if I asked some of my own?

i. Have you devised a diplomatic exit strategy, which enables you to walk away from meaningless debates, without damaging your witness to people who are not yet Christians, but who might be more amenable to believing?

ii. Do you pray for the Holy Spirit to endue you with the same wisdom that He gave Jesus, in order to effectively deal with these situations?

iii. If you're not yet a Christian, are you intentional when engaging with believers in relation to matters of faith?

Forgiven, So Forgive!

"If thou therefore count me a partner, receive him as thyself. If he hath wronged thee, or oweth thee ought, put that on mine account (Philemon 1: 17 & 18)."

Paul's shortest recorded correspondence has an interesting context, in that it was written to a believer in Colossae, by the name of Philemon, whose slave, Onesimus, had absconded to Rome, where he encountered Paul, heard the Gospel and accepted Jesus as Lord and Saviour. It may be surprising to hear of a Christian, such as Philemon, owning a slave, but the context was different to what we're used to hearing about in more recent centuries. In first century Rome, most people who would now be regarded as employees were actually indentured slaves, including professionals, such as doctors. For example, Luke, who wrote the penultimate Gospel, in addition to the Book of Acts, was a slave to whom his owning family granted release, in order that he could accompany Paul on his missionary journeys. Although there were considerable abuses, there were nonetheless many honourable slave owners in that era, including people in the church, who frequently adopted their servants into their families, as 'bondslaves'. At this point of adoption, the relationship became a voluntary contract, and Paul uses this terminology, in describing himself as a "servant of Jesus Christ (Romans 1:1)," where the word translated as 'servant' is 'duolos', or 'bondslave'.

The message of the Gospel shines most radiantly from Paul's brief letter to Philemon, and the verses upon which we're reflecting represent a heartfelt intercessory plea, as Paul entreats Philemon to regard Onesimus as he would himself. Just as Moses's intercession for the people of Israel (Exodus 32: 31 & 32) prefigured Calvary, Paul's plea on behalf of his brother in Christ,

Onesimus, takes us back to Jesus's sacrifice, on the sole basis of which He confidently asks the Father to accept His believers as though they were the Son. In dying for us on the cross at Calvary, taking the punishment for our sins, and rising again from the grave, Jesus has offered to redeem us from our own appointment with eternal death. Even this term of 'redemption' has its origins in the slave market: a mechanism existed for slaves to be purchased and set free, which is exactly what Jesus has done for us; provided, of course, that we want to be set free! As agents with free will, we have the option of remaining bound if we want to, but our bondage in this scenario will be to the cruellest of taskmasters, who will never give us a moment's rest. Surely it would be far better to serve the Saviour Who is offering to redeem us, which is exactly what Paul wanted for Onesimus, as he petitioned Philemon for his release, in order that he could join him in the ministry (verse 13).

As Christians, we can certainly see ourselves in Onesimus, due to the fact that we found Jesus in the midst of our rebellion, thereby being released from our guilt and shame. However, we should also be able to see ourselves in another brother, Philemon, who, along with Paul and Onesimus, we will encounter in heaven! In addition to invoking Calvary from the perspective of redemption, Paul's letter also emphasises the forgiveness we find in Jesus, which confers upon us a responsibility to ourselves be forgiving. When we consider that we've been released from the grip of every sin we ever committed, it would surely be churlish to hold petty offences against others, especially when the person who has offended us is a brother or sister in Christ. This forgiveness isn't merely a trait that we're suggested to exhibit: it's something we're commanded to display, in Luke 11:4, where Jesus urges His followers, including ourselves, to beseech the Father to "Forgive us our sins; for we also forgive every one that is indebted to us." Note that the instruction isn't to forgive some, but *every one*. Part of the reason for this requirement is undoubtedly the responsibility we have to represent Christ to the watching world, meaning that, through the grace and power of the Holy Spirit, we're expected to behave as He would. Moreover, it's also an instruction given for our own benefit, because unforgiveness causes far more physical and emotional distress to the person who refuses to forgive than it does to the individual against whom our grudge is held.

If including this instruction in His model prayer wasn't sufficient to emphasise the importance of forgiveness, Jesus reiterated it by using the hard nature of the Pharisees as the backdrop for further teaching on the topic, in Luke 7: 36 - 50. If you're not familiar with the passage in question, it's well worth checking out! The implication is clear: we've been forgiven of a monumental debt we couldn't even begin to dream of repaying, so how can we possibly dwell on the comparatively minor debts of others?

I'll conclude with three questions, which are intended to provoke thought or inspire discussion.

i. Do you view your relationship with other people, including your decisions relating to forgiveness, in the light of what Jesus did for you at Calvary?

ii. Have you considered that, as a believer, you should no longer do as you wish, but be subject to the desires of your Master in heaven?

iii. If 'freedom *from* Christ' seems like an attractive reason for not becoming a Christian, have you considered the freedom you can find *in* Him? This includes freedom from sentences such as: sin, guilt, shame, (spiritual) death, hell, judgement, condemnation, misery, despair and discouragement, to name just ten!

What Is Faith?

"Now faith is the substance of things hoped for, the evidence of things not seen (Hebrews 11:1)."

Isn't chapter 11 of Hebrews an inspirational passage of Scripture? We're taken on a whistle-stop tour through Biblical history, chronicling the extraordinary feats of ordinary men and women, made possible by their faith in our awesome God. In essence, faith is believing God's promises before we see their fulfilment, which is the common denominator connecting the heroes and heroines of Biblical times and beyond, who served God in a variety of different ways, notwithstanding their obvious flaws. The call on our life today is precisely the same: to place our trust in the Lord and be willing to be used by Him, knowing that, "without faith it is impossible to please Him (Hebrews 11:6)." This faith has to be in Jesus; not merely, in some abstract sense, in faith itself.

The most fundamental type of faith we can ever exhibit is the trust we place in the Lord for our salvation, following which we must continue to "walk by faith, not by sight (2 Corinthians 5:7)." This is the faith for the accomplishment of God's plans for our lives and the fulfilment of His promises. Throughout our lives, we may exhibit 'little', 'regular' or 'great' faith. In Matthew 8:26, Jesus lovingly admonished His disciples for being "of little faith," when they cried out to Him in the midst of a storm on the Sea of Galilee. The reason for this description, as I've mentioned previously, is that they'd already seen Jesus perform great miracles, meaning that it wouldn't have required much faith, in relative terms, for them to believe He would calm the waters. In contrast, He praised a centurion (Matthew 8:10) for his great faith, when he believed that Jesus could heal his servant, without physically visiting him. The people of Israel had been given the revelation of Jesus's power, but here was a Gentile with the faith to believe for an extraordinary miracle! Regular faith comes somewhere in between, and might be described as living in accordance with the revelation of God's power that's been manifested to us, whereas little faith is believing for less and great faith means believing for more (many thanks to Pastor Randal Cutter of New Dawn Community Church, Coral Springs, Florida, for these definitions). As with salvation, this faith needs to be practical and not merely theoretical: we might theorise that, as the omnipotent Creator God, there's no reason why He can't restore a broken heart, whether it be physical or emotional, but do we really expect that He'll do it, laying claim to His promises and travailing in prayer until we get an answer?

Jesus doesn't expect us to have blind faith: He built the faith of His disciples by performing progressive miracles, leading up to His resurrections of Lazarus, Jairus's daughter and the son of the widow from Nain (Luke 7: 11 - 17), then ultimately His own triumphant emergence from the grave. He does exactly the same with us: not only do we have the revelation we receive from Scripture, but Jesus also leads us on a journey of increasing faith, as we place our trust in Him, observe the way He changes our character, then see the way in which our changed lives are impacting others. If we feel Jesus begin to curb our temper, can we not trust Him to heal our marriage, and if we can trust Him for this, why not believe for physical healing, too, or financial deliverance? Then, when He's provided for us in one area of our lives, why not believe that He'll do it again, maybe increasing our ministry from local to national to international!

Numerous wonderful promises are made to people who exhibit faith, most significant of all being our inheritance of eternal life. However, we risk missing out on these by not using the faith that God has given us, as the people of Israel found to their cost, when they were promised a wonderful inheritance, but failed to possess it, because of the unbelief they displayed in Kadesh-Barnea. Even the generation which did enter Canaan failed to step into anything near the entirety of what God had promised them. The explanation has resonance for Christians today, who fail to inherit everything He's made available to us: His promises are conditional, and one fundamental condition is that we exhibit the requisite level of faith to lay claim to them! This is different to the 'name it and claim it' fallacy discussed previously: we're considering here our failure to claim blessings that have already been promised to us, either personally or through God's Word.

Not only does our failure to exhibit faith directly displease God; it also underpins much of everything else we do that displeases Him. For example, our wilful sin, or transgression, is founded upon a conscious decision to over-ride God's will for our lives, due to the mistaken belief that we can achieve greater success or happiness by doing things our own way, than we can be yielding to His purpose for us. If we had that bit more faith, surely we'd trust God to accomplish everything He'd promised and allow the Holy Spirit to work through us, empowering us to achieve infinitely more than we ever could on our own! If we genuinely believed that God would provide for us financially, we wouldn't need to even contemplate making a false claim for expenses or withholding our offering from the church collection. Similarly, if men put God's word into practical action by loving their wives as Christ loves His Church, they'd enjoy far happier marriages, with greatly reduced temptation towards infidelity, for either party. Why don't we do these things? It surely has to be because, all too often, we don't believe His promises, thereby exhibiting 'little faith', as opposed to the faith Jesus would expect of us.

Faith isn't an abstract concept, but something that emanates from our relationship with Jesus. This is surely what He meant when He exhorted His followers to have "faith as a grain of mustard seed (Matthew 17:20)," in order to move mountains. Note, He didn't say to have faith *the size of* a mustard seed! How does a mustard seed move mountains? It abides where it's been planted, receives nourishment from the soil, drinks in the water and pushes aside a veritable mountain of earth, relative to its size, as it pokes its head above ground and grows into a herb-yielding plant. How do we move the mountains in our lives? We remain rooted in fellowship, receive nourishment from the Word and drink from the Living

Water of the Holy Spirit, thereby naturally producing a bounteous harvest, through our relationship with God.

Taking a step back, much of our failure in this regard can be attributed to our decision to focus too much on ourselves, or our circumstances, and not enough on our Saviour. We're inclined to criticise the Israelites for having insufficient faith to enter the Promised Land, after God miraculously delivered them from Egypt and led them across the Red Sea, but we're frequently guilty of an even greater sin: unbelief in the face of Calvary and Jesus's resurrection! If we focus on the God Who created the world, the Saviour Who died for our sins and the Holy Spirit Who raised Him from the dead, before coming to live within us, we can surely have faith as a grain of mustard seed, at the very least!

Will your faith stretch to answering some more questions?

i. Do you consider yourself to have 'little', 'regular' or 'great' faith?

ii. Is it your habit to maintain a journal of prayer requests and answers? This can be a good way of building up our faith.

iii. Do you ever pray for increased faith? In Mark 9:24, we see a distressed father asking the Lord to help his unbelief, and there's no reason why we can't do the same!

Resist And Grow!

"Submit yourselves therefore to God. Resist the devil, and he will flee from you (James 4:7)."

At the moment we gave our lives to Jesus, we entered into a spiritual battle, but the good news is that Satan is absolutely no match for God! He doesn't have anywhere near the same level of power, he doesn't possess any of the 'omni' attributes that only God does and, while he'll inevitably snarl, in an attempt to persuade you that defeat is inevitable, he's a liar (John 8:44)! By the same token, we have to actively resist him, rather than allowing him to have dominion over our lives: Jesus purchased our victory at Calvary, but we still have to enforce it! The key to doing this, as with everything, rests in our relationship with God. James tells us to submit ourselves to God, thereby placing ourselves in the centre of His will, which is always the safest place to be! It's interesting to see these two complementary instructions in such close juxtaposition: we must submit to God and resist the Devil but, if we refuse to submit to God, we are by definition resisting him, meaning that, even if only by default, we're submitting to the Devil. In the very next verse, we receive the reassurance that, if we draw near to God, He will draw near to us (James 4:8), emphasising that we ourselves determine the closeness or otherwise of our relationship with Him.

Jesus successfully resisted Satan in the wilderness, and one of the reasons He has given us His Holy Spirit is for us to be able to do the same. In defeating Satan in this way, Jesus provided a model for us to resist the temptations we ourselves encounter, emphasising the importance of prayer and our knowledge of the Word. As we develop an interactive relationship with Him, rather than a one-way channel of prayer requests, we'll begin to witness for ourselves the truth of His promise that we won't be tempted beyond our capacity for endurance (1 Corinthians 10:13). Over time, however, that capacity should grow, meaning that we're able to bear others' burdens, as well as our own.

The epistles we've been considering aren't theoretical treatises, but letters written to real believers, many of whom were experiencing serious trials. The Christians to whom James was writing had dispersed throughout the known world, following the execution of another James, the brother of John. We should never underestimate the significance of the circumstances we're currently experiencing, because we're fighting against a spiritual adversary who is intent on causing destruction. However, when we appreciate that the advice given in James's epistle helped a group of displaced, persecuted Christians to take the Gospel to their adopted communities, then we can have absolute confidence in the results which will follow, if we apply these principles to our lives today.

The primary result James was looking for in his readers, and which the Holy Spirit would like to see in us today, is that of spiritual growth. Just as a raw recruit wouldn't be thrust onto the front line, a new believer wouldn't be expected to resist the Devil on his or her own. Certainly, Jesus endues us with His Spirit, meaning we're able to do far more than we think, when our circumstances are viewed through spiritual eyes, but there is also a pathway to maturity that we need to travel. Throughout our Christian life, we're expected to study God's Word, engage in fellowship and seek the Lord in prayer: anyone who believes they've outgrown these disciplines needs to take heed, lest she or he falls (1 Corinthians 10:12). However, as we grow in our faith, it's natural to expect a degree of progression, from solely being recipients of spiritual advice and encouragement, to being net providers. Our relationship with the Lord in prayer should also mature, as we begin to see how our earnest intercession can change the spiritual destiny of the world around us, rather than simply looking to pray for our own needs. This same principle applies with regard to our resistance of Satan: initially, when we experience a spiritual attack, it's likely to come as quite a shock, and we'd be well advised to seek the support of an experienced believer, who will hopefully pray both with us and for us. Although we will never outgrow the need for such support, because we are part of one Body, it is anticipated that, through time, we will become less dependent on others and more equipped to be someone to whom fellow believers are themselves able to turn.

Much as we might like it to, this level of maturity doesn't automatically occur over time: as with our academic studies, or our relationship with our spouse, it's something that has to be worked at. Regrettably, there are Christians today who are no further forward in their walk than when they accepted the Lord ten or fifteen years ago. This may be for a number of reasons, including the nature of their church fellowship, which denies them an opportunity for serving (the best way to grow is to serve), spiritual laziness in matters such as prayer and Bible study, or the mistaken belief that our mandate is purely defensive. When Jesus taught His disciples to "Occupy until I come (Luke 19:13)," this has to be seen in the context of the parable He was teaching, and also His instruction to "Go ye into all the world, and preach the Gospel to every creature (Mark 16:15)." How about your world? Does everyone in your office, university, tower block or community centre know the Lord? If not, there's work for you to do! As we've previously mentioned, Satan won't be thrilled at the prospect of us attempting to snatch his victims from the fires of hell, but we have James's assurance that, when we resist him, he will flee. Because this promise appears in God's inspired Word, we have His assurance, too!

Are you ready for a few challenging questions?

i. How effective are you in your attempts to resist Satan?

ii. Do you seek to draw near to God, when He seems distant from you?

iii. Are you further forward in your walk with the Lord than you were five years ago, and where do you envisage yourself being, from a spiritual perspective, in five years' time?

Be Ready!

"But sanctify the Lord God in your hearts: and be ready always to give an answer to every man that asketh you a reason of the hope that is in you with meekness and fear (1 Peter 3:15)."

If you're a Christian, does the way you live your life serve as a witness to those around you of the wonderful hope that you have, emanating from your faith in Jesus? We know only too well that life is far from easy, whether or not an individual knows Jesus as Lord, but we have so much going for us that we should naturally exude the joy which proceeds from knowing He has saved us. Even when we're negotiating a valley, we should be walking rather than trudging, knowing that we have the Holy Spirit guiding us and are destined for heaven! Christians, of all people, should be looking up, instead of down!

The essence of Peter's first epistle is summarised in the verse which forms the centrepiece of our current reflection: our attitude, allied to the way we treat people, should prompt individuals in our circle who aren't yet Christians to ask what's different about us, thereby earning us the right to be heard, in relation to matters of faith. The present age provides us with a wonderful opportunity in this regard! We'll inevitably meet men and women who are fearful about the pandemic, economics, job security, racial tension, political developments and a host of other matters. Even though most individuals are preoccupied with their own lives, they'll frequently cast more than a passing glance in the direction of Christians, to see how we are reacting to the steady stream of unsettling developments. Should they see us being similarly fearful, they'll conclude that the faith we've been espousing has no substantive value, but if we exude a calm confidence in the God we profess to know, it will inevitably open avenues for conversation, as friends and colleagues ask why we appear to be different to the majority of their acquaintances. While we always need to be responsive to the particular situation, and the needs of the individual(s) before us, it's highly recommended that we are prepared with a defence of our faith. This doesn't mean being defensive *of* Christianity, but having credible answers for the questions our peers are likely to pose, relating to the existence of God, creation, salvation and the chequered history of the church in the world.

Although our reflection taken from Titus urges us not to waste time on meaningless debates, the majority of people who aren't yet Christians have honest questions, and it's always a privilege when they come to us for some answers! Before responding, we should always listen carefully, taking the time to hear a person's story. Simply rattling through a list of apologetic statements will leave the other person completely bewildered and sincerely regretting ever having sought us out! Jesus provides the perfect example, in the form of His conversation with the Samaritan lady at the well, in Sychar (John 4: 5 - 30). He was perhaps the only Man ever, up to that point in her life, who had valued her as an individual, and He took the time to address her concerns, before revealing more about Himself. Our revelation of God comes in the form of our personal testimony, and it's important we have this ready to share, whether in a bus queue, over a meal, or in a more formal setting. Our testimony enables us to weave the Gospel message into our own story, which is invaluable in an era when personal stories are valued above proclamations of objective truth. As well as being responsive to the person or people we're talking to, we need to be conscious of the constraints of time, so it's important to have a testimony which can be tailored to the needs of the occasion, while always containing four essential elements:

SPIRITUAL REFLECTIONS - I

1. An outline of your life before you met Jesus. Resist the temptation to glorify the past, but be authentic. This enables you to make a connection with the person you're talking to, showing them that you, too, are on a journey. Help them to see that becoming a Christian was a natural response to the circumstances you were facing, and the best decision you've ever made.

2. A description of how you came to Jesus. You might relate the tug you felt on your heart, which is something with which many people can identify, or your dissatisfaction with the life you've just described. Alternatively, it may be that Jesus 'found you', as you responded to an invitation to attend a church service which changed your life forever. In either case, emphasise the fact that it was necessary for you to make a definitive response to the Gospel message, and that Christianity isn't something you were simply born into; at least, not from a natural perspective!

3. Why you needed Jesus. Here is your opportunity to weave in the Gospel, although this can be done separately, if time permits. Explain that it wasn't possible for you to transform your own circumstances, however hard you tried, and that you also desired the security of eternal life, which only Jesus can give. Summarise the way in which Jesus bridged the gap between heaven and humanity by living a perfect life, dying for your sins on the cross at Calvary, and rising again from the grave, to give the promise of eternal life to everyone who chooses to believe in Him.

4. A description of the way in which Jesus has transformed your life! It's important for people to see that becoming a Christian represents a new beginning to be embraced, rather than an end to be feared. Be genuine and emphasise that the eternal life you've inherited is something which begins here on earth,

rather than being a deferred hope for the future, while never creating the false impression that Christianity provides a passport to an easy life. Most importantly, make Jesus, and not yourself, the Hero of your story!

Instead of simply leaving the conversation there, ask your acquaintance what they think: this might provide an opportunity to allay their concerns that Christianity 'may not be for them'. In an era where there is so much spin, people will appreciate you making yourself vulnerable in this way, and there is every chance that you will open up a dialogue, moving forward into the future. If the person you're sharing with isn't someone you're likely to meet again, you will hopefully at least have planted a seed, although there's no reason why you can't exchange contact details, provided that it's appropriate to do so.

Never be afraid to ask people if they'd like to accept Jesus as their Saviour, and always be prepared to pray with them. Examples of the types of short prayer you could use are provided throughout this book, but the essential points are the confession of sin, an expression of repentance, and an invitation for Jesus to come into the person's heart. Don't worry if you get tongue-tied: Jesus values sincerity over performance!

In many cases, it will take longer for your acquaintance to make a decision, and you may never see the outcome, but you'll have been faithful in doing your part, which is all you're expected to do. Keep the dialogue going, for as long as the other person wants to, without exerting undue pressure. Be prepared to answer any questions they may have, doing whatever research is necessary to provide a sound, Biblically-based response. It's also good to remember that people's journeys of faith aren't an immediate rush to a destination, as we see from the lady at the well, who first saw Jesus as a Man, then perceived Him to be a Prophet, and finally recognised Him to be her Messiah (credit to Canon J. John for this insight!). We can never force people to make a decision, and neither should we seek to do so. As Mitch from Crown Jesus Ministries taught me during a recent on-line School of Evangelism, "It's our job to tell the truth, the Holy Spirit's role to convict and the other person's responsibility to make a decision. Things go horribly wrong when we get these roles confused!"

The following questions will hopefully enable you to translate our reflection to the context of your own life.

i. Does your life reflect the hope that you have, as a Christian?

ii. Are you ready to share the reason for this hope with others?

iii. Do you know what you'd say if someone asked you to pray with them, to accept Jesus as their Saviour?

God's Will May Not Be Done!

"The Lord is not slack concerning his promise, as some men count slackness; but is longsuffering to us-ward, not willing that any should perish, but that all should come to repentance (2 Peter 3:9)."

The promise Peter speaks of here is of our Lord's return, which is something he prophesied, just a few verses previously, that our society would call into question as the time approached (see 2 Peter 3: 3 & 4). The reason for Jesus's apparent delay, as referenced by Peter, is His longsuffering nature: in other words, He is giving you, if you're not yet a Christian, every opportunity to accept His offer of salvation, before the eternal drawbridge to Calvary is finally pulled up. Something else our culture can have difficulty with is deciding whether we serve a God of love or a God of judgement, but this dilemma itself indicates that we're considering Him from the wrong perspective! We know that God *is* love (1 John 4:8), but we've also seen, throughout our series of reflections, that it's necessary for Him to administer judgement. There are at least four reasons for this, but I'm sure you'll be able to think of many more.

1. God's judgement can serve to protect others from evil, just as prisons give society rest from serious criminals.

2. If God doesn't administer judgement, people will become so hardened in their sin that they enter into a state of imperviousness to His Holy Spirit, meaning they won't be able to receive His conviction and begin the journey towards salvation.

3. The judgement that one person experiences will serve as a warning, or wake-up call, for others. We see this on numerous occasions in Scripture; for example with the company of Korah (Numbers 16), Nadab & Abihu (Leviticus 10) and Ananias & Sapphira (Acts 5).

4. A world without any eternal consequences for our actions would give people free rein to perpetrate all kinds of evil, without any final accountability. Allowing this to happen would not only be contrary to God's nature, but it would also offend our own innate sense of justice.

Ultimately, while it may not be a reality we wish to think about, judgement has the form of permanent exclusion from heaven for anyone who has dismissed the revelation of Scripture and rejected the conviction of the Holy Spirit. This isn't something God ever wants to impose, however much we may have hurt Him, and His heart in this respect is made clear in the verse we're currently reflecting upon. As believers, it is both exciting and challenging to realise that we have a role to play in the fulfilment of God's will, on behalf of people all around us, which is that they be awakened to their need for a Saviour and pray to accept Jesus as Lord. We see here the reason for the exhortation given in Peter's first epistle, that we always be ready with an explanation for the hope we have. When our lives serve as a witness, and our words point to Christ, we're inviting the Holy Spirit into the scenario, figuratively 'teeing things up' for Him to convict a person of sin and rescue them from a lost eternity. Although Jesus's sacrifice at Calvary occurred approximately two thousand years ago, it is a very present reality: one which is brought to life for individuals who, this very day, are being resurrected from spiritual death, just as Jesus was resurrected physically.

Taking a step back, we might question why God allows anyone to be lost, given that it isn't His will for this to happen. The reason is another gift He's given us, which we've frequently chosen to abuse: that of free will. God has done everything in His power to save us from a lost eternity: He not only sent His Son to do what we couldn't do, and live a perfect life on our behalf, but He accepted

Jesus's payment for our wrong thoughts, deeds and actions, which are all the things which separate us from God. We therefore have the offer of redemption, just like the slaves we considered recently, but we have to want to be redeemed! If we're absolutely determined to go to hell, we can do, but it will literally be over Jesus's dead body, and in the face of increasingly desperate overtures from His Holy Spirit. Thus, we have the power of thwarting God's will, both for our lives on earth and our eternal futures, but I have to wonder why anyone would want to do that!

If you're reading this and you don't yet know Jesus, please be assured that He's not waiting to judge you, but to welcome you into His eternal family. If He'd wanted you to enter into a lost eternity, He'd have remained in the glory of heaven, rather than coming to earth, knowing that He'd be rejected, tortured and crucified. He willingly did all this for you, and He wouldn't have done so if He didn't love you more than anyone ever has or ever will. Jesus's sacrifice wasn't a selfless act of solidarity with a sinful world, but a necessary and sufficient precondition for the salvation of humankind. If you reject Jesus's sacrifice, there is no other way for you to be saved, meaning that you arrive at judgement by virtue of your rejection of Jesus, as opposed to having lived an inherently sinful life.

Should you be reading this reflection as a Christian, my prayer is that it will convict you of any tendency to sit back, basking in your own salvation, and instead motivate you to labour for the harvest, while we still have time to gather it in. We can't save anyone in our own strength: salvation is a sovereign act of the Holy Spirit. However, we can make it our lifetime's mission to share the Gospel with people who don't yet know Jesus and intercede for their eternal destinies!

I hope you'll find the following questions to be thought-provoking:

i. Have you been guilty of sitting back, waiting for God's will to be done, rather than playing your role in ensuring that it's accomplished?

ii. Do you pray for people who, as described in 2 Peter 3, verses 3 & 4, mock the prospect of the Lord's return?

iii. Have you ever reflected on the spiritual significance of Jesus's miracles? Just as His resurrection miracles speak of our need for spiritual life, we also require the restoration of spiritual sight, unblocked ears to hear the Gospel (a point repeatedly made in Revelation) and cleansing from sin (leprosy)!

The Way Back!

"If we confess our sins, he is faithful and just to forgive us our sins, and to cleanse us from all unrighteousness (1 John 1:9)."

Have you ever been in a situation where you thought you'd really blown it? Perhaps you'd been given a letter by your teacher to deliver to your parents, which you knew contained a bad report, and you spent the walk home dreading what their reaction might be. Or, it may have been that a mistake you made at work cost the company money, resulting in an invitation to meet with the board of management. The best course of action in these scenarios is always to admit our mistakes, rather than making excuses, or seeking to blame someone else. Accepting responsibility in this way will earn us greater respect in the long run, and it will also enhance our Christian witness, even from the shadows of an unpromising situation. While we may have an angst-ridden day, anticipating the reaction of our parents, or a sleepless night, pondering the likely response of our managers, we need never fear God's reaction, when we come before Him to confess our sins.

It would be wonderful if we instantaneously became sinless upon accepting Jesus as our Saviour, but it's only in eternity that we'll be able to enter into such a level of sanctification. In the meantime, we're still prone to sin, although by walking closely with the Holy Spirit we'll hopefully become more sensitive to Him, thereby reducing our predilection for doing things which would grieve Him and hurt others. As John says in the verse immediately prior to the one we're reflecting on, "If we say that we have no sin, we deceive ourselves, and the truth is not in us." We know from Scripture that "the wages of sin is death (Romans 6:23)." This is true both physically (when Adam and Eve sinned they brought a curse upon the earth, from which death originated), and also spiritually. Without any intervention, our sin separates us from God and results in a lost eternity, but we have an infallible antidote, in the form of Jesus's sacrifice at Calvary. It is therefore true to say that, for people who don't yet know Jesus, God will be faithful to forgive their sins, if only they confess them before Him and accept Jesus's offer of salvation. However, John's epistle was actually written to individuals who had already accepted Jesus as their Saviour, meaning that they were Christians, who were assured of their places in eternity. We therefore see that, just as Jesus is the only Way to salvation, He also provides the only Way back to God, once we have sinned as believers.

Although we must always be faithful to our marriage vows, our motivation should be our love for our spouse, rather than the formality of the contract into which we've entered. Similarly, our love for Jesus, as opposed to any burden of obligation, should be what inspires us to strive to keep His commandments, relating to our relationships with God and those around us. As John goes on to say, in the opening verses of chapter 2 of this epistle, anyone who claims to be a Christian, but has no desire to keep God's commandments, "is a liar, and the truth is not in him (1 John 2:4)." Thus, the genuineness of our heart, in accepting Jesus's offer of salvation, is revealed by our desire to honour Him, and we demonstrate this honour by endeavouring to do what pleases Him. This isn't legalism, but love!

When we fall short of the standards God expects of us, we have two options, which are quite similar to the ones we encountered before we accepted Jesus as our Saviour. The first is to do nothing! This may seem quite attractive: referring to one of our previous examples, we may have been tempted not to deliver that fateful letter to our parents. However, we knew such a course of action would be futile: the letter would be followed by a telephone call, and we'd end up in far more trouble than if we'd initially been obedient. Trying to hide anything from God is even more futile, because He knows everything, which may prompt us to wonder why He requires us to confess our sins at all. The reason is the same as the explanation underpinning the need for any kind of prayer: God knows what we have need of before we ask (Matthew 6:8), whether it be healing or forgiveness, but He desires a relationship with us, so waits for us to come to Him. In the same way that our repeated failure to call, text or e-mail someone can harm our friendship, so our reluctance to come before God negatively impacts our relationship with Him. This is especially so when we knowingly do something which offends Him, but don't repent, or unwittingly grieve Him, and ignore the Spirit's conviction. Recognising the folly of doing nothing brings us to our second option, which is always the right one: to confess our sins before the Lord. Just as our relationship with our parents is restored by apologising for whatever we did which precipitated the letter home, our standing with God is rectified when we come before Him in a genuine spirit of repentance, knowing that He will always be faithful to forgive us!

The following questions are intended to add a further dimension to our reflection.

i. Can you recall an occasion when a mistake you made actually provided you with an opportunity to enhance your testimony, by accepting responsibility for your actions, in a way that someone who isn't yet a Christian may not have done?

ii. Does your desire to honour God inform the decisions that you make?

iii. How do you respond to people who claim to be Christians, but who don't exhibit any outward signs of change in their lives?

Exercise Discernment!

"Whosoever transgresseth, and abideth not in the doctrine of Christ, hath not God. He that abideth in the doctrine of Christ, he hath both the Father and the Son. If there come any unto you, and bring not this doctrine, receive him not into your house, neither bid him God speed (2 John 1: 9 & 10)."

I'm sure you're familiar with Jesus's instruction, often quoted as "Judge not, lest ye be judged," which we find in two of the four Gospels (Matthew 7:1 & Luke 6:37). The context here is that we have no right to condemn anyone else, because we ourselves are only saved from condemnation by the fact that Jesus gave His life for us on the cross at Calvary, and we exercised a modicum of faith to accept His offer of salvation. We can't even boast of having possessed the faith to believe, because this itself is a gift from God, as Paul points out in his letter to the Ephesians (chapter 2; verse 8). Some people erroneously teach that this means anyone who doesn't believe has been pre-destined to hell (due to not having been given the requisite faith), or can't be held responsible for their rejection of Jesus. However, as with any gift, the recipient has the responsibility to appropriately utilise the faith she or he is given. I may give you a new phone but, if you leave it in the box, you won't be able to use it for the purposes of making and receiving calls, sending text messages, receiving e-mails and accessing the internet. It's exactly the same with our saving faith: it has to be 'taken out of the box' for the express purpose of believing in Jesus.

This saving faith isn't to be confused with the spiritual gift of faith, which is one of the gifts that the Holy Spirit may give believers, should we request it, once we have been saved (see 1 Corinthians

12 for a full exposition of the spiritual gifts). In addition to faith, another virtue God has given us is discernment, and it is this quality which John is exhorting us to deploy in the verses quoted above. While we have no right to judge in a condemnatory manner, God expects us to be discerning, in terms of the people with whom we closely associate. If you're a parent, you'll be very familiar with this idea, as you no doubt seek to ensure that your children mix with friends who you anticipate will exert a positive influence, while keeping a distance from known troublemakers.

Exactly the same concept applies in our spiritual lives. It's important that we have friends who aren't yet Christians (we wouldn't be able to be salt and light to them if we didn't), but we also need to be discerning, by ensuring that we don't grieve the Holy Spirit, on account of spiritual compromise, caused by our desire to 'remain in with the crowd'. We obviously can't expect acquaintances who aren't yet Christians to behave as Jesus would want His followers to do, but when professing believers in our circle exhibit a flagrant disregard for Christian values, this has to cause us concern. Association with such people can be dangerous for a number of reasons, of which I will list four.

1. The individual concerned may be persuaded that they are right with God, due to the fact that they're welcomed into fellowship with other believers. This is the point Paul was making, when he urged the Corinthian church to exclude a member who was living in a manner unworthy of his Saviour (1 Corinthians 5).

2. Other believers, who are less mature than ourselves, might conclude that the system of heretical belief being espoused by our acquaintance is doctrinally sound, by reason of our continued association with them.

3. Our children are likely to be influenced by people they see us associating with in a church setting or, especially, in a house group, believing that anything they do or say should be taken on trust, because 'they must be Christians'.

4. Over time, there is a danger that we, too, may depart from the truth. This is one reason why Paul urged Titus to make two attempts to reason with a heretic, before leaving him to his own devices (Titus 3:10).

Thus, while we must never judge, we are called to always be discerning!

Will your levels of discernment stretch to the consideration of three questions?

i. Why might it be a gracious action to, perhaps temporarily, disassociate yourself from a professed believer, when their words and actions are inconsistent with their putative faith?

ii. How would you explain your decision, in a culture that sees 'tolerance' as a higher virtue than integrity?

iii. What criterion, or criteria, would you use for accepting such a person back into fellowship?

Walk In Truth!

"I have no greater joy than to hear that my children walk in truth (3 John 1:4)."

The apostle John, who was a venerable age when he wrote this letter, clearly derived significant encouragement from the fact that his spiritual children - people he'd brought to the Lord - were continuing to follow Him. This certainly wasn't something to take for granted, because there were considerable pressures on believers at the time, who endured persecution from Rome, resistance from the Jewish establishment and repeated attacks from false teachers, who actively sought to deflect them from the truth. It doesn't matter to Satan how he diverts us from following Jesus, as long as he manages to do so, and it takes considerable character to faithfully serve the Lord in an era when, as in the first century, our Christian faith is increasingly unpopular.

The secular world bombards us with lies, proclaiming Christianity to be a 'religion of hate' and, if nothing else, my hope is that this book has demonstrated that our faith is neither a religion nor hateful! The very concept of objective truth is continually under attack, and the damage emanating from this strategy is evident in the erosion of the fabric of our society. Individuals who believed that they'd been released from the constraints of 'religion' find themselves trapped in a meaningless existence, which entices them to cry out to anyone other than the God Who loves them. It's not only Christians who make this assertion: the narrative is made by the statistics which point to ever-increasing rates of hopelessness, despair and suicide. These aren't mere numbers, but heartbreaking testimonies of the natural outworking of lives lived without God. Our education system indoctrinates people into believing that there is no universal standard of judgement, then we wonder why they rebel against governmental legislation. We're persuaded that everyone has the right to do what's best for themselves, but react in horror when others seek the same level of freedom, leaving us as victims of fraud or infidelity. Then, ironically, the society that claimed there is no God, and which invested all of its emotional, physical and financial capital in trying to eradicate any trace of Him, returns to blame Him for the condition in which we find ourselves! We can't have it both ways: we either believe in God and accept that His will is best for us, meaning that a departure from it must cause us harm, or we effectively make ourselves 'gods', as a consequence of which we will ultimately become subservient to the people or groups with the greatest physical, financial and political strength.

If the preceding paragraph paints a depressing picture of our collective departure from truth, then we needn't despair, because healing and restoration are in the hands of the One Who Himself is the Truth (John 14:6). John obviously appreciated the significance of Jesus's statement, especially in the light of His miracles and resurrection. The truth embodied by Jesus is the reality on which our eternal destinies hinge: we can choose to make our own way to hell, or we can follow Him to heaven. Our Lord claimed to be the Way to eternal life and His resurrection validates that claim beyond all doubt. Perhaps it does us no harm that the disintegration of our society is giving us an insight into the implications of life without Jesus, while we still have the time to make a decision in relation to where we stand on a personal level. Our collective rejection of Him has resulted in hell on earth, but this may be the very thing that's needed for people with spiritual discernment to cry out for something better, knowing that we were created for more than this. Once we do so, let's not stop there, but corporately repent and call out to Him, for revival and the healing of our land. Our decision to follow Jesus assures us of a future more wonderful than we could ever imagine: let's bring as many people with us as we possibly can!

How about a few quick questions?

i. If you're a Christian parent, how are you preparing your children for the onslaught they'll face from teachers, professors and colleagues, in relation to their faith?

ii. Do you, like John, seek to ensure that people you've led to the Lord continue to walk in the truth?

iii. Have you given thought to how you might be able to use your influence, either at university, work or on social media, to proclaim the truth, and ultimately lead people to the Truth Himself?

Diabolic Dialogue

> "Yet Michael the archangel, when contending with the devil he disputed about the body of Moses, durst not bring against him a railing accusation, but said, The Lord rebuke thee (Jude 1:9)."

This must have been quite an exchange! In Deuteronomy 34, verses 5 & 6, we read of God Himself superintending Moses's burial, and it seems that He despatched Michael, His faithful lieutenant, to take care of matters on the ground. There are two possible reasons for God giving Moses such an unusual send-off, and they needn't be mutually exclusive. In the short-term, there would have been a significant prospect of Moses's tomb having been turned into a shrine by the Israelites, given the reverence they had for him, and the proclivity they'd previously demonstrated towards idolatry. In this respect, God would have been counteracting, in advance, the plans Satan had for Moses's body, demonstrating the advantages of omniscience and foreknowledge! Of course, Satan always seeks to oppose God's plans, but he invariably comes up short, unless we allow him the victory. We know that God had a purpose for Moses during the Transfiguration (Matthew 17: 1 - 8), and it's also entirely possible that Moses will be one of the two witnesses He uses to warn the world of impending judgement (Revelation 11: 3 - 11). Satan usually underestimates God's power, so perhaps erroneously believed He'd need Moses's body to perform a resurrection! It's reassuring to know that the Enemy is no match for God, whether physically, spiritually or intellectually!

We can frequently fall into one of two alternative traps, so far as Satan is concerned: to credit him with either too much power or too little! We must never be overawed by him because, unlike God, he isn't omnipotent, meaning that his power is limited. Furthermore, he's constrained to one location, in contrast to our omnipresent God, which means that, when we're under attack, it's likely to be his demons who are opposing us, rather than the Devil in person. Moreover, Satan cannot read our thoughts: he isn't omniscient, and his knowledge is restricted by God Himself! Notwithstanding these limitations, he has been around for much longer than we have, and has been successful in persuading countless people to follow him to a lost eternity, so he shouldn't be contemptuously dismissed. To a considerable degree, Satan has as much power over our lives as we allow him, and the entry points we provide are either through sin, which is an alignment of our will with his, or prayerlessness, which denies the Lord the authority to intervene in our circumstances. This is why repentance and prayer are so important: both to evict the Enemy from the domain of our lives, and to restore the hedge of protection provided by fellowship with our Heavenly Father!

One way of inviting Satan into our lives is to talk to him, because that opens up a dialogue, and we don't want to be dialoguing with the Devil! It's most instructive to observe that even Michael didn't take Satan on directly, but said, "The Lord rebuke you." This is as far as he went, despite the fact that Michael and Satan are combatants of equal rank, whereas we, in our own strength, are no match for a demonic adversary who has been around for several thousand years, and who is intent on destroying us. That's not to say that we should be afraid of him, either: our sanctuary is found in the Lord Jesus Christ, Who is infinitely more powerful than Satan, and He holds the key when we come under demonic attack. Rather than contending with Satan directly, affording him an opportunity to respond, it's imperative that we invite Jesus into the situation through prayer, thereby authorising Him to release an angelic host to come to our aid. Endeavouring to launch a counter-attack in our own strength is the spiritual equivalent of kicking a hornet's nest, whereas we'd be far better served by calling for heavenly pest control!

If you're still tempted to start a conversation with Satan, it might be instructive to consider the sons of Sceva, in Acts chapter 19,

SPIRITUAL REFLECTIONS - I

whose fraudulent attempts at exorcism elicited the dismissive retort that, "Jesus I know, and Paul I know, but who are ye (Acts 19:15)?" We may not be fraudulent (I certainly hope not!), but we frequently don't have the reputations we believe we do! This is especially true in the spiritual realm, where there are clearly defined hierarchies, of which we are not at the head. The power of demonic spirits is illustrated by the events described in Acts 19:16, which have echoes of an account found in Mark 5, verses 3 - 20. The answer to these men's problems, as with ours, lay with Jesus. If a single angel could slay 185,000 of the Assyrian Army (2 Kings 19:35), then think what He can do for us! In that passage from Mark's Gospel, we read of demons leaving a man bound and living in a cemetery, which is where their master would have us all, both temporally and eternally. By means of absolute contrast, Jesus died to give us eternal liberty, and He's only waiting for us to call out to Him, before it's ours!

While accepting absolutely that our ultimate answer lies with Jesus, there may come a time when the attack we're experiencing is something we're unable to deal with on our own, in which case it's essential that we seek assistance from the leadership within our church. As members of a global Body, we're blessed to have brothers and sisters who are expertly trained in the fields of spiritual warfare and deliverance, and these are the people to whom we need to turn, when we're experiencing intense attack. Rather than railing against the darkness, it's always far better to turn on the light, which we do by calling out to Jesus. If we can't find the switch, then there's never any shame in enlisting the help of a trusted believer who can!

The following questions are intended to help you consider how you can develop your own defence mechanism in this important area of our lives.

i. Do you have a trusted Christian to whom you're able to turn, when you're experiencing spiritual attack?

ii. What kind of relationship do you have with Satan? Do you dismiss him, fear him or, as Michael did, respect his relative authority, without respecting his character?

iii. Why do you think God allowed Lucifer to continue to play a role in the world, rather than destroying him immediately after he fell?

SPIRITUAL REFLECTIONS - I

Revelation!

"The revelation of Jesus Christ, which God gave unto him, to show unto his servants things which must shortly come to pass; and he sent and signified it by his angel unto his servant John (Revelation 1:1)."

If we were to conduct a poll relating to the most misunderstood Books of the Bible, then there's a very good chance that Revelation would come out on top. However, the introduction should leave us in no doubt as to the fact that this is not only a Book we can understand, but also one we should study rigorously. A blessing is promised (Revelation 1:3) to everyone who reads or hears the text, which is described in the same verse as being a prophecy, thereby dispelling any notion that the Book is merely allegorical. The designation of Revelation as being a prophetic Book also refutes the suggestion made by some that the events it chronicles occurred historically, perhaps when Jerusalem was destroyed by the Roman Emperor Titus, in 70 AD, because it wasn't written until the very end of the first century, when John was exiled on Patmos.

The Greek word from which we derive our English noun 'Revelation' is 'Apokalupsis', which obviously gave us 'Apocalypse'. However, the meaning of the latter word has changed over time: whereas it is now associated with calamitous destruction, the original interpretation was 'unveiling', hence the name of 'Revelation'. This is an important point, because it informs us of the reason for the Book having been written: God the Father unveiled the events that would occur at the end of the current world age and revealed them to Jesus, Who shared them with John, in order that we wouldn't be ignorant of end-times events. Numerous Bible critics claim that Revelation is a 'sealed

SPIRITUAL REFLECTIONS - I

book' which cannot be understood, but nothing could be further from the truth! When we see the phrase "must shortly come to pass" in the middle of the opening verse of chapter one, we might be inclined towards discouragement, wondering if God's prophecy had failed, but the concept being elucidated is that the events outlined in the following twenty-two chapters will occur in quick succession, once they begin to take place. God's prophecies never fail and He is always in control, to which end it's worth noting that we're contemplating "The revelation of Jesus Christ," and not the revelation of the Antichrist!

As with any of the Bible's sixty-six Books, Revelation should be read literally, unless the meaning of a word or phrase is clearly figurative. The occurrence of the past tense of the verb 'signify' in the opening verse prepares us for the fact that we'll encounter a considerable amount of symbolism, but this is nothing new for students of God's Word: taking an example from elsewhere in Scripture, Jesus described Himself as "the door of the sheep (John 10:9)," thereby illustrating the fact that He is the Way to eternal life. The importance of following that Way is emphasised in Revelation, as the incomparable majesty of our Saviour and the indescribable glory of heaven are revealed to us, in complete contrast to the misery of hell. People often focus on the death and destruction when discussing Revelation, but there's considerable hope and optimism, too! Highlights that believers can eagerly anticipate include:

1. The Marriage Supper of the Lamb (Revelation 19: 6 - 9), where Jesus's followers feast with Him, prior to entering into their glorious inheritance.

2. The return of Jesus Christ to earth (Revelation 19:11), accompanied by us, His followers (Revelation 19:14)!

3. Satan being bound for a thousand years (Revelation 20:3), during which time Christ rules the earth and we reign with Him!

SPIRITUAL REFLECTIONS - I

4. The unveiling of a new heaven and a new earth (Revelation 21:1) and the new Jerusalem (Revelation 21:10).

5. A future with no more sorrow, crying or pain (Revelation 21:4).

6. The glorious inheritance of the overcomers (Revelation 21:7).

7. The river and tree of life enjoyed by believers in a future free from the curse that has plagued our time on earth, as we finally see our Saviour face to face (Revelation 22: 1 - 4).

The extent to which we should look forward to the literal period of time described in Revelation is therefore determined by whether or not we have accepted Jesus Christ as our Eternal Saviour. If we have taken this simple step, Revelation describes the fulfilment of all our hopes and dreams; if we haven't, it's the culmination of our worst possible nightmares. The good news, however, is that it still isn't too late! All of our reflections to this point have been pointing us to Jesus, and in Revelation we see Him as we've never seen Him before, but He's still inviting us to spend eternity with Him!

Would it shock you if I said that the Bible isn't the most important Book of all time? Before you classify me as a heretic, let me explain! In Revelation, we're introduced to the Lamb's Book of Life (chapter 13, verse 8), which contains the names of everyone, throughout history, who has accepted Jesus as their Saviour. Bible study is extremely important, in order that we get to know God and understand His purpose for our lives. However, what matters far more than how well we know our Bible is how well we know its Author: in other words, have we given our lives to Jesus, and are our names written in the Lamb's Book of Life? If you're not sure whether or not yours is, you can make sure today: all you have to do is pray to accept Jesus into your heart, just like this:

> *Heavenly Father, thank You for the revelation You've given us of Jesus, and of the future that's in store, both for people who accept Him as their Saviour and those who reject Him. Lord Jesus, I've rejected You for too long, but today I want to confess my sins before You,*

and accept the payment You made for them on the cross at Calvary. I humbly ask You to enter my name in the Lamb's Book of Life and adopt me into Your eternal family. Holy Spirit, please help me become the person You always intended me to be, enable me to honour You, and endue me with the power and wisdom I need to serve my Saviour Jesus, in Whose Name I pray. Amen.

If you've prayed this prayer, please let a trusted Christian know, in order that she or he can encourage you in your new life of faith!

Finally, here are a few questions for further reflection:

i. Have you been put off reading Revelation by the complexity of the symbolism? If so, why not give it a try, and see what you've been missing!

ii. Are you confident that you have an invitation to attend the Marriage Supper of the Lamb?

iii. Does the fact that the church isn't mentioned between chapter 4 and chapter 19 of Revelation suggest to you that genuine believers won't endure the Tribulation?

Open The Door!

"Behold, I stand at the door, and knock: if any man hear my voice, and open the door, I will come in to him, and sup with him, and he with me (Revelation 3:20)."

Have you ever seen a tract quoting this sentence, or something similar? The verse we're reflecting on is frequently used in evangelistic circles to prompt people who don't yet know Jesus to open their hearts to Him. The imagery perfectly lends itself to this purpose, because the sense of conviction wrought when the Holy Spirit begins to awaken an individual to their need for a Saviour can often make it feel as though Jesus is knocking on the door of their heart. It may well be that, as you read these words, you are aware of the Holy Spirit drawing you nearer to Him and, if that's the case, I would implore you to respond to His loving embrace, rather than forcing Him to walk away with a broken heart, knowing that it's your heart which will ultimately be broken. There's absolutely no danger of being asked to pay a penalty, like a delinquent schoolboy who once ran away to Liverpool! Jesus is waiting to welcome you home, just as the father did in the parable of the prodigal son. You may feel you've left it too late, but Jesus told another parable to demonstrate that this isn't the case. In Matthew 20, we read of a man who hired labourers at various times between the third hour (9 o'clock in the morning) and the eleventh hour (5 o'clock in the evening), and gave them all the same reward for their faithfulness in their endeavours. The implication is clear: while it's always better to come to Jesus sooner rather than later, everyone who sincerely accepts Him will enter into the Kingdom of Heaven, irrespective of when they come! More than that, we will literally eat (sup) with Jesus, as we participate in the Marriage Supper of the Lamb!

Having said all this, the actual context of the verse we're reflecting on is a letter that Jesus wrote to the notoriously 'lukewarm' church in Laodicea. Do you remember one of our reflections from Ezekiel, in which we read of the glory of God departing from the Temple in Jerusalem, then ultimately from the city herself? Now, in correspondence with a specific fellowship, which also signifies the current age in world history, we see Jesus knocking at the door of *His* church! Such a scenario is incredibly tragic, but for many of you reading this it may not be surprising. It could be that you were terribly hurt by your experience of church and wondered why there was no discernible presence of God in the sanctuary you attended. Well, it may possibly be that He wasn't there! Many churches today are spiritual mausoleums: the life having been extinguished by bureaucratic and judgemental attitudes, which have grieved the Holy Spirit to the extent that He's been compelled to leave. This doesn't only happen in apparently moribund churches, but in fellowships where there appears to be vibrant life, as in the church of Sardis (Revelation 3:1), which Jesus lamented as being dead, despite having the appearance of being alive! It can be exciting to walk into an auditorium where people are praising God to the sound of melodious music, against the backdrop of radiant lights but, if these things are being done for the wrong reasons, the hypocrisy of the show is an offence to God. He therefore absents Himself, preferring to attend a simple service where believers are meeting with humble hearts, and genuinely gathering in His Name (Matthew 18:20).

Mercifully, even when we reject God, He continues to love us, and invite us into a relationship with Him. Despite her numerous imperfections, He continues to love His Church, too! This isn't only for her intrinsic value, as the vessel He's chosen to use to reveal His love to the world, but because of His love for those faithful individuals who, as in Sardis (Revelation 3:4), continue to live for Him, while others are living for themselves. Isn't it gracious of Jesus not to give up on us, but to courteously seek entry into His Church? As with our hearts, before we were believers, God will never force His way in and, even now, it's imperative that we invite Him into every area of our lives. This should prompt us to contemplate, both on an individual and a corporate level, whether Jesus is at the centre of *our* worship. When we praise, are we focusing on Jesus or on the lights and music? When we pray, are we inviting the Holy Spirit into situations, or merely anxious for our voices to be heard? When we preach or teach, are we pointing people to Jesus, or seeking to enhance our own reputations?

Extending this concept further, it may not only be our church sanctuary which finds Jesus at the door, knocking to get in. Could it be that He's forced to wait on the outside of our homes, as we watch inappropriate television programmes, or ignore His Word for days on end? When an individual goes to hell, it's always because of a sin of omission: failing to respond to the Holy Spirit's witness of Jesus as Lord and Saviour. However, it seems that many of us as believers are guilty of something similar, as we omit to invite the Holy Spirit into our lives, homes, cars and workplaces. Who knows how different things might be if we allowed Him to play the role in our lives that He truly wants to? It may well be at this time when our acquaintances who aren't yet Christians see such a change in us that they, too, are enticed to answer the knock on the doors of their own hearts!

Time now for a few questions!

i. Are there any areas of your life, even in the deepest recesses of your thoughts, from which Jesus is excluded?

ii. Is your church or home a place where someone who doesn't yet know the Lord will be able to encounter His presence?

iii. If, on an individual level, you intend to close your heart to Jesus, do you know for sure that you'll get another chance to invite Him in, and are you prepared for the consequences, should you never do so?

The Final Warning

"And I saw another angel fly in the midst of heaven, having the everlasting gospel to preach unto them that dwell on the earth, and to every nation, and kindred, and tongue, and people, saying with a loud voice, Fear God, and give glory to him; for the hour of his judgement is come: and worship him that made heaven, and earth, and the sea, and the fountains of waters (Revelation 14: 6 & 7)."

We've reached our ninety-ninth and penultimate reflection, and have almost come full circle. Having begun with the creation of the earth, we are now given a preview of the time when everyone who dwells on this beautiful planet will be given one final opportunity to accept Jesus's free gift of salvation, rather than facing into eternal separation from the light, rivers, trees and hills that make life worthwhile. Some amongst us go so far as to worship creation, but to do this is to miss the point that the splendour we see all around us serves as a testament to the One Who created the world in which we live, and everything it contains. It is for this reason that secular culture has so aggressively attacked the reality of creation; seeking to supplant it with empty theories designed for the sole purpose of deflecting our thoughts from our Creator. God formed us in His image (Genesis 1:27), in order that we could enjoy a relationship with Him, and we initially have to fight hard to resist the gravitational pull of our hearts towards the One Who created us. If we hold out for long enough, resistance becomes easier, until it takes a major miracle to open our eyes to our need for a Saviour. Should we manage to live to the very end of our lives, without requiting the love Jesus demonstrated towards us at Calvary, we won't be invited to enjoy the next phase of His creation, revealed in the restoration of this planet and the new heaven and earth (Revelation 21:1). We may consider it unfair that not everyone will be able to enter into eternal life, but the reality is that the invitation *has* been extended to us all. In Romans 10:13, Paul assures us that, "Whosoever shall call upon the name of the Lord shall be saved," and here, in God's final, impassioned plea to humankind, we see Him reaching out to every nation, kindred, tongue and people. In the same way that, if you were hosting a lavish house party, you would only permit entry to people who wanted to be there, God only grants us admission to His eternal party if we've signalled our desire to be there, by accepting the privilege of entrance which was painfully purchased by His Son.

Many people view Revelation as a Book of judgement, but we are seeing that God will do everything in His power to spare us, right up until the very end! In chapter 11 and verse 3, we read of the two witnesses He will send to prophesy during the closing three and a half years of this age, for the express purpose of awakening the earth's inhabitants to the consequences of living life to a conclusion without accepting Christ. Even during the most challenging times, whether of our personal lives or world history, we have a choice between serving God and ultimately prospering, or serving Satan, believing that we're actually living for ourselves, and reaping the consequences. Eventually, we reach the stage when we reject Jesus for the last time, no further opportunities are afforded to us, and we enter into eternal judgement. This isn't God's will for any of us, but we have to be aware that the warning is real: God wouldn't invest the time and effort in alerting us if the prospect of judgement wasn't genuine, and we've considered historical precedents in this book; related to the Flood and, especially, Israel and Judah, prior to their respective Assyrian captivity and Babylonian exile.

In the current era, our fate of entering into eternal judgement is confirmed when an individual takes their final breath on earth, having consistently rejected Jesus's offer of salvation. However, during the Tribulation, it's possible for people to be eternally condemned while they are still alive on the earth. This occurs when they reject Jesus and proclaim undying loyalty to Satan by accepting the mark of the Beast (Revelation 13:16). This mark isn't something which can be acquired by accident, but the preceding verses, particularly 12 - 15, reveal that those who accept it will have been deceived by the miracles of the Antichrist, demonstrating, once again, how vulnerable we are to believing a lie when first we choose to reject the truth. Although it will require a conscious decision to accept the mark, doing so places you in a state of spiritual death, meaning that you literally have no hope of redemption, even while your body remains alive. If you're reading this book after the Rapture, having finally given credence to what Christians were saying for all these years, **please, please** don't make the mistake of accepting the mark. Once you've done so, there's no opportunity to turn back: you'll be condemned to a place of eternal judgement which was reserved for Satan and his demons (Matthew 25:41). It's far better to face martyrdom in this life, which is likely to be the consequence of rejecting the mark, than to be tortured for all eternity. If you're reading this before the Rapture, then you still have time to accept Jesus as your Saviour, with the result that you won't need to endure the Tribulation or worry about the prospect of accepting the mark of the Beast!

Throughout this book, we've seen that the counterpoint to God's judgement is His immense love, and His desire for you, if you're not yet a Christian, is that you will find a place for Jesus in your heart and participate in the wonderful scene of Revelation 19:11, when He returns to earth, accompanied by everyone who has placed their trust in Him. This scene represents the fulfilment of the hope believers have had for the past two thousand years, as Jesus returns to establish His Kingdom on earth. This Kingdom will last for a literal Millennium, before the creation of the new earth, described in Revelation 21. The disciples were wanting Jesus to set up His reign when He first came, but He tarried in order to give you and me the chance of salvation. Even now, He is imploring you to come to Him, feel the embrace of His love, and be saved from the failed ideologies of this world, which ultimately lead only to destruction. As I've previously emphasised, there is no middle ground: we are either released into glorious liberty as followers of Jesus Christ, or trapped in the hopeless state of everyone who has rejected Him. Even on earth, life without hope can't really be called 'life', but imagine what it would be like to spend the whole of eternity in darkness, knowing that you missed the opportunity to enjoy the beauty of a whole new creation. In case you were under any illusion that it might be possible to stand against God, we see that He ultimately destroys His enemies with a single word (the sword of Revelation 19:21). The Antichrist can't compete with Jesus, and nor can we, but we don't have to: whoever you are, and whatever you may have done, He's calling you to be a part of His future, and in the closing chapters of Revelation we see just how glorious this will be!

There's only one question at the end of this reflection, which is for anyone reading it who hasn't yet accepted Jesus as their Lord and Saviour: can you give me one good reason why you would prefer to enter into a lost eternity than to enjoy the majesty of the new heaven and the new earth? If you want to receive the blessings God has prepared, specifically for you, the only thing you need to do is to call out to Him now, and invite Jesus into your heart. You'd make His day if you did!

No More Pain!

"And God shall wipe away all tears from their eyes; and there shall be no more death, neither sorrow, nor crying, neither shall there be any more pain: for the former things are passed away (Revelation 21:4)."

The promise contained in this verse holds immense personal significance for me, as someone with a medical condition which causes chronic pain. However, it should be a promise that every believer treasures: all the things which spoil our life on earth will soon be gone! It's worth reiterating that the following things will be done away with: death, sorrow, crying and pain. The absence of tears also means an end to everything which causes them: heartache, illness, loneliness, fatigue, stress, calumny, depression, poverty, regret, disease, ageing and failure, to name just a dozen! Our explanation for this glorious state of affairs is found in Revelation 22:3: the curse which came upon the earth when Adam and Eve first sinned will be revoked! The only people entering into this glorious eternity will be those whose sanctuary is found in Christ, who will finally attain the sinless state of sanctification previously referenced. As a consequence, we won't be capable of causing emotional or physical pain to others, and no-one else will be able to cause pain to us! The only people who won't be sanctified are those who have rejected Jesus's gift of salvation, and they won't be sharing our eternal futures with us, for the very reason of their decision. This has to be an immensely sobering thought for those of us who have loved ones who don't yet know the Lord: a realisation which will hopefully motivate us to do everything we can on their behalf on this side of eternity, while remembering that it is the Holy Spirit's job to convict and their responsibility to make a decision.

Amazingly, the final tears we ever shed will be wiped away by God Himself! One obvious question is why there would be any tears at all on what should be such a glorious occasion, when we meet God in Person, enter our eternal home and have our expectations wildly surpassed by the river and tree of life (Revelation 22: 1 & 2). I can think of five possible reasons, but don't have any special revelation in this area, so could be well wide of the mark!

1. Particular comfort may be afforded to our brothers and sisters in Christ who have suffered profoundly on earth. We often cry with relief when a horrible ordeal is over, and life on earth is exactly this for many believers, who are persecuted for their faith.

2. There will be initial heartache on the part of believers who reach eternity to find that someone they loved dearly will not be joining them. Rather than leaving it too late, let's make it our lifetime's mission to fast and pray for people who don't yet know the Lord.

3. We will almost certainly be moved to tears by the realisation of the depth of Jesus's suffering, when we see the scars on His body, which were inflicted so that He could take our sins upon Himself, allowing us the communion with God that had been reserved for Him. Although we are likely to understand this to a greater extent during the Millennial Kingdom, which precedes the events described in Revelation 21:4, we may receive a deeper level of insight, as we enter into this new phase of our lives.

4. It is entirely possible that we'll be struck by a sense of regret that, if only we'd had the faith we ought to have done, we'd

have achieved so much more, both during the current phase of our lives on earth and, perhaps, during the Millennium.

5. Meeting God in Person and observing the majesty of the new heaven and new earth will be so utterly amazing that our only instinctive response will be to cry, in the same way that an overjoyed mother spontaneously sheds tears of happiness when her daughter marries someone who would give his life for her without a moment's hesitation.

In this particular scenario, it is we, the Church, who are the Bride, and it is Jesus Who unquestioningly gave His life for us. Now, we will finally be able to enjoy life as it was always meant to be, with boundless joy, no unhappiness, no more tears...and no more pain! All of these glories, with innumerable others besides, are waiting for us, provided we've done the only thing we've been asked to do during our time on earth, and yielded our lives to Christ. As my Master said Himself, "He that findeth his life shall lose it: and he that loseth his life for my sake will find it (Matthew 10:39)."

It's your decision.

What's it to be?

I hope you've enjoyed journeying with me through the Scriptures, and that your faith has been strengthened as you've done so. I've posed a considerable number of questions, throughout the course of this book, and what you've read may well have prompted some questions of your own. If that's the case, please feel free to get in touch with my publishers, using the contact details provided.

Finally, let's conclude in prayer.

> *Heavenly Father, thank You for the enduring and infinite nature of Your love for everyone who has read this book. I thank You for the wonderful plans You have for their lives and the fact that it's not too late for destinies to be changed and communities transformed. Lord Jesus, thank You for Your amazing sacrifice at Calvary, which is our only pathway to eternal life. I pray that You'll reveal the truth to everyone who doesn't yet know You, and strengthen the faith of those who already do. Holy Spirit, I'm immensely grateful to You for enabling me to write this book, and I commit it into Your hands. Please use it in whatever way You consider appropriate, to release spiritual captives, bring revival to our world and continuously exalt our incomparable Saviour Jesus Christ, in Whose Mighty Name I pray. Amen.*

ingramcontent.com/pod-product-compliance
Source LLC
urg PA
980526
0010B/922